W9-AVR-555

WITHDRAWN

WRITING HORROR

WRITING HORROR

Edited by
MORT CASTLE

WRITER'S DIGEST BOOKS
CINCINNATI, OHIO

Writing Horror. Copyright © 1997 by the Horror Writers Association. Printed and bound in the United States of America. All rights reserved. No part of this book may be reproduced in any form or by any electronic or mechanical means including information storage and retrieval systems without permission in writing from the publisher, except by a reviewer, who may quote brief passages in a review. Published by Writer's Digest Books, an imprint of F&W Publications, Inc., 1507 Dana Avenue, Cincinnati, Ohio 45207. (800) 289-0963. First edition.

This hardcover edition of *Writing Horror* features a "self-jacket" that eliminates the need for a separate dust jacket. It provides sturdy protection for your book while it saves paper, trees and energy.

Other fine Writer's Digest Books are available from your local bookstore or direct from the publisher.

01 00 99 98 97   5 4 3 2 1

Library of Congress Cataloging-in-Publication Data

Writing horror / edited by Mort Castle.
    p.   cm.
ISBN 0-89879-798-5 (alk. paper)
1. Horror tales—Authorship. I. Castle, Mort.
PN3377.5.H67W75   1997
808.3'8738—dc21   97-17493
                                                          CIP

Edited by Mort Castle
Content edited by David Borcherding
Designed by Angela Lennert Wilcox
Cover illustration by Gerald Brom, Brom Illustration

The permissions on pages vi–vii constitute an extension of this copyright page.

This one is for brothers-in-arms:

Big Brother Jerry Williamson, The Hoosier Sage of Horror; The Bobs, Twin Brothers of Different Parents: Robert Lightell and Robert Weinberg; Baby Brother David Campiti, Uncrowned King of Comics.

Thanks to all contributors, of course, of course, and thanks a double portion to the gracious Harlan Ellison; to the Amazing Mark Squad: Mark Evans, Mark Valadez and Mark Powers; to the Madias, Mudbone, Mudmom, Mudbaby; to Adam Post and his electric pushcart; to all those fine young writers at Bloom and Bloom Trail High Schools and their fine teachers, too; to the Gang of Old Kids and Young Kids at Crete-Monee and the crew who helped make C-M Press a reality; to my own wife, Jane, who now speaks three foreign languages; to James Gormley, who decided this book ought to be and worked to make it happen; and to all those who write the words and hear the voices.

TABLE OF CONTENTS

HORROR
GENRE AND SUBGENRE

INNOVATION IN HORROR
TODAY AND TOMORROW

MARKETING HORROR

AFTERWORD

A Shockingly Brief and Informal History of the Horror Writers Association

Stanley Wiater

As with most great ideas, the concept for a horror writers association originated in the fevered imagination of one individual—in this instance, one Robert R. McCammon. In an interview with *Publishers Weekly* in 1984, the author (who had already published six horror novels) first publicly expressed his desire for a professional organization specifically geared to the needs of fellow writers of fear. At that point, however, his decidedly colorful name for the then nonexistent organization was "HOWL" (Horror/Occult Writers League). Even so, reasoned McCammon, mystery writers had their professional organizations, as did science-fiction writers. Wasn't it past time that the equally honorable genre of terror, fright and the supernatural be formally recognized?

Perhaps more than anyone, McCammon was shocked at the subsequent—and often sincere—interest of the media in his remarks, including *The New York Times* and *The Washington Post.* Then the B. Dalton and Waldenbooks chains wanted to know more. Horror writers began to "hear the HOWL" and wrote McCammon to ask where to sign up, though it had always been his intent to first survey every writer he could contact before ever making a formal announcement about the proposed organization. Nevertheless, McCammon was deluged with still more letters of support from writers, editors and scholars both stateside and overseas—my own enthusiastic response as a self-styled "horror journalist" included.

Before long, McCammon enlisted the support of two colleagues who were instrumental in bringing the concept of HOWL snarling into reality: Texas author Joe R. Lansdale and his wife, Karen. They in turn sent out a formal letter of invitation to some 177 writers, of whom 88 responded with suggestions or a willingness to join.

Working by phone and letter with McCammon, the trio committed themselves to the insane task of creating what they believed could be a nationally—perhaps even internationally—recognized writers organization. Thanks primarily to Karen's unflagging energy, they then drew up the constitution and bylaws, formulated mailing lists, took out ads, issued press releases—whatever it took to ensure that from the outset, HOWL would be recognized as a *professional* writers organization, not a "fan club" for side-show horror buffs.

Other new volunteers contributed in numerous ways, most notably in the production and content of the early newsletters. We took our organization seriously—right from the bloody start. Why not? Stephen King and Peter Straub, among others, were becoming increasingly known as "brand name writers." For the first time "Horror" was being labeled as a separate category in most bookstores. The entire field was riding a growing wave of popularity in the 1980s; it was only logical that those of us exploring this increasingly recognized genre would desire to have our own legitimate organization.

The goals of HOWL were stated simply and directly in the preamble to its constitution and bylaws:

> Be it known that the Horror and Occult Writers League is a non-profit organization of professional writers of fiction and non-fiction pertaining to or inspired by the traditions, legends, development and history of horror and occult. Its members are together for their mutual benefit in an earnest effort to further a more widespread publicity, promotion, distribution, readership and appreciation of the literature of horror and occult.

The lack of high-profile authors like King was one of the stumbling blocks early on, even as the organization was searching for recognition by its peers precisely among those most successfully working in our genre. (Dean Koontz and Robert Bloch were among the first to respond favorably to the concept and to volunteer their aid and reputations.) Regardless, new members from all across the country and overseas were being added to the growing roster. It was obvious from the burgeoning newsletters that, for many writers, editors and critics, the fledgling organization was being taken quite seriously.

Unfortunately, HOWL was not being taken seriously by some colleagues . . . nor by much of the mainstream media. (If *I* can easily poke gentle fun at the acronym "HOWL," just think how anyone less than sympathetic would describe the virtually unknown group and its membership.)

Nevertheless, history was made when the first formal meeting took place on November 3, 1985, at the World Fantasy Convention held in

Tucson, Arizona. (Subsequent meetings have taken place at both the World Fantasy Convention and the World Horror Convention.) No more than two dozen people attended that fateful meeting, led informally by founder Robert R. McCammon and Joe R. and Karen Lansdale. Outside our fledgling meeting, of course, there were hundreds of writers, agents, and other professionals at the convention.

Dare I say it: there, yours truly took note of the small number of the faithful in attendance that glorious Sunday morning.

And so I made a brief yet heartfelt speech imploring those present to change the name from the undeniably memorable "HOWL" to, say, the *Horror Writers of America* . . . with the obvious intent to bring our name recognition to the public more in line with such well established groups as the Mystery Writers of America and the Science-Fiction Writers of America. By unanimous vote, my suggestion was approved.

After that initial gathering, others were inspired to make our new organization truly viable and far more visible. McCammon formed a steering committee with Melissa Mia Hall and Joe R. Lansdale to tackle (as described in an open letter to members) "the toughest part of putting the HWA together—the trial by paperwork, if you will—and after these hurdles are overcome with your help and support, we'll have a stronger organization that will benefit authors in our field for generations to come."

Dated July 1986, Volume 1, Number 1, the first HWA (Horror Writers of America) official newsletter appeared. Entitled *Our Glass* (after a famous medieval statue in which a corpse is admiring itself in a pocket glass), the professionally printed first issue was eight pages long. It featured timely news items, a letters page, a market report, the first ballot for the formal election of officers, and brief interviews with artist Phil Parks and founder Robert R. McCammon. Only two issues appeared with this title, even as a search was launched for a permanent logo for the organization. (While the admiring corpse was suggested as one possibility, the logo would ultimately be a tastefully stylized haunted house.)

Later that year, early supporter Dean Koontz was chosen as the organization's first president. In a statement to the membership, Koontz declared his belief that the HWA could "add dignity and publicity to the field, as well as giving horror fiction a focus." Koontz further suggested an annual anthology to be composed of contributions from the membership ranks. (The first of several such anthologies to subsequently appear would be *Under the Fang*, edited by Robert R. McCammon.)

Through the volunteered help of legal counsel Sheldon R. Jaffery, the HWA was legally incorporated in March 1987. The initial board of trustees was also in place, which included at that time McCammon, Lansdale and Koontz. The HWA was formally on its way, anxious and ready to make its unique voice heard.

Koontz furthered, fostered and promoted the idea that the HWA was a serious organization for writers, and damn well should be taken seriously by all concerned. Before he left office, there were some 300 members—many of them among the most popular and respected authors in the business. As many are aware, the most recognized horror authors in the world have become members, including Ray Bradbury, Stephen King, Peter Straub, Clive Barker, Richard Matheson and Ramsey Campbell. The membership of the HWA today numbers well over 600 and is growing.

It was under Koontz's administration that the formation of an annual award for "Superior Achievement" was initiated. At the time, Koontz was chief among those who believed the award should be named after a famous—and deceased—writer. His short list of dead-on recommendations: Mary Wollstonecraft Shelley, Edgar Allan Poe, H.P. Lovecraft and Bram Stoker. The membership ultimately voted on the "Bram Stoker Award," to be issued in the form of a magnificently wrought haunted house designed by Stephen Kirk.

Charles L. Grant ably succeeded Koontz as president; he would be succeeded by such acclaimed authors as Chelsea Quinn Yarbro, Craig Shaw Gardner, Dennis Etchison, Lawrence Watt-Evans and Brian Lumley.

In 1988, the first Annual Bram Stoker Awards Banquet and Business Meeting took place in New York City. Since then, the officers have attempted to satisfy both the West Coast and East Coast members by swapping coasts from time to time.

In 1993, to further involve its international membership, the name of the organization was changed once again, from the "Horror Writers of America" to the "Horror Writers Association." Whatever the name, the horror genre it proudly champions continues to be more widely recognized and increasingly appreciated as we approach the new millennium.

Just as the HWA continues to flourish—and be taken seriously— by both publishers and the public alike.

If I may close on a personal note, it's been my singular pleasure to be a dues-paying member from the earliest origins of the HWA. My highest honor in the literary field undoubtedly has been to win the Bram Stoker Award in 1991. Without the HWA, it's difficult to say where the career of at least one writer might have ended up. In fact, one might be sorely tempted to say it's too damn frightening to even contemplate . . .

Editor's Introduction

Mort Castle

The questions are out there.

> *Horror? What—exactly—do you mean by that?*
>
> *Where do you get ideas?*
>
> *Do you know Stephen King?*

In a typical year, in addition to writing, I give readings; speak at writing conferences; conduct writing workshops; serve as a writer-in-residence hither, yon, and over there; and put on a customized literary dog and pony show at schools, libraries, bookstores, coffeehouses—any place that wants this worker in the literary vineyard to share some of his (often dark) grapes.

So I can attest that inquiring minds do want to know—about horror. Then there are questions related to the craft of horror, to the methods employed to put down the right word, then to find the right word to follow it, then to find the right word to follow *that*. As a long-time teacher for Writer's Digest School, I frequently hear from WDS students:

> *But how can you make* credible *what is plainly* incredible?
>
> *If you are creating mood, how can you keep the story's plot moving briskly?*
>
> *How do you make your horror story characters* act *right,* talk *right,* think *right,* undergo demeaning, spiritually destroying, agonizingly messy, maiming deaths *right?*

And—

> *Do you know Stephen King?*

Most writers—and most certainly anyone who is associated with the horror field (editors, agents, artists, etc.)—have heard some of these questions, or most of these questions, or all of these questions, *and* plenty of others.

And you try to answer questions . . . . Just like Mom told you, it's simple politeness.

But there is something more. Each of us human beings, each in a unique way, is a teacher. It's an altruistic thing that Freud never got around to disdaining and that no major psychic hot line has yet figured out how to exploit.

People honestly want to share their knowledge of—I've *got* to use the word—of what they *love*.

I've seen my father, who is retired now but was an on-the-street salesman deluxe for fifty-plus years, explain to sales novices over the decades: Keep notes on customers, including births, nicknames and back injuries; follow through on order fulfillment, even when no one in the warehouse is at all familiar with any written language; manage to get in touch with your personal, interior cheerleader when your order pad has been empty for too many days in a row and even the jokes you're hearing from prospects are pretty stale.

My father did his teaching not because a "boss" said, "Shel, show this newby some stuff, OK?" and not because the local junior college asked, "Mr. Castle, would you teach a night course in 'Principles of Successful Selling'?" but because my father *loves* selling, the people part of it, the strategy part of it, the organization, the . . . he loves the unique vocation that is *selling*. The totality of it.

And he taught people who came to him and said, "May I ask you a question?"

Now you have come to this book, *Writing Horror*.

You have brought your questions to us, the members of the Horror Writers Association. Each of the contributors to *Writing Horror* has made a serious time, energy and creative commitment to putting words on the page with the calculated intent to make *horror* happen.

And one of the contributors to this book, Elizabeth Engstrom, has penned a novel called *When Darkness Loves Us*.

I believe it no less true that *we* love the darkness.

So bring on your questions.

Where do you get ideas?

Wayne Allen Sallee walks you to your window and shows you how to *see*. Bob Weinberg waits to take you on the grand tour of the forbidden library.

Where is horror going?

Jeanne Cavelos envisions a more literate *and* literary horror. Robert Walker observes the mainstream becoming more horrific, even as horror becomes more mainstream, even as . . . *Ultra-Horror comes to the comics!* proclaims David Quinn, one of the folks who put it there. Horror goes multimedia, says Matt Costello, the very best friend of the *7th Guest*, who's invaded more than two million computers!

How do you . . .

Fine-tune your ear for dialogue? Maestro David Morrell lends you his tuning fork. *Figure out what comes next?* Join the secret plotters, Nancy Holder and Alan Rodgers, as they divulge their schemes and solve your puzzles.

What about style?

Norman Partridge introduces you to the Super-Surgeon of Style, none other than the good Dr. Frankenstein. It's Joe Lansdale's hand on your shoulder guiding you to the strangely familiar regions not so far from home where horror abides.

But just being practical, you know . . . How do you sell *horror?*

Benjamin Adams, Lawrence Watt-Evans, James Gormley, Edo van Belkom and Paula Guran will field that question, with all due practicality—and they have more than a few real-life horror stories on *this* subject.

And listen! There, so quiet that it demands to be heard, Harlan Ellison whispers the "Quiet Lies the Locust Tells."

Come in, come in now to our realm of dark imaginings and enlightening realities. Come in, and we, *all of us* together, will explore the strange art and demanding craft that is *Writing Horror*.

DEVELOPING
HORROR
CONCEPTS

———

The Madness of Art

Joyce Carol Oates

> *When you consider what a slight part the weird plays in our*
> *moods, feelings and lives you can easily see how basically minor*
> *the weird tale must necessarily be. It can be art, since the sense*
> *of the uncanny is an authentic human emotion, but it is obvi-*
> *ously a narrow and restricted form of art . . .*
>
> —H.P. LOVECRAFT

> *The Brain, within its Groove Runs evenly—and true—But let*
> *a splinter swerve—'Twere easier for You—To put a Current*
> *back—When Floods have slit the Hit And scooped a Turnpike*
> *for Themselves—and trodden out the Mills*
>
> —EMILY DICKINSON (#556, 1890)

Since the start of my writing career as an adult—I should acknowledge that, before I published my first short stories in national magazines, let alone my first novel, I'd written literally thousands of pages of prose fiction—I have been fascinated by the fluid and indefinable boundaries between "realism" and "surrealism." What are the "Gothic," the "grotesque," "horror"—as literary genres? What is the distinction, if there is a distinction, and if it is significant, between the art of Franz Kafka—that extraordinary tale of unspeakable horror, "In the Penal Colony," for instance—and the art of H.P. Lovecraft—that extraordinary tale of unspeakable horror, "The Shadow Out of Time," for instance? Is there any significant distinction, in terms of depth of perception or quality of vision, between Henry James's *A Portrait of a Lady* and *The Turn of the Screw* by the same author? Is Edgar Allan Poe, our most martyred American Gothicist, now a "mainstream" writer, as a consequence of the literary canon that has enshrined him as a "classic"? Perhaps, to transcend categories others have invented for us, we have to be both dead—long dead—and "classics."

In art, such extravagant, experimental movements as expressionism, symbolism, surrealism and Dada freely obliterated restraining and defining categories. The numinous and frequently nightmarish image lay at the core of the artist's inspiration.

Consider such work as "Rape," by the Belgian surrealist Magritte, which combines features of the female anatomy and the female face in a nightmarish conflation that possesses its own logic, and other works of Magritte's in which the human form is distorted or dismembered, or melted into other, inanimate objects; or those most powerful horror images of Egon Schiele in which the human figure, Schiele's own in some paintings, is imagined as a living skeleton, an animated embodiment of Death; or the flamboyantly decadent art of Aubrey Beardsley, in which sexual organs seem to have acquired sinister lives of their own; and works of Klimt, and Munch, in which Death cavorts with life in scenes of arresting visual beauty.

The visual arts are perhaps the most radical of arts, for there seems to be no mainstream, no "convention," exerting its gravitational pull upon individual artists, at least since the time of Cezanne. In music, the "great, abiding classics" of Mozart, Beethoven, Brahms, et al. continue to be played incessantly, to the despair of contemporary composers who are forced, however against the grain of their ideologies and temperaments, to "compete" for a relatively small, conservative audience. In literature, the canonization of "classics" has resulted in the relative demotion of other writers and other kinds of writing; the elevation of "mainstream" and predominantly "realistic" writing has created a false topology in which numerous genres are perceived as inferior to, or at least significantly different from, the mainstream. If Edgar Allan Poe were alive and writing today, he would very likely not be accorded the acclaim given the putative "serious literary writer," but would be taxonomized as a "horror writer." Yet talent, not excluding genius, may flourish in any genre—provided it is not stigmatized by that deadly label "genre."

Speaking as a writer predisposed to reading and frequently to writing what I call "Gothic" work, I should say that this so-called genre fascinates me because it is so powerful a vehicle of truth-telling, and because there is no wilder region for the exercise of the pure imagination. The surreal is as integral a part of our lives as the "real"; one might argue that, since the unconscious underlies consciousness, and we are continuously bombarded by images, moods and memories from that uncharitable terrain, it is in fact more primary than the "real." The Gothic work resembles the tragic in that it is willing to confront mankind's—and nature's—darkest secrets. Its metaphysics is Plato's, and not Aristotle's. There is a profound difference between what *appears* to be, and what *is*; and if you believe otherwise, the Gothicist has a surprise for you. The strained, sunny smile of the Enlightenment—"All that is, is holy"; "Man is a rational being"—is confronted by the Gothicist, who, quite frankly, considering the history and prehistory of our species, knows better. That there should be a highly conscious, rigorously crafted art of the grotesque, in the very service of such painful revelations, seems to me a tribute to our species, a check to the homogenization of culture, in which a single vision—democratic, Christian, liberal, "good"—has come to be identified with America generally.

Of course, horror fiction has its weaknesses. But so does "serious, literary" fiction. If there is any problem with the Gothic as an art, it is likely to lie in the quality of execution. In the literature of horror, a handicap has frequently been that of verisimilitude, the relative weakness or flatness of character. H.P. Lovecraft spoke of the "weird" rather than the Gothic, which seems to me, for all my admiration of Lovecraft's masterly work, unnecessarily restricting. To Lovecraft, too, "phenomena" rather than "persons" are the logical heroes of stories, one consequence of which is two-dimensional, stereotypical characters about whom it is difficult to care. Situations and plots may be formulaic, language merely serviceable and not a vehicle for the impassioned inwardness of which "weirdness" is one attempt at definition, but only one. The standards for horror fiction should be no less than those for "serious, literary" fiction in which originality of concept, depth of characters and attentiveness to language are vitally important.

Gothic fiction is the freedom of the imagination, the triumph of the unconscious. Its radical premise is that, out of utterly plausible and psychologically realistic situations, profound and intransigent truths will emerge. *And it is entertaining; it is unashamed to be entertaining.*

Those of us (how many of us!) who have given our souls to the activity of writing are obviously engaged in a lifelong quest. Perhaps, though we experience ourselves as individuals, our art is communal, like our language and our histories. We write in order not just to be read, but to read—texts not yet written, which only we can bring into being. Is this quest quixotic, perverse or—utterly natural? Normal? Do we have any choice? Henry James, one of our exemplary beings who understood the lure of the grotesque, the skull beneath the smiling face, as well as any writer, has characterized us all in these words:

We work in the dark—we do what we can—we give what we have. Our doubt is our passion, and our passion is our task. The rest is the madness of art.

A World of Dark and Disturbing Ideas

J.N. Williamson

Throughout my professional writing career I have thought of an "idea" as a "useful premise," and my impression has a worthwhile history. Mary Wollstonecraft Shelley, in a dream influenced by a long, eerie conversation and perhaps John Milton's *Paradise Lost*, conceived the notion of a living human being created by a man. Bram Stoker remembered reading about people who genuinely believed in creatures called "vampires." Because neither author actually became immortal on the strength of individual inspiration, the originality we respect in them resides in the uses they made of these concepts. Dr. Victor Frankenstein might instead have been a mere neurotic whose innocent, horrifying being existed solely in his mind. Dracula could have been an insane woodcutter or book editor whose only interest to readers depended upon his abnormal but not supernatural lust for human blood.

The numerous tales since then in which writers have used man-made monsters or vampires in different forms, with different agendas and a variety of endings, have been made possible by virtue of *ideas*. But when dealing with the urge to create fiction that's a twist on what was already written—on primary conceptions existing before Mrs. Shelley or Mr. Stoker were born—the originality demanded of you or me is both centered on and discovered elsewhere: on the setting or date of the yarn, on new characters, on more modern science and contemporary beliefs or on the opponents and pursuers of our particular versions of the monster.

Defining a Useful Premise

Why do I like the term "useful premise" instead of "idea"? Writers' ideas that won't sell are useful only as practice. I define a useful premise as a concept that (1) may be new, or not developed into a plot for quite awhile, (2) that the writer is comfortable with, (3) one for which it can be reasonably assumed an accessible market exists.

These three numbers correspond with the following clarifications:

1. Entirely new ideas are as precious as gold and thus rarely discovered.

Most people argue with this; I know *I* did. But consider some of the alleged ideas annually developed by droves of new writers who haven't read nearly enough: people who are injured and find out they're man-made or from a different planet; mirror stories, magic and otherwise; vampires who have AIDS or steal blood from blood banks; little girls who turn out to be little boys, and vice-versa; short-shorts written in one sentence; lovers who discover they are sister and brother; grandparent-ghosts who save a grandchild; sentient, malicious machines and vicious vehicles; and, more recently, abused women who mutilate and humilate men.

No, these are not new or original ideas; they have not gone undeveloped for a long period of time, and they decidedly are *not* useful premises.

2. Contrary to what college (and other) writing teachers once instructed, it is not necessary for new dabblers in the great fictive sandpile to make castles based on the backs of their houses and populated by characters who resemble the people who live inside them. If that were true, there would be precious little science fiction and, I think, not much horror fiction. Most of us aren't related to monsters of any kind, including the serial killer variety.

However, unless a writer has experienced an amazingly checkered life and held dozens of unrelated jobs—and unless said paragraph collector has the luxury of spending all the time required in extensive research—there are ideas for fiction that won't make the writer feel very comfortable in his or her development of a plot.

I've had a dozen or more appealing ideas I have sadly had to judge as "somebody else's," as if the mysterious creative process erred and got the imaginative right hemisphere of *my* brain confused with some other author's.

Are you ready, comfortably and credibly, to sustain characters of very different age, background, sexual lifestyle and outlook on life long enough to write a commercial story or novel?

The question is particularly important in learning to write effective dark and disturbing fiction, which is often fantastic or at least improbable and demands that a higher premium be placed on characterization than that required by mainstream fiction. When we ask readers to believe the impossible, we have a greater likelihood of cooperation if we're comfortable with our characters and if *they* remind our readers of people they know.

3. Often, new writers simply excited at getting a story idea, just sit down and see where the "story" takes them. Although spontaneity may be underrated, impulse tales have a way of meandering out of the mood set at the start and wandering into other genres. The product is the most difficult of yarns to place: a mixed-genre or genre-straddling piece.

You see, one of the criteria for creating fiction a writer can reasonably assume has a chance to sell is honoring the demands of the kind of story being written. Clever endings that clash with the type of yarn one just wrote should be saved in a folder for use at the close of a new, appropriate tale.

Study the fiction currently being bought, and attune your imagination in those directions.

An accessible market might conceivably mean almost any active one, whether in books, magazines, TV or film. But reason tells us it is much more limited than that. With the exceptions of a few "name brand" authors, I know only two who have sold to *Playboy*. The overwhelming majority of us begin with immeasurably smaller financial successes.

The accessible commercial market is one that reads your tale, likes it, and has the honest intention of doing something toward getting it into print in return for a sum of money spelled out in a contract legally signed by you and the purchaser.

Engaging the Hypnagogic State

Everything you've read to this point is wrapping paper on the gift I'm about to give you. Under the heading of "How do you dream up all those ideas?" is my reply that I *do* "dream them up."

The somewhat pompous term for the source of my useful premises is *the hypnagogic state*. The gift you get is a description of how I first "visited" that state, what I took from it, what I've managed to do with it for two decades, and my belief that *you*, imaginative, talented, ferociously wanting to write, can go there and find similar success.

In the mid-1970s I'd had a few stories sell but working as a sales manager and raising a large family, I was not writing at all. One night I had a Mary Wollstonecraft Shelley-like nightmare and was up early, fascinated by its content. It may be important that I stayed put; rising might have chased it away. I was astounded to find that there was so much detail, I reconstructed it as a novel, laid out for me chapter by chapter! I didn't know the names of the children or the monster living down the hall from them, but I saw each of them clearly as I lay on my side, remembering this strange intruder into my dreams.

I got up, located a notebook and pen, and began jotting down the whole nightmare just as my unconscious mind had presented it to me. The first names of the girl and boy, Peg and Eric, leapt instantly to mind; otherwise, it was an exact replica of my dream, and I decided to start writing it that weekend. I named it *The Offspring*, and while it didn't sell until I'd become the published author of seven other novels, the book won me my first agent, who sold novel two.

That was the one in which I *consciously tried* to do what I'd done before—lie in bed and attempt to coax my creative right hemisphere into telling *me*, the author, a story. But there was a significant difference: I had seen the movie *The Omen* and liked it but sensed that I had an entirely different "take" on the Antichrist theme. So my unconscious mind knew what I wanted—I had programmed it to that degree—and the magic happened again! I wrote several chapters plus an outline of what, once more, I had "seen" in my thoughts, and in 1979 *The Ritual* became my first published novel.

I had no idea that there was a name for what I was doing with my imagination, or that there was anything unusual about it, until my wife, Mary, gave me Colin Wilson's marvelous book *Mysteries* on my birthday in 1979. By then I had visited the hypnagogic state often enough to have conceived all or part of the other seven novels and a few I eventually decided not to finish. Since novel eight, *The Offspring*, I've written and sold (at this date) 29 more novels and 126 of my 155 short stories.

In *Mysteries*, Wilson, arguably the most versatile writer of our time, wrote, "As you pass into unconsciousness, you linger briefly in a twilight realm that has been labeled the hypnagogic state." It also happens, apparently, in such realms *before* you awaken; although for all I know, the basic seeds for *The Offspring* and *The Ritual* were "planted" as I fell asleep, my unconscious mind developed the plots while I slept, and they were just "there" in the morning.

In my article "Releasing Creativity" (*The Inkling*, January 1984), I asked:

> Can you tap such an inexhaustible source? Read Wilson's next sentence: "Everyone has experienced these states, if only for a few seconds." They seem, he points out, independent of you, even thrown at you; they are often representational. He cites the psychologist, (Wilson) Van Dusen: "One doesn't explore these things for long without beginning to feel there is a greater wisdom in the inner processes than there is in ordinary consciousness."

Colin also alluded to research at the Menninger Foundation suggesting that all "states of creativity" may involve theta brain rhythms produced by individuals having hypnagogic imagery. Perhaps the idea for any story you have written came to you this way.

For your voyage to the twilight realm, you need to make arrangements not to be disturbed even for the usual important call or visits. Unless you do it at night and your bedmate is never restless, you'd be wise to choose a part of the day when your home and your neighborhood are customarily quiet. A vital point: *Never* is this a case of forcing anything. Your conscious mind should be void unless your need is to get an original, useful premise for a specific "theme" anthology or issue, or to find a way to complete chapter six, or perhaps to begin a book or story for which you already have a basic concept. Wandering off mentally in *those* instances to thoughts on what to have for dinner or how well your team's draft choice will fit in is the equivalent of asking your neighbors in for a party!

But then, you surely know the world must seem still for you to write at all. Visiting the hypnagogic state calls for a serious approach, even if you appear to be staring into space.

It seems to me the proof is in the pudding, and in what I can draw from my right hemisphere for *this chapter*. Truth is, in recent years I have resorted to "hypnagogis" mostly for short stories I was invited to create. Even when I wrote "Releasing Creativity" more than ten years ago, it had become possible for me to imagine novel ideas basically at will, sitting upright in my chair. *Bloodlines*, my 1994 hardcover, was born while my wife Mary and I were playing canasta late at night.

So, now—the man and his self-appointed challenge—ten ideas in twenty minutes!

I don't know if the ideas I'm about to seek while I sit before my typewriter will be good short story or novel ideas, or possibly just subtext (lesser ideas to be drawn from my file to make a more useful premise more substantial). All I can say beyond that is I wish the little girl speeding by my window on her tricycle would go home for dinner!

The clock is running:

1. A White House politician illegally requests files from the FBI detailing the private lives of more than one hundred people, including the President. Our pol discovers "facts" about the Prez that he knows are lies! Some research, and it becomes clear that the Chief Executive was *replaced* at some point by an impostor who *has no past*. Who and what is the President? Oh, by the way, because our pol has broken the

law to obtain these files, he cannot tell the FBI—and certainly not the man in the Oval Office!

2. A meeting of the best meteorologists at the Weather Network. The newest and youngest scientist, a chic woman, rises to announce her findings: It's late winter, people want to know when spring is coming— but her readings show no sign of a warming trend *anywhere*. "Yet I have this memo saying I must say there are temps in the middle sixties due over the next ten days." Jane is told, "There are." She asks boldly, "By whose authority?" A white-haired weatherman murmurs, "The government of the United States." Honest, she says, "Gentlemen, my long-range readings indicate that spring may not come at all this year. Nor summer. *Something's* wrong." The old weatherman says to an underling, "Willard, lock the conference room door until the Secretary arrives for our next briefing." Jane stares at them in shock. (Story might be called "Spring Will Be a Little Late This Year.")

3. A mid-teenage girl who has "felt funny" for weeks awakens in the hospital. Nurses treat her well but answer no questions, particularly the one about what was wrong with her—and why does she have a white bandage over her stomach. The nurses leave the fearful girl. She wants to see her boyfriend, Willie, and we find she is a virgin. She peels back the bandage and finds the remnant of an umbilical cord trailing from her navel. (I don't know what it means, no.)

4. A man is trying to quit smoking. One morning he hungers badly for a cigarette and locates a pack of his brand he had concealed. Tearing off the cellophane, he tries to tap one cigarette into view. A creature never seen before by any living man crawls out and eats its way through his chest into the closest lung. The last thing the man sees is the warning label on the edge of his cigarette pack and the words: *May be injurious to your health.*

5. Another man—*Jack*, that's what we call him—collapses in a seizure, then awakens to hear he has a brain tumor. It's benign and it's operable; surgery is planned in a month. But when he next undergoes an MRI, the tumor hasn't grown and surgery is not needed. The same test results occur six weeks later and again in another eight weeks. Now, amazingly, the tumor is shrinking! The neurosurgeon tells Jack it is incredibly rare, but isn't it wonderful? Jack attempts to go on with his life but the thought recurs and won't leave him, *What if I'm just imagining this and I'm in a vegetative state?* Everyone is thrilled for him but their reactions begin to seem abnormal to him. He wants to know, suddenly, where he *really* is. He starts to contact hospitals, then tells

people who care about him what he's doing. Afraid he will harm himself, Jack's wife puts him in a mental ward. Jack sees he has been a fool, but it may be too late. Then a huge door is left ajar! Jack escapes into a corridor, finds himself outside a door with a window. Inside, in a bed, head swathed in bandages but face exposed, lies . . . Jack himself! Staring at nothing. Jack tiptoes back to the psychiatric wing, claims he's well now, and is ultimately released. He and his wife lead an idyllic existence but sometimes Jack opens his eyes around 3 A.M. and imagines he's staring out a window at a hospital hallway.

6. A child-proof lighter drives aging, rich Margaret into a screaming breakdown. Her younger husband (number four) takes control of her funds. He throws away the lighter in which he had substituted water for lighter fluid and orders a new car.

7. A small boy is always told he must eat all his veggies or he might "get like Uncle Sydney." The kid loathes green food but obeys. For the first time he meets the great-great uncle, who comes for a holiday meal. The frail, emaciated man eats no turkey. Amazingly, he covers his plate with vegetables! Then he chokes, has a terrible coughing fit, and gasps his last words to the little boy: "I was as healthy as a horse 'till I turned ninety and your mother threatened to put me in a home unless I started eating more damn vegetables. As you value your life, boy, consume no more green food!" He dies with a racking cough, and one new pea rolls from his lips. Come spring, the boy pulls up everything Mom plants, always looking at her with suspicion. He stands a chance of growing up to become a veggie serial killer.

8. *The Bully* (a novel). Prologue: A young, bright student is teased, then beaten, by the high school bully. Asked to identify his attacker, he refuses. Worse, the boy knows he wouldn't squeal because he wants *personal* vengeance on the huge kid someday.

The novel takes place in the present and the bully hasn't changed, just grown. He beats his wife and child and commits crimes. Our protagonist, the ex-victim, is now a police detective. Evidence in a murder points to the bully; in an interrogation, the latter still verbally abuses the detective. Arresting the bully would be easy but the detective is not convinced of his guilt. Knowing the cop's wife from school, the bully phones her to say "*hi,*" beginning a sequence of taunts. Then the officer learns from Domestic that the bully battered his (the bully's) wife and she refuses to press charges. Our hero goes to her in the hospital, begs her to make a complaint. In retaliation, the bully actually visits the cop's wife and, without touching her, says what he'll do to her "one day"—

but it's his word against hers. This psychological thriller has the suspense note: *Which of these former students will break first and physically attack the other?* Each underestimates the other's commitment—to good *and* to evil.

(I may just decide to use this useful premise!)

9. Just like in many old and extremely politically incorrect jokes, a southern Baptist, a Catholic priest and a Jewish rabbi are on a plane when the pilot dies, and there is only one parachute. My creative right-mind tells me this is a serious story that explores an interesting point: Having heard the jokes before, which man will bring them up first and (mainly this) will all three plunge to certain death instead of quibbling over who gets the parachute?

10. UFO aliens are actually vampires. They abduct people for their usual bloody reasons, and the experiments the people remember are merely false "screen memories" for the bloodlettings they suffered. The aliens are gray in color for the obvious reason that they are the "un-dead." They have no intention of taking over the world beyond what they've already done because nobody capable of stopping them *believes* in them, and their food supply is, with Earth densely populated, unlim-ited. But one of them, a leader, makes the mistake of falling in love with his abductee . . .

Ten ideas!

But, a *confession* before closing this chapter.

It took over an hour for these ten ideas—not all useful premises—to appear on paper. In planning for twenty minutes, I did not allow for the time it would take to type my ideas into understandable form. Be-sides, by the time I'd put down premises as lengthy as the fifth and eighth, it got harder to slide back into my unconscious thoughts.

What turned out to be most remarkable to me was the disappear-ance of the little girl who was riding past my window back at the begin-ning of this exercise.

Bonus time for you—and *me*:

11. Useful premise: A writer getting in touch with his creative side wants a child on a trike to stop disturbing his concentration and go home to eat. Next day, she has vanished.

He finds her, red ribbon in her hair and all, the next time he needs to write a story about a little girl who interrupts a writer busily getting in touch with . . .

Mirror, Mirror

Wayne Allen Sallee

There are no vampires or werewolves in my world. The terrors I create usually come from the boy/girl next door or from my own mirror.

Isn't it always *the* question? New writers approach me at conventions or book signings and ask where I get my ideas. Each and every time, I reply that I live in Chicago, where the most vile deeds do occur, often for the most absurd reasons.

Where do I *not* get ideas?

But there are those writers who live in small towns or supposedly safe suburbs who do not have the benefit of witnessing odd characters acting out cathartic scenarios unless relatives are over for Thanksgiving dinner. (And, that is not to say that senseless crimes and squalor only occur in the Big City. In recent years, I have found increasing amounts of "fiction-fodder" in my father's hometown of Shelbyville, Kentucky, where several events rival any Chicago claim of a monopoly on wickedness.)

Newspapers are good sources, and television is even better. One local news station touted itself as "your window to the world." Watch any given edition (or episode, depending on your level of cynicism) of your local news. Then stop and think about just how you can possibly startle someone with your prose when the anchorpersons at five, six, and ten o'clock are doing a bang-up job of it already.

Put Yourself in the Picture

I had never planned to look into the mirror and bastardize my own life experiences as a native Chicagoan. But it is the easiest groove to fall into, particularly because I choose more often than not to write in first person-narrative point of view.

What I found hard, though, was the story itself. I had the setting; the love/hate relationship every area writer has with this city had long ago invaded even my dreams. My first dozen or so stories, written in about six months, I approached as I would scribing a confessional (another mirror of sorts).

Going back to the evening news and its "If It Bleeds, It Leads" standards, I projected myself as an invisible bystander to actual occurrences in Chicago's passing parade. On paper, I let it all play out differently, the character's actions answering, or at least defining more clearly, my darkest questions about myself.

Only the fates have been changed to protect the innocent.

Those early stories, about a woman murdered beneath an elevated platform as one lone man looks on, a drunk who disappears from a strip joint and is found at the bottom of a quarry the next day, and several more from the vantage point of commuter and/or observer, were all heavy on atmosphere. In fact, the first three stories I wrote had not one line of dialogue. But the reader was given smells and sights, from the shape of the downtown skyline to the amount of dirt beneath a little boy's fingernails. From the manner of dress of people on the street to the type of reading material each chose for the train ride home. Describing something as common as a man bending down to tie his shoelace or something as patently absurd—to some people—as a young woman applying mascara while sitting on a lurching bus.

My images from public transportation notwithstanding, each of the scenes I've just described can be dreamed up by a writer living in the smallest of towns, in which the skyline is a water tower set against a billion stars.

"Sometimes, people cannot detach themselves from the original circumstances and see the ways in which the writer has had to, for aesthetic reasons, transform not only the circumstances but also the characters." So says Richard Stern, a much lauded novelist living in Chicago's Hyde Park neighborhood. I cannot agree more. Whether you are writing about your Uncle Vern and Auntie Nurleen, your first employer (only you changed his name to *Jerry* Mizel, see), or a camp counselor from your childhood, someone out there might take umbrage at being described as a tyrant or buffoon. You cannot let yourself think of these matters. There is a potential tale to be told in the eyes of any single person you encounter. Life is a game you learn as you go, even if the playing board is tattered and worn. If you can think of writing in those terms, you will see we're *all* in the game, all on that same board.

And the thimble game piece is as interesting as the top hat or the race car.

Getting in the Game

Carry a pencil nub and a notepad, or lug that laptop to the corner tavern or coffee shop and choose a "game piece." Write a thumbnail sketch about that person, describing his appearance, mimicking his speech pattern, or making mention of his body movement. What is your subject eating or drinking? What song does he play on the jukebox?

Mentioning brand names or models of cars or rock groups indige-nous to 1997 America might get you be labeled "contemporary," and there is nothing wrong with that. And do not think that using contem-porary icons to describe your characters and situation will soon make your work seem dated and muddled. This is not so. Lovecraft never gave us the exact address of his Shunned House, though it does exist and is part of the Providence, Rhode Island, guided tour. But Stephen King gladly tells us the beer of choice for every Maine inhabitant from Jerusalem's Lot to Castle Rock.

I mention the icons of our everyday lives, I suppose, to give you a sense of something familiar. Surround yourself with the commonplace and the prosaic, and you'll find that replacing "fast food restaurant" with McDonald's or WaffleSteak will give both you and the reader de-cidedly different settings.

Now, the flip side of this advice—reasons *not* to use an actual place, be it franchise or national chain. Simply put, if you invent your own commercial abattoir, anything and everything goes within its con-fines, with no threat of maligning a corporation or, even worse, fostering reader disbelief. All right, we know acts ranging from murder to embez-zlement to the unimaginable have occurred at late-night mini-marts across the country, but it might still be in your best interest to make up a place if, say, it featured circus clowns wrestling Sumo style with wagers taken on the side. The sole reason Chicago was never specifically an-nounced as the setting for the 1980s cop show *Hill Street Blues* was that Police Captain Frank Furillo's city was *entirely* corrupt. The net-work needn't have worried; come Election Day, our unofficial motto is "Vote Early, and Vote Often!" If written distinctly enough, the ficti-tious can be made into an icon, too.

The icons, real or invented, are part of the ritual: the ceremonies of our workday and our nightlife.

Several years ago, *New Blood*, a horror paperback anthology of works by mostly first-sale writers under the age of thirty, was published. The book made me reminisce about my college writing workshops. *New Blood* was filled with tales like the stories we shared in that University of Illinois classroom—stories by young writers who were working hard to bring readers into their—the writers'—familiar surroundings. Into the formalities of their—the writers'—lives. If the story focused on a clerk in a mail room, you could bet that the writer once held such a job, if he were not still employed as such. That held true in my 1982 workshops. The college stories were about frustrations with classes, the opposite sex, even tuition and the transit system.

Perhaps I had no social life back then, and certainly found no horrors in working for a retail clothing store, because my story was about the attack beneath the elevated tracks. The impetus for such a tale came equally from my habit of devouring the morning newspapers and from the fact that my father was a Chicago police officer. (Something to keep in mind, close family members or even co-workers can provide a jump-start to your story if you believe your own experiences to be less than spectacular.) I said earlier that my first three stories contain no direct dialogue. I wanted the reader to be overwhelmed by the sputtering neon and angular shadows, the smells from the street mixed in the autumn air with sounds of both impatience and complacency.

I guess this approach worked. The late Karl Edward Wagner chose that first story, "Rapid Transit," for DAW's *Year's Best Horror* despite, in his words, "the less-than-polished writing," and because I had created (also in his words) "images that he could not get out of his mind."

Certainly, my approach to that story today would make it better constructed, but most new writers would agree that the impact of images that will stay in an editor's memory is a necessary and great boon.

No, the murder of my fictitious victim, Quita McLean, never occurred, yet aside from her killing, *every* sight and sound that filtered through my protagonist, Dennis Cassady, was witnessed by me one October night in 1982. The descriptions you will create are always just an arm's-length to infinity away.

The Horror of the Mind

I've mentioned characters and settings. I've talked about carrying those blank scraps of paper around, of writing everything down, no matter how seemingly banal. You can sort through it all later. But exactly what is it you will be discarding? What truths will remain? What *horrors* will remain?

When asked why I write psychological horror, I always reply that this form is the most intimate way to reach a reader. Think about it. Whether it is an aversion to spiders or a shadowy figure in the alley behind an apartment building, you've got your readers, and you've got 'em *good*, even if they have a "Been There/Done That/Bought the T-Shirt" feeling of superiority. The true and pristine horror is that of the unknown, and so those latter readers who look at the genre with condescension are still showing a reaction, be it in denial at being frightened, or in ignorance of today's indignities.

Most of us write about what moves us most. And I believe that this is true particularly in the field of horror.

Horrors, real or imagined, are all around us. In an increasing number of instances, they can be both real *and* imagined. Welcome to the realm of the inner demons. With the increasing awareness of different behavioral traits, new writers may have a fresh angle on terror. Things that go bump in the night are no longer ghosts or succubi, but the heightened heartbeat of someone suffering from OCD (obsessive-compulsive disorder) and its attendant cousins; or, as at least one well-known horror novelist has written of, repeated alien abductions.

New Directions

Earlier I mentioned the difficulties of coming up with more terrifying story ideas than true-life incidents that can be virtually witnessed on a television news program. Think about it. With whom, or what, did Poe or Lovecraft have to compete? Perhaps I oversimplify the matter, but I might suppose the only competition for both were the public's memories of The War of 1812 and World War I respectively. Even the infamous Jack the Ripper wasn't a terror to be reckoned with until the advent of the pulps, forty years after he murdered the women of Whitechapel.

Conversely, the world we now live in allows new writers to embrace a broader range of topics. At the turn of the century, Stephen Crane wrote on how he was too busy running from demons (the way he did this was in making sense of his world in his prose) to attempt to find out why they'd singled him out in the first place. Now, in our time, those demons, or their hosts, are appearing on talk shows daily.

My own ideas of horror have changed. I have accepted that there will always be the vampire, either romanticized or brutal, still as big a cash cow as the next installment of Must-See-TV. In the decade I've been professionally published, vampire novels have consistently appeared, along with shared-world anthologies and role-playing game tie-ins. But, whereas my leanings are not towards vampires or anything supernatural, I do realize that to write successfully about the undead, I would have to treat each one as I would a living human being. In fact, giving your supernatural characters certain human traits or afflictions, as I did when I wrote of a werewolf with Huntington's chorea, may propel your story further, as well as make it more memorable.

On most any convention panel, the question will be brought up regarding "the direction horror is headed." To concern yourself with this is as potentially destructive as equating the money you make per story with the amount of time spent writing it. No matter "directions," categories, genres, subgenres, whether your terrors are archetype or topical—your characters must be timeless.

As long as you can look into and through the mirror, whether real or pretend, be it atop your dresser plastered with postcards and family photos or a bus or train window tagged with graffiti, if you can look and see the humanity, the common struggles and the little victories, then you will always be able to place your own signature, your style, on your work.

As Richard Stern said, "The best and worst readers of your work are those who provide stimulus, even partial models, for it."

If you want my spin on it, I always recall Roy Scheider portraying Bob Fosse in *All That Jazz.* He'd take a long look in the mirror and say, "It's Showtime!"

It's Showtime!

Now go to it.

Dark Light Focus: Karl Edward Wagner

Robert E. Weinberg

While there are a number of fine writers in the horror field, and a much smaller number of fine editors, there is just a handful of individuals who do both well. The task becomes twice as difficult when those tasks span several genres. Without question, one of the very best at managing both careers simultaneously was Karl Edward Wagner.

As an author, Karl made his mark in two genres. His sword-and-sorcery stories featuring Kane, the mystic swordsman, were incredibly popular, earning him a huge following among the fans of Robert E. Howard. Equally successful were his straight horror stories in the horror genre, many of them focusing on Karl's own background in abnormal psychology. His fiction won numerous awards, and he was considered one of the finest short-story writers in the fantasy and horror fields in the 1980s.

Karl Edward Wagner possessed a unique and powerful fictional voice. His tales of Kane were not heroic fantasy adventures with a noble hero venturing into far-off lands. Instead, Kane was a cursed, amoral killer who wandered a nightmarish earth filled with demonic creatures and half-mad gods. Based on the Gothic villain, Melmoth the Wanderer, Kane was much less a hero than a survivor. Though publishers classified the Kane stories as heroic fantasy, they are unquestionably evocative and powerful works of horror.

Just as intense were Karl's modern horror stories. Much of his work was based on his own dreams and nightmares, and tales like "Sticks" and "Neither Brute Nor Human" evoked haunting images that were not easily forgotten. Karl used his background in psychology in many of his most frightening tales. His "River of Night's Dreaming" is one of the most unsettling horror stories ever set down on paper.

During the years he was writing, Karl was also editing anthologies in the same two genres. He helped assemble three volumes of Conan stories for Berkley Books, and later put together several excellent sword-and-sorcery collections for Tor. In the horror field, he served for more than a decade as the editor of the DAW Books annual series *The Year's Best Horror Stories*. Karl possessed the knack for finding unique short stories in the strangest places. Always a friend to the small-press publisher, he did more to publicize their efforts than any other editor who ever worked in the horror genre.

Karl Edward Wagner died comparatively young. His output compared to that of many other writers in the genre is small. But what he wrote shines among the very best. It will not be forgotten.

Honest Lies and Darker Truths
History and Horror Fiction

Richard Gilliam

L et us start with an observable fact: Many commercially success-ful novels and motion pictures pay only slight attention to his-torical accuracy. This is true in horror fiction just as it is in other types of historical storytelling. Let us also observe that these inaccuracies are found in many outstanding works of literature and drama, and that faithfulness to history does not by itself create compelling stories.

This places me at somewhat of a quandary. I've always valued accuracy in writing, and the skillful use of historic facts to enhance a story. Yet I concede to being a fan of the motion picture *Braveheart*, which uses the names of actual persons and places but which grossly violates both the facts and the issues surrounding William Wallace. Nor do the events in the film conform to the known history of the era. Nor was the historic Isabella the likable person we find in the film. (She caused her husband, King Edward II, to be murdered and then, with her lover Roger de Mortimer, ruled England corruptly until her son Edward III overthrew them and assumed power in 1330.)

Accuracy vs. Relevance

Does it matter that *Braveheart* has only a tenuous relationship to the era of history in which it's supposedly set? What's more important is that *Braveheart* has relevance to today's world, and that its central issues resonate with current audiences. It's very likely that the film *Braveheart*, historical inaccuracies and all, spurred a significant part of the recent increase in interest in Scottish history. It's probable that because of *Braveheart* many more people have taken the time to read about William Wallace than would have done so otherwise.

And perhaps most important, particularly to us, as writers: As a story, *Braveheart* is outstanding. There has long been a place in litera-ture for the "pseudo-historical" fable that tells its lies honestly, and *Braveheart* occupies that place well.

There is, though, a danger that the fictional image may overwhelm the historical one. Certainly there are many examples of inaccurate propaganda being advanced to further unworthy political or social agendas. It's a dangerous game to tamper with history for the sake of convenient storytelling. Still, every work of fiction in some way must deviate from objective history; it is the nature of fiction to do so. Each writer must determine individually the standards and limits for abstractions from the objective world.

Researching Your Lies

What methods, then, should a writer use for historic research—assuming that the writer is interested in an honest recreation of a historic setting? There isn't any "one size fits all" answer—you'll find a wide range of successful methods and successful authors. For the help it might be, here are some of my experiences in researching historical fiction.

The first historical fiction I attempted was "Caroline and Caleb," a 20,000-word novella written for the Civil War anthology *Confederacy of the Dead*. I primarily used the reference books in my personal library and supplemented that with research at the public library in Clearwater, Florida, where I was living at the time.

The story is set in eastern Tennessee following the end of the U.S. Civil War. I grew up in northern Alabama, had visited eastern Tennessee often, and already had a pretty clear idea of what the geography was like; I didn't need a new research trip to the area. There were three primary areas of research I felt were needed for this project.

The Historical Setting

The first area, obviously, was the Civil War itself. For example, in today's military, recruits from all parts of the country serve together, but that wasn't the case in the 1860s. Individual states raised their own armies, which meant that most of the persons from a particular region of a state would likely be known to have fought in a specific set of battles and campaigns. Even though the story begins some months after the end of the war, that was the sort of historical detail I wanted to make the story more interesting. Most people are probably unaware that Tennessee raised armies for both the Confederacy and the Union. To get these elements and the characters introduced, I started the story with Caleb and his father attending a Sunday church service as part of a congregation whose members included both Northern and Southern veterans. Thus I was able to get a good bit of the historical exposition out of the way early, which is often a good thing to do in storytelling:

Once the setting is established, the writer can then get on with building a strong narrative flow and sharpening character development.

The Environmental Setting

The second area that required research, was plants, animals and geology. This was pretty much a matter of going to the Clearwater library and using natural history books to verify information. Nonetheless, in early drafts I made one mistake in flora and fauna—I had grizzly bears instead of black bears living in the Smoky Mountains. Fortunately, a friend caught the error while proofing the story and it's correct in all print versions of the story. For reasons of storytelling, I made a deliberate decision to include a red wolf and a raven in the story even though neither species is thought to have still inhabited eastern Tennessee by the 1860s. The reason I did this ties in with the third area of research.

The Religious Setting

A major theme of "Caroline and Caleb" is the contrast between the religious beliefs of the Cherokees, who were indigenous to eastern Tennessee, and those of the white settlers who displaced them. I knew plenty of Protestants, so researching that history was easier—I called my sister and asked a few questions, mostly having to do with how the annual church calendar (Easter, Christmas, etc.) affected the themes of sermons. For the Cherokee religious beliefs, I turned to my friend Owl Goingback, whose story "Spoils of War" also appears in *Confederacy of the Dead*. Owl, who has lectured throughout the country on the customs and folklore of Native Americans, explained that not until the 1800s, after about three centuries of cultural contamination, did the Cherokee begin keeping written records of their ceremonies. That made its way into the story both in an expository section that foreshadowed later developments and again symbolically through the Cherokee spirit the Raven Mocker, who is himself corrupted after being exposed to the Christian concept of damnation.

You may find interesting one small decision I made to deviate from Cherokee symbology. According to Joseph Campbell and other writers, the sun is primarily a female Cherokee symbol, though there are some examples of Cherokee representations of the sun as male. I used the sun as a male symbol for Caleb and plant life as the female symbol for Caroline. I probably would have been uncomfortable having one of my male Cherokee characters represented by the sun, but I think it was appropriate for the story and for Caleb.

How does all this historical background relate to horror writing? The plot of "Caroline and Caleb" is pretty simple: Boy meets girl. Boy marries girl. Monster threatens community. Monster is defeated.

My idea was to use setting and background to build to a horrific event that could only be overcome by the defeating of the Raven Mocker. In Cherokee beliefs, the Raven Mocker tears people's hearts out. While many dark events are mentioned in the story, there's only one horrifically graphic portion of "Caroline and Caleb," and that occurs just prior to the final confrontation. Some people believe horror stories should maintain a horrific tone from beginning to conclusion and end on a downbeat note, and certainly I'll agree that many fine stories follow that structure. Even though by the end of "Caroline and Caleb" all the major characters have been killed, the story has a redemptive conclusion. If horror fiction tends to have unhappy endings, then I suggest that horror fiction set during unhappy periods of history tends to have "even less happy" endings, and that the unhappy periods of history are often the most interesting.

The What-if Story

One form of historical story is the "what-if" story based on one deliberately selected deviation from history. The reader knows up front that this is an "alternate history," that the writer is speculating on what might have occurred.

A possible problem with this structure is that the premise is often more interesting than the story. Another is that the personality of the subject may be at odds with the premise. I once proposed to Timothy Leary a story in which, instead of leaving the West Point cadet corps, Leary would remain in the military and become the commanding U.S. general during the Vietnam War. Leary loved the idea, and someday I may write the story—*if* I can figure out how to be faithful to the person Timothy Leary was while presenting the story as a credible premise. After all, Leary's conflicts with the inflexible rules at West Point and his later similar problems at Alabama and Harvard are central to why he became an icon of his era. Iconoclasm and civil disobedience are traits rarely sought in military commanders. Indeed, almost by definition, anyone who rises to command an army cannot have them.

I had a much easier time envisioning an alternate history about the Roman emperor Caligula, "Phantoms of the Night," for the anthology *Phantoms of the Night*. The "what-if" here is that rather than being assassinated by his guards, Caligula escapes into hiding, returning to Rome only decades later when he becomes haunted by the ghosts of his past. The point gets back to honest lies—it's easily believable that Caligula might have escaped and that he would continue to be ruthlessly insane just as he was when he ruled Rome. Timothy Leary as a military commander would not be an honest lie. If that idea worked at all, it would most likely be at a gimmick or exploitation level with the premise more interesting than the story.

It's probably easier to write a credible "what-if" horror story about a horrible person, or perhaps about a nice person who lives in horrible times. While there have been several excellent horrific alternate-history stories and novels in recent years, it continues to be an under-utilized form that is perhaps more popular with readers than with authors.

The Parable

Yet another sort of historical story is the parable that substitutes a historical situation for a contemporary one. For examples we can look to the "McCarthy Era," the shameful period in the United States in the 1950s when accusing someone of being a "Communist" was sufficient evidence to ruin the person's career. Those who spoke out against McCarthyism were often investigated for supposedly being unpatriotic or, worse, sympathizers to the Communist cause. This created a chilling effect that stifled both political dissent and the creative arts. It was decades later before Hollywood was willing to make movies about the McCarthy era. Nonetheless, some writers used historical stories to criticize the social and political climate. *The Crucible*, *Inherit the Wind*, and *High Noon* used historical events—the Witch trials of Massachusetts, the 1925 Scopes trial, the American West—to mirror the problems of the contemporary era. Such metaphoric stories are rare in horror fiction, perhaps because horror fiction is so seldom concerned with political events.

What About Gothic Horror?

I have thus far not discussed what is commonly called "Gothic" fiction, partly because entire books have been written about Gothic fiction and also because Gothic fiction encompasses far more than historical fiction. It is worth noting, I think, that when Mary Wollstonecraft Shelley wrote *Frankenstein*, the setting was contemporary to her—as was the setting for Bram Stoker when he wrote *Dracula*. Most commercially successful horror fiction has a contemporary setting, and this is true of both nineteenth century and twentieth century horror fiction. The primary current exception is Anne Rice, whose novels frequently use both historic and contemporary settings. Rice uses vivid historical detail to establish mood and draw the reader into the world of the protagonist. Creating that world for the reader is at the heart of good historical fiction writing.

Methods of Research

The methods writers use to research vary drastically. The great "true adventures" writer Daniel Mannix felt that experiencing the event was part of the process of writing. Thus when asked to write an article on vampire bats, Mannix obtained several vampire bats and wrote about how it felt when they bit him and fed from his arm. On the other hand, Bram Stoker wrote *Dracula* without ever traveling to Transylvania—indeed, he seldom left Ireland during the period when most of his work was published.

It's also worth noting that authors often change methods of research. When writing *Memos from Purgatory*, Harlan Ellison joined a street gang so he could write about the subject convincingly. The result was one of the landmarks of Ellison's career and led to his career in Hollywood as a writer for film and television. Some years later when writing *Mephisto in Onyx,* he spent hours on the telephone interviewing the warden at Alabama's death row prison and then wrote about the prison so convincingly that he continues to receive letters from inmates asking when he visited there. With all respect to the younger Harlan who rumbled in the Bronx and to Daniel Mannix and his vampire bats, there are easier ways than personal experience to research a story, particularly if you're writing about what it's like to be a death-row inmate. Raymond Chandler said it nicely: There are only two professions where you need to know how to rob a bank—and one of them is being a writer.

Are there absolute maxims specific to the writing of historical horror fiction? I think not. The elements of good writing important to any form of fiction are important to all horror fiction and to all historical fiction. Readers want to be taken someplace they haven't visited—or perhaps someplace they've visited before and enjoyed. Writers create historical fiction for many of the same reasons. And horror writers? Creating horror from history takes us on an intriguing search for those darker truths that reside amidst the honest lies.

What You Are Meant to Know

Robert Weinberg

Breaking into the horror field isn't easy. Even if you use every tip, every suggestion in this book, there is no guarantee you'll make it. Markets expand and contract, change and disappear all the time. Still, it's always toughest for a beginning writer to sell that first story. There's lots and lots of competition. Plenty of people want to become rich and famous like Stephen King and Anne Rice. Others just want to see their name in print.

No matter your answer to the question, *Why do I write horror?*, you need to convince an editor to buy your masterpiece.

And to accomplish that, you need to be original.

When editors say they're looking for the next Stephen King or Anne Rice or Dean Koontz or John Saul, they don't mean they want to find someone who writes exact imitations of those authors' works. Instead, they're hunting for authors who bring that same spark of originality and excitement to their work.

Anne Rice writes about vampires and witches—such monsters have been a popular staple in fiction for a hundred years. John Saul writes about children in dire peril—another oft-used theme since fiction was invented. Both of these authors though, have given new life to old concepts. They've taken basic themes and ideas and looked at them in different ways. Creativity sells.

The biggest problem faced by many new writers is not lack of skills. They've learned how to write, know the basic structure of a story, understand the rules of grammar and punctuation. However, there is one area of their education that has been sorely neglected. They don't know much about their subject. It's difficult—nearly impossible, actually—to be original if you do not know what else has been written.

Horror fiction did not begin with Stephen King. There's no doubt that he is the most popular practitioner ever to write in this particular field. But there are plenty of other important and influential writers. Here is a checklist of twenty-one books anyone who wants to write horror should read. It's not everything worth studying. There are books aplenty; and plenty more. This list is just a starting point. The more familiar you are with your subject, the better. But without *these* books, you're beginning the race a lap behind the competition. (This list is arranged in roughly chronological order.)

1. *Frankenstein* by Mary Wollstonecraft Shelley: Forget the Boris Karloff movies, and the Hammer adaptations. Read the book itself to see what it says and does not say about the meaning of being human. At least one major critic has called *Frankenstein* the first science-fiction novel. It may be that, but it is also a horror novel that has endured for over 150 years. A great book, it raises important questions about life and death, good and evil that are still being debated today. Though slow-moving by today's standards, *Frankenstein* remains one of the cornerstones of horror fiction.

2. *Dracula* by Bram Stoker: Again, "no" on the movie versions—all of them. They are distinctive and flashy and reflect various directors' and actors' interpretations of the novel. Seeing a film is like getting your news secondhand. If you want to be a horror writer, you *must* go to the original source material: the horror writing. Anyone who dreams of being a horror writer must read *Dracula*. The book, though overwritten and melodramatic, is filled with powerful images. The action scenes are fast and furious, the horror intense and replete with strong descriptions. *Dracula*, though written a century ago, still moves well. It stands as the most important book ever written in the horror genre.

3. *The Ghost Pirates* by William Hope Hodgson: Hodgson was a sailor before he became a writer. His promising career was cut short when he was killed in a major battle in World War I. Much of his reputation rests on his short stories of the sea, which are atmospheric and filled with menace. He wrote four novels, three of which are more fantasy than horror (*The House on the Borderland, The Nightland,* and *The Boats of the Glen Carrig*). All of them are worth reading. Hodgson had a gift for describing ominous, gruesome monsters that few writers even today can match. However, his novel, *The Ghost Pirates,* is not about monsters but about ghosts. It tells in straightforward, almost journalistic manner how a ship is overwhelmed by ghostly invaders. Hodgson makes no effort to identify the menacing figures—they could be the ghosts of dead pirates or beings from another dimension. All that counts is their gradual capture of the boat. It is one of the finest examples of the "tightly written" novel ever published.

4. *Collected Ghost Stories of M.R. James:* Montague Rhodes James was a Don at Oxford University who delighted his friends by telling

old-fashioned ghost stories. When put down on paper, these tales formed the most popular collection of ghost stories ever written in the English language. While not the first English ghost-story writer, James is the most famous and the best. His stories are perfectly told, meticulously crafted, building slowly but steadily to the inevitable climax. James never failed to deliver, and his tales are filled with malevolent ghosts, ancient curses and demonic creatures. James's fiction influenced numerous writers, and for decades after the publication of his work most ghost stories were written in his style.

5. *Burn Witch Burn* by A. Merritt: Abraham Merritt's roots were in the pulp magazines of the 1920s and 1930s, and it shows in his fiction. He was one of the most famous writers of those publications, and his novels were extremely popular. Though regarded by most as a fantasy author of "lost race" adventures, Merritt wrote several novels that crossed over into the horror field. Of these, *Burn Witch Burn* was the most successful and most important. The story deals with an evil crone who turns people into demonic dolls to commit crimes for her. What raises the book above standard pulp fare is that the witch's nemesis is a crime kingpin, a typical gangster of the 1930s, and his band of hoodlums. In an interesting reversal, a lesser evil battles a greater evil as the modern world fights a menace from ancient times. Merritt knew more about pacing and narrative than just about anyone. This novel sweeps the reader along in the best pulp tradition. In *Burn Witch Burn* Merritt wrote a horror thriller that works as well today as it did sixty years ago.

6. *To Walk the Night* by William Sloane: In the 1930s, genre fiction was not so clearly defined and writers were more willing to bend the rules for the sake of a good story. Think Dean Koontz and Stephen King were the first to write science-fiction novels that were also horror stories? Read Sloane's *To Walk The Night*. This book combines horror, science fiction and mystery into one of the smoothest presentations ever set on paper. The secret at the heart of the story is no surprise now, but in its time the book set the pattern for all those that followed. The author's other horror novel, *The Edge of Running Water*, is equally recommended.

7. *The Dunwich Horror & Others* by H.P. Lovecraft: Lovecraft turned horror fiction away from the ghosts of M.R. James and focused attention on the huge, unknown universe that surrounds us. The concept of "cosmic horror" perhaps was not invented by Lovecraft, but he popularized it. His stories work best at novelette length: "The Dunwich

Horror," "The Thing on the Doorstep," "The Call of Cthulhu." But all his fiction is worth reading. Lovecraft had his weaknesses (lack of characterization and dialogue are the worst), but his talent at hinting at the monstrous horrors lurking in the dark corners of our world remains unmatched more than a half century after his death.

8. *Fear* by L. Ron Hubbard: Many newer writers believe psychological horror was invented just a few years ago. Not true. Back in 1940, L. Ron Hubbard wrote this short novel about a professor searching for an hour of time he cannot remember—and the dire consequences of his actions. Is this the story of a man haunted by demons of the supernatural, or by the demons within his own mind? *Fear* is overwritten in spots but still packs a real punch. It is one of those trend-setting novels that helped redefine modern horror.

9. *Darker Than You Think* by Jack Williamson: Werewolves are the stock and trade of horror fiction. There have been numerous werewolf movies, even werewolf comic books. But most people can't name the great werewolf novels, because in a field filled with memorable vampire books, horrific serial killer novels and terrifying visions of cosmic horror, memorable werewolves are in woefully short supply. The title that stands above the rest is Jack Williamson's *Darker Than You Think*. It brought werewolves into the twentieth century and is filled with dark, powerful images. It remains the definitive werewolf novel, even though it first appeared in print in 1940.

10. *Conjure Wife* by Fritz Leiber: In the early 1940s, the pulp magazine *Unknown* (later titled *Unknown Worlds*) pulled horror out of the English manor house and into mainstream urban America. *Fear* and *Darker Than You Think* both appeared first in *Unknown*, as did this novel by Fritz Leiber, who was one of the first authors to postulate that ghosts and witches would change with the times. His short story "Smoke Ghost" told of new spirits, unfriendly spooks, that haunted big cities. In *Conjure Wife* he mixed witchcraft and black magic with college campus politics. It remains one of the most influential novels ever written.

11. *I Am Legend* by Richard Matheson: Matheson is one of the true giants of our field. Though known primarily for his short stories, his few novels are equally well crafted and important. This tale, a blend of science fiction and horror, could be labeled *the* ultimate vampire novel as the entire population of the Earth are turned into monsters. It demonstrates that a horror novel can be more than just a series of

shocks. Matheson explores the importance of legends and horror in a manner unique to the genre.

12. *Rosemary's Baby* by Ira Levin: Horror broke out of the pulp ghetto due to the popularity of several books. This novel, by a writer not previously associated with genre fiction, was one of the works that led the escape. It is subtle, well-written and quite frightening. The movie made from the book is excellent, but the novel stands nicely on its own. Again, it takes horror out of the countryside and haunted manors and puts it right in New York high-rise apartment buildings.

13. *The Collected Short Stories of Richard Matheson*: Much of the finest horror writing is done in short-story format. If you want to know how to do it, study two writers: Ray Bradbury and Richard Matheson. This book, filled with startling images, horrific visions and waking nightmares, is a textbook on how to write a horror story. Matheson can be subtle or shocking, but his work is always innovative, literate and challenging. What makes it so spectacular is how often he is able to catch the reader completely off guard with his endings. Many people think Matheson is the finest horror short story writer ever. This book offers strong evidence to support that claim.

14. *Hell House* by Richard Matheson: Haunted houses have been a standard device in horror and supernatural fiction for well over a hundred years. But, a good writer can take a well-worn device and make it seem new. This book is very scary, without being overly gory. Matheson knows how to push all the right buttons, and does exactly that in this modern horror thriller.

15. *The October Country* by Ray Bradbury: Before he mellowed with age, Ray Bradbury was one of the finest horror writers of the 1940s and early 1950s. Mellowed or otherwise, he is also one of our finest living short-story writers. *The October Country*, a collection that includes many of his best pieces from his early days, is another sustained lesson on how to do it right.

16. *Something Wicked This Way Comes* by Ray Bradbury: Bradbury is much weaker as a novelist than a short story writer. But that does not mean he doesn't know how to write a long piece. This book, with its wonderfully evocative title (taken from Shakespeare's *Macbeth*) works on many levels. But most of all, it is scary and literary at the same time, a trick rarely accomplished.

17. *The Exorcist* by William Peter Blatty: More than any other book, this novel is credited with popularizing modern horror fiction.

The Exorcist returned religious themes to horror and clearly defined the ongoing battle between good and evil. Though filled with shock after shock, the story primarily works because Blatty makes you care about the characters. As in all such novels, the evil proves to be much more cunning than first realized, and the menace is much greater than expected. The movie version of this novel helped make this one of the best selling horror novels of all time.

18. *Falling Angel* by William Hjortsberg: Horror and mystery fiction are close companions. However, it is a rare combination that combines supernatural horror with the private eye genre and makes it work. This novel takes some old ideas and twists them into something new and compelling. The horror is frightening; the mystery is well presented; the ending is both shocking and yet logical. Perhaps the best hardboiled horror novel ever written.

19. *Salem's Lot* by Stephen King: Undoubtedly Stephen King is *the* most popular horror writer ever. His books have sold millions (and millions and millions) of copies and he is one of the favorite authors of this generation. King's success is no fluke. He writes books that people want to read. His characters are ordinary people facing extraordinary circumstances. How they deal with the nature of good and evil makes fascinating reading. In *Salem's Lot*, King employs a standard horror theme and combines it with mainstream fiction techniques. Instead of focusing on the monster, King presents many different stories. By shifting emphasis from one or two main characters to the entire community of the town of Salem's Lot, he makes the evil all-pervasive and much more believable. King knows that the more *believable* a horror novel is, the more frightening it becomes.

20. *The Stand* by Stephen King: The end of the world as envisioned by Stephen King. There were other horror novels before *The Stand* that described a global holocaust. Lots of science-fiction novels did exactly that. But King was the first to link science fiction as the cause and supernatural horror as the aftermath. Again, mainstream fiction techniques are responsible for the book's success. Readers cared for the characters—whether they succeeded or failed, lived or died. The book was the first epic horror novel. It worked. There have been other epics since. *The Stand* remains the best.

21. *Watchers* by Dean Koontz: Dean Koontz over the course of several decades took the horror thriller of the 1920s and 1930s and reshaped it into a product for modern readers. Tough, competent heroes and heroines engage in life-or-death struggles with sinister forces,

from secret government agencies to science gone berserk, in a mad scramble that keeps readers flipping the pages of one best-seller after another. *Watchers*, though basically a science fiction story, works equally well as a horror novel. More important, it works as a gripping drama with characters readers care about. Those people who think horror novels can't be anything more than light entertainment have not read *Watchers*.

There you have twenty-one books. Read them all and you'll have some idea of what horror fiction is all about. Not a complete grasp of the field, since there are plenty of writers who are extremely important who don't have one defining book but a whole body of work that should be read and studied. Robert Bloch and Harlan Ellison are two authors who immediately come to mind.

But this list serves as a good starting point. Read these books; see what the authors did to make them work. Then take that same drive, that same ambition, that same vision, and apply it to your ideas.

The editors are waiting.

HORROR CRAFTING:

PLOT, CHARACTERS, MOOD AND MORE

Such Horrible People

Tina Jens

If you have carefully plotted your story from beginning to end and you are now planning to plug your characters into this so cleverly woven plot, you are *doomed*! That is, your story is doomed to failure.

But I'm the master puppeteer! I'll make my characters do whatever I want. I am in charge!

Wrong. Your people, the characters of your horror story, are not puppets. If you want to play with two-dimensional, paper-doll characters, you can *force* them to jump through your hoops. But if you want three-dimensional, "Is it live or is it Memorex?" characters, no way. Writing with three-dimensional characters is kind of like herding ducks. You can guide them in a general direction, but they're going to go where they want to.

That sounds like a lot of work. Why should I go to all the bother, if two-dimensional characters are so much easier to work with? After all, horror is about plot.

No it isn't. Horror is about how people react when they encounter the plot.

Even the coolest monster gets dull fast without a protagonist we can really care about, someone who acts in an intelligent, realistic way.

Take the movie *The Creature From the Black Lagoon*. The Gill Man. One of the *coolest* monsters ever created.

One of the dullest movies ever made.

Why? Because the supposedly intrepid and scientific exploration team was dull and dumb. They jumped through plot hoops instead of acting as individuals.

"Plot hoop," a definition: When a character does something really dumb, or so far "out of character" that the response is:

Yo! Why *are you chasing the zombie motorcycle gang into the dark room by yourself when backup's on the way?*

Why *are you going into the vampire's lair at midnight, when you could wait a few hours and do it safely in daylight?*

Plot hoops are what make people put down your book and turn on the TV, walk the dog or call up Auntie Em for a long chat. No one wants to read about puppets jumping through plot hoops.

So what can you do?

Find the Character First

Start by rearranging the steps in your writing project.

Don't plot, then create character. Start with your basic idea: Vampires invade small town. Man creates monster. Tornado carries girl to fantasy world.

Now, before you take your premise another step, find your characters. I like to start with "the bad guy." Put flesh on his bones, attitude on his lips and a driving passion in his brain.

Okay, back to plot for a moment. What is the monster's goal? To find a mother for the brood of teenage vampire boys? To seek revenge against an uncaring creator? To capture the girl with the magic shoes? Time! That's plenty of plotting—for now.

Back to characters.

Who is this monster likely to run up against? Who's going to be brave enough, smart enough, likely to happen by in your story's particular geographic location or fantastic milieu?

If your vampires live under a 1970s seaside boardwalk, your choices for a hero are going to be very different than those you would encounter in seventeenth century Rumania or the merry old land of Oz. But not all heroes are chosen by geography or historical era.

Sometimes careers determine monster and hero. If your story takes place on another planet, you're probably going to be dealing with astronauts and aliens. If your story is about a ghost riding the cyber waves of the Internet, chances are there's a computer expert somewhere nearby. If the people in your story are being mugged in back alleys and their internal organs taken when they were still using them, you can bet there's a doctor on call.

You know where your hero lives. You know that person's profession. Ready to return to plotting?

Nope. Don't. Not yet.

It's time to make a new best friend. Actually, a couple. It's time to get to know both your hero and your villain, painfully, intimately, well.

Borrow From Life

There are several ways to do this. One is to borrow a character from real life: your step-mom, your husband's boss, your second cousin's mechanic. This is a quick and easy path to characterization, and one fraught with peril. If real-lifers recognize themselves in story characters, and do not like what they see . . .

Best case scenario: You have a rift in the relationship.

Worst case: A libel suit.

Generally, I only use this technique when I'm in a hurry or I want to give a "present" to a close friend or relative. I follow two strict rules. I take bad habits or character flaws only from myself. If I'm borrowing from anybody else, I play up the good side. My friends and relatives are almost always cast as good guys.

I had a tight deadline and was doing a family crisis when I was trying to write a story for the anthology *The Secret Prophecies of Nostradamus*. I had problems bringing my heroine to life. So I borrowed—very liberally—from *me*, and then exaggerated those characteristics. Agent Charlie (don't ever call her Charlene) and I have the same taste in wine—though I don't drink as much as she. We both hate housework—though my bedroom isn't *quite* as messy as hers. And while I can be, let's say, "outspoken," Charlie can be downright rude. Of course, she's probably a little smarter, a little funnier and a little braver than I am, too.

As a Christmas gift to the family, I once "cast" two cousins as the fictional audience to an old woman's storytelling. "The Princess and the Frog," a modern retelling of the Cinderella story, can be found in *100 Wicked Little Witches*. Cuz One and Cuz Two provided nice dialogue and added depth and ambience to the story. And the family still likes me.

I suggest you do not cast your mother-in-law as the bitchy old neighbor lady. Don't cast your pastor as a demon from hell. And just to be on the safe side, don't cast your hometown as a generations-old warren for mangy, man-eating dogs. Not if you want to stay on good terms with family, friends and neighbors.

Start a Picture File

Another way I sometimes develop my characters is to pull out "the picture file." I clip interesting pictures of people, from magazines mostly. My best sources are *Rolling Stone* (really creative photographers!) and *People* (because of its profiles of such, ah, "odd" human specimens). But sales catalogs and *Newsweek* have provided interesting photos, too. Certain snapshots present a fully realized, flesh and blood, full-of-attitude character. If you look closely, you can almost see the lips move as the pictures talk to you and the photographees tell you all about themselves. When I need a character, I'll flip through the pictures until one stops me to say, "I can take on that monster. Just give me a chance."

Those are the fairly easy ways. But when they don't pan out . . .

Create a Character Sketch

A third and usually reliable way to create a living, breathing character is to create a "character sketch."

I generally start with basic personality type: Joker. Class Clown. Optimist. Pessimist. Rebel. Eco-warrior. Artist. Musician. Activist. Politician. Worrywart. Ant-sized self-esteem. Hippo-sized ego. Paranoid. Schizophrenic. Lovesick. Sick of love. Power-hungry. Computer nerd. Bimbo. Beauty queen.

Next, the name. Names can convey a great deal about the character. You didn't have the choice of your own name (at least, not way back then!), but you can pick your character's name. Make the choice count. Don't name your hero John Smith unless he's a Pilgrim or a wallflower. Give him a nickname. You may never use it in the story, but nicknames do a good job of highlighting the essence of the character.

What does the character look like? Tall, short, skinny, fat? Truly attractive or double-ugly? What does the character think about how he looks? Do others agree?

These choices can lead to excellent plotting possibilities for the story. The character stands four feet eight inches tall, the antidote is on the top shelf, and there's no chair or ladder in the locked room. How does she get it down? Or does she die trying?

What mode of transportation does the character use? Bicycle, moped, skateboard, El train, chauffeured limo? He drives a car? What make and model? A back-firing beater (two-tone job, primer and rust) or that near-silent purring Jaguar? Does it have a nickname? Is it clean or messy?

Clothing: New, used, wrinkled or torn, starched and pressed? Designer boutique, outlet mall, Am-Vets resale shop, or Aunt Gertrude hand-me-downs? Fashion: Anne Klein, Gothic, punk, corporate or grunge? How long does it take to get ready in the morning? Quick, because "I don't care how I look"? Or "I am obsessively efficient and manage my time well, thank you"?

Family history: Character needs a mom and dad with full names and occupations, even if mater and pater won't appear in the story. How does the character relate to these parents?

Best friend.

Home town.

Home town . . . Time to ask some questions: Did you grow up

there or did you move away? How do you feel about that? What religion were you raised in? Do you have a job, or a career? Either way, what—exactly—is it that you do? When you were a kid, what did you want to be "when you grew up?"

More questions: Where do you live? An apartment, condo, half-way house, mental ward, retirement village, high rise, beach shack, abandoned car, or tree house in aunt's backyard? Oh, you share a houseboat with a cousin? A college dorm room with your best high school buddy? Do you own or rent, live on the street, or crash in the back room of a pool hall?

What are the character's political leanings? What political issues press the hot buttons? How do you feel about gun control, abortion, environmental protection laws, peacekeeping forces sent to other countries, draft registration, drinking age, welfare, social security, gay rights, feminism, assisted suicide?

Hobbies? Talents? (The latter might not play a part in the former.)

What kind of pet do you own? Chia pet or pit bull? What kind of pet would you like to own? Why do you hate pets?

A general philosophy of life: Don't worry, be happy. Don't sweat the small stuff. Details, details, details. Be prepared. Be kind to others. Beware of strangers. Never trust anyone over thirty. You can't always get what you want. It's only rock and roll (but I like it.) When the going gets tough, the tough go shopping. The one who dies with the most toys wins. The one who dies is dead ...

The character's favorite music is _____.

This is one of the first questions I answer for my characters. Often, I give them a theme song or "theme band." A character who likes only classical may be quite different from someone who worships Aretha Franklin, Bob Dylan, David Bowie, Joan Baez, Joan Jett, Thelonius Monk, The Who, The Go-Gos, Guns and Roses, Hootie and the Blowfish, The Kingston Trio, Captain and Tennille.

Eating well—or ... Eating? Well ... How and when your characters feed themselves will tell you a lot about them. Do they count calories or grams of fat? Do they cook gourmet meals or order pizzas in? What's their favorite junk food? Which vegetables do they hate? Do they binge when they're unhappy, or starve themselves when they have a date? What do they drink? Are they caffeine addicts or alcoholics? Do they carry Evian everywhere they go or drink milk right from the carton?

What do they do when they're upset? This is a very important question. If you're writing horror, we must assume your characters will be upset, scared, frightened or ticked off on a fairly regular basis. Do they listen to music, exercise until they're exhausted, yell, cry, brood, complain, shadow box, make crank phone calls, play Nintendo, play guitar, slam dance, write nasty letters, call Grandpa, break pencils, break dishes, punch holes in walls?

Now, the fun part.

Give your characters flaws. Lots and lots of flaws. (Just like us real-lifers!)

Are they messy, neat freaks, grumpy in the morning, grumpy all the time? Can't remember people's names, always hopelessly lost?

You say you are jealous of others, you hate dogs, you're rude to strangers? You hang out in biker bars, read horror books instead of doing housework, have no table manners, burp in public, can't color-coordinate your clothes. You're so clumsy that friends won't let you in the house. Why are you always losing your keys? You sing off key, snore, sleepwalk. You're stingy, always overdrawn, generous to a fault . . . You won't answer the phone and there are stupid messages on your answering machine.

What is the character's worst habit? What is the character's worst habit—in *his* opinion?

What does he do that drives others crazy?

What is he afraid of: airplanes, heights, dogs, snakes? Enclosed places, exposed places, dying while asleep, dying while awake, dying and being dead? Monsters under the bed, monsters in the bed? The building collapsing in an earthquake, a meteor hitting the house, an inferno raging through the high-rise?

Be sure to spend as much time giving your bad guys *good* traits as you do giving your good guys *bad* traits. A bad guy with no redeeming qualities is no fun to beat. And a good guy who can't lose is no fun to root for.

By now, you should have a two- or three-page character sketch.

Am I going to use all this stuff?

Of course not.

So why'd I do all this work?

To get to *know* your character. At some point, you should have stopped making up random answers to those questions and the character should have started answering for himself. Your character has attitudes and opinions, a philosophy and bad habits, moods and a physique. Your character should be talking back to you by now. Which is what the character sketch work is all about.

Listen to Your Characters

That's a lot of work for one story!

Yes, it is. And in the beginning, I did it for each of my major characters for every story I wrote. I don't have to do it for every character anymore. I'm in the habit of asking those questions, almost subconsciously, so the details come to me without having to put it all down on paper. But when I get stuck, when a character won't talk to me, I pull out that list and start interviewing the shy character.

And now, *finally*, back to plotting.

Only now, you aren't doing it by yourself! Your hero and your villain are sitting beside you. Your villain throws up an obstacle and your hero tells you how he will overcome it. Your villain observes your hero's weaknesses and fights dirty! Your hero cleverly finds a way to turn his own weaknesses into strengths, spies the villain's fatal flaw, and devises a plan that cannot be beat.

But your villain beats it.

Your hero learns from his mistake, and comes up with an even better plan! As a writer, your job is not that of Master Puppeteer.

It's more like Office Stenographer.

Once you've created your characters, trust them. They will whisper in your ear and tell you what they need to do. Even if what they suggest wreaks havoc with all your plots and plans, listen to them!

For my story "Preacherman Gets the Blues" in the anthology *Phantoms of the Night*, I had carefully created a character sketch of my heroine, a single mother who runs a haunted blues club, my anti-hero, a young and cocky guitar player, and my villain, a demon from hell. I listened to them as I plotted the story.

But as I was plotting "Preacherman," two minor characters—a grizzled old barfly, used-to-be-musician, and the ten year old daughter of the club owner—teamed up and told me *they* knew how to save the day. They were only supposed to have a couple lines each; I'd tossed them in for atmosphere and color. They took over the story—and wrote a far better one than I had outlined on paper.

Listen to your characters. It pays off.

Use Anecdotal Evidence

Once your plotting is done and it's time to start writing, you will of course refer to your character sketches. You're looking for voice and details. But don't drop chunks of your character sketch into the story like a brick into a fishbowl.

Yiri the vampire was a shy type whose motto was "never trust anyone over 300."

Don't *tell* us. *Show* us. That's why you did all that work, so you would know your creations well enough to provide anecdotal evidence, instead of surface observations.

To return to "Preacherman Gets the Blues" (yes, I like the story—that is, I *really* like the story people I created): My character sketch for Suzy establishes that she's ten years old, has blonde hair and blue eyes, and was raised in the club, getting to know some of the greatest blues musicians in Chicago. Her nickname is Little Mustang. She's precocious, racially colorblind (her best friend is an old black man who frequents the club). She helps her mom out a lot in the bar, and wants to be a blues musician some day.

But those are just surface observations. They have to be turned into anecdotal evidence. Here's how we first meet her in the story.

Her daughter came bounding over to the waitress station and climbed up on a bar stool.

"Hey, Little Mustang!" The grizzled patron winked at her over his snifter.

"Hey, yourself, Old George!"

Old George let out a laugh that was equal parts wheeze and chuckle.

Sarah shook her head. "Sweetheart, put out the ashtrays will you?"

"'Kay, Mom."

Sarah smiled as her daughter grabbed the stacks of ashtrays and started distributing them to each table, stopping to greet the regulars.

At ten years old, Mustang's nose barely reached the rail of the bar when she stood up. Sarah had bought the club while she was pregnant. Unable to afford a sitter, she took the child to work with her. Mustang had grown up on the knees of the Blues greats: Buddy Guy, Koko Taylor, Son Seals, Junior Wells.

They'd played checkers with her between sets, sung her lullabies, even changed her diapers in an emergency. When the musicians weren't playing with Mustang, Jayhawk was. And if the baby started fussing in the middle of a set, all the band had to do was break into a rendition of "Mustang Sally." It calmed her down and put her to sleep every time. Sarah had named her daughter Suzy, but she doubted if even Suzy remembered that.

If you spend time doing your research up front, getting to know your characters until they are truly living, breathing people, the rest of the writing process is easy.

Wooden puppets may seem easier to work with, but they're stiff and brittle, and they tend to break when it comes to issues of believability. That's when you lose your readers.

If you know your characters as well as you knew your best friend in high school, every secret dream and desire, every pimple, every wart, then your characters will be as loyal and devoted as your high school buddy. Trust them, and there's no writing obstacle that they can't help you overcome. They'll lead you back to the plot when you wander off the trail, they'll lower a rope ladder to you when you paint yourself into a plot corner, and they'll goad you back to your computer and nag you to finish *their* story when you're being lazy and watching football on the couch.

Know and trust your characters. They will stick by you every step of the way.

Guerrilla Literature
Plotting the Horror Short Story

Nancy Holder

It's the hour of the wolf. There's a hush over the forest and everyone's sitting around the campfire shining flashlights on their faces to make themselves look sinister. The guitars are put away. The fire's crackling.

It's time for ghost stories.

Someone pipes up and asks you, the resident horror writer, to tell the first one.

"Yes, yes," everybody says excitedly. They all wait with anticipation for you to start. Your best friend protests (also excitedly) that she *hates* to be frightened.

A burning log pops and three people jump and giggle nervously. An owl hoots. Someone else shifts and arcs a flashlight around the circle and calls your name.

And finally the others notice that you aren't even at the campfire.

You're off among the skeleton trees, away from the light and the warmth, plotting your commando raid.

Because writing short horror fiction is more about attacking the people around the campfire than sitting benignly beside them with a blazing marshmallow on the end of a coat hanger and a flashlight under your chin. On your elbows (or your broom) in the icy, dank dark, you are closing in on them on a rapid-fire stealth mission. You're going to deliver your payload into their brains in a low-level tactical strike before they have the slightest idea what hit them.

You're going to give them the creeps.

You're going to make them scream.

Then you're going to return to base.

It's all in a night's work for a teller of horror tales. How do you accomplish your mission? As with any war, there are rules of combat. They can be learned and they can be used, and they can do a lot of damage.

Finding Common Ground

First, you need to find your common ground. For horror fans, it's a love of the darkness. Reader and author, we're both proud to be soldiers in the army of the night as we traverse the terrain of rough edges and deep shadows.

Knee-deep, chin-deep, we cross a battlefield in some wise familiar, in others tantalizingly, frighteningly new: the place where evil dwells.

Horror writers, like all writers of speculative fiction, labor under a peculiar burden. Our plots, when told aloud to others, sound childish and rather silly:

"A guy rises from the grave every night and sucks people's blood."

"This evil hotel comes to life and makes a guy go nuts."

The horror writer's basic weapon is primal fear, which we either discover or develop in childhood—of the dark, of the bogeyman, of being alone, being hurt, being killed. People spend lifetimes hiding these fears, and hiding *from* these fears, but horror aficionados admit their existence and gaze at them with fascination, both close up and from afar. Sometimes scouts are sent out. As Clive Barker has put it, horror writers are the ones who venture into the caves and dark places and return to tell the rest of the tribe what they saw. As are horror artists, horror film directors, and composers of horror music.

Horror writers who worry that they won't march with their readers on common ground, that their short-story plots will be deemed unsophisticated or ridiculous by their readers, get into trouble by editing out what they see in the dark landscape and focusing instead on what it means. What the story is about. The theme or the subtext, if you will.

This is dangerous because you were invited to the campfire to tell a scary story, not to discuss, for example, the existential notion of evil. A frightening short story that includes a theme or subtext about the existential notion of evil may have an added dimension of richness, but a piece of writing light on plot and long on anything else is a thought piece, an essay or a vignette. It's not a *story*. This seems to be a problem for horror writers; one highly regarded editor and anthologist in the field observed that nothing happens in many of the stories submitted to her by beginning authors. Their work is all *mood*, she says. All *atmosphere*.

It's not enough to hide behind a tree, leap out, and shout, "Boo!" So, let's assume that the notion of common ground has been verified. We have met the horror fan, and he is us, and we're both dangling over the abyss.

Structure

Now we move on to the next rule of combat. Usually, a satisfying short story has a beginning, a middle, and an end, and a logical progression of causation from start to finish:

Because the Japanese businessman fell in love with a vampire, he completed his suicide pact with her.

Because the cannibal rock star discovered that his best friend ate his girlfriend, he killed him.

Where some writers get into trouble is assuming that a succession of unnerving events is all there is to creating a plot for a horror short story. That to win the battle, you just turn on your tank and let it run from the valley to the hill, shoot off a volley and take the village. A story that reads like a simple battle plan isn't satisfying because it simply runs its course. It doesn't strafe. It doesn't explode. It has no sense of causality, intention or motivation. It feels inevitable. Rejection slips come back with the criticism that the story was predictable.

Many horror writers confess that structurally, they have the most difficulty with endings. Perhaps this is because most horror short stories move forward under the stress of a highly dramatic conflict. Horror is an emotional, reactive genre, and the reader is seeking a feeling of solution or, at the least, *resolution* at the conclusion. An episodic storyline works in some novels, and it may also work in short stories for children, who are new to the idea of story to begin with. It may be enough to discover that the monster was Uncle Bud in his Halloween costume, or it was all a dream, or an initiation for a school club. But for a more sophisticated reader, there must be a more sophisticated ending. Beginning writers assume there are only two: The protagonist triumphs, or the protagonist fails. How many of us have read stories where the hero stakes the vampire as the sun rises and that's the end of it? Or embraces the heroine and declares, "We have destroyed them forever," only to discover that the heroine is now a (A) vampire (B) pod person (C) thing from another world?

Endings are probably the most difficult part of making a horror short story work, and this, I believe, is where a writer's strong belief in the horror world he has created can set the work apart. The more completely you're immersed in a world, the easier it is for you to manipulate it.

I remember a conversation I had with a writer friend who was having trouble with her ending. I said, "Okay, what if Robert doesn't die?"

She replied, "But he does."

I repeated, "What if he doesn't?"

And she argued that he does, he does, he *does*—until it occurred to her that *she* was the one who had killed him off in the first place. Feeling sure of your universe gives you the ability to manipulate and change it, as any god can. This sense of authority can translate into the ending, where you now have command over events, and not they over you. Perhaps Robert dies after turning the heroine into a pod person, but he never knows it. Perhaps his death frees the heroine from her vampiric state, or his disintegrating corpse releases the virus into our atmosphere that allows the pods to grow.

The ending is the place where the guerrilla nature of short horror fiction can really shine. Where you can defy expectations and execute a surprise attack. Instead of the anticipated atomic bomb, you drop leaflets impregnated with poison. Instead of Harriers, you send Zeppelins. You find your own twist, moving one step beyond what the ending might or could have been, and carve out new territory for yourself.

Know Your Readers

We'll talk more about endings in a moment. For now, let's discuss the third rule of combat: *Know thy enemy.* Understand your readers and consider them when you set up the plot. Are you writing for seasoned horror fans who will appreciate the nuances of a twist on an old theme? For young adults eager for surprises and chills? Or Gothic readers who love slow pacing, seductive demon lovers and fog banks of atmosphere?

Adjust your plot to take advantage of their typical defenses. You can't take down a thick wall with a firecracker. You don't need to take down a flimsy shack with a neutron bomb. Don't lose an audience of sophisticated, cutting-edge readers with a predictable tale of "ironic retribution." Conversely, reel kids in with stories where justice is meted out and the punishment fits the crime (preferably, in a way that is larger than life): The greedy little boy eats so much candy he blows up. The cruel, demonic substitute teacher is thrown into the Pit and forced to do multiplication tables for all eternity.

Fourth, inventory your armaments. What are your tactical strengths? Are you able to suspend your own disbelief in the type of horror story you've chosen to tell? Do you feel you're attacking a worthy adversary or swooping down on a village of defenseless peasants?

I once knew an author who was quick to tell other writers that she was actually a literary writer who was using horror as a metaphor for the themes she wanted to explore. She found the work of most horror writers "silly," and she steadfastly wrote her literary horror stories without venturing beyond her own self-imposed boundaries. This very successful writer was wise to fire her salvos of similes and metaphors at readers who could appreciate her style, and to avoid attempting other types of stories, which surely would have revealed her lack of enthusiasm and respect.

On the other hand, I know another, less successful writer who continues to receive rejection slips for his stories of ironic retribution, who would probably be well served by sending them to children's magazines or young adult horror anthologies. He doesn't realize that his warheads are detonating before they hit the "I've-read-this-a-dozen-times-before" atmosphere of various editorial desks.

Promise a Good Scare

The fifth rule of combat is to marshal your troops. Your main objective in telling a tale of horror is to frighten your readers. To lead them through your sentences, paragraphs and pages, you have to make sure they're following you. They need to be sufficiently motivated to break camp and strap on their equipment. You can assure them the trip will be worth it by setting the scene, either by the use of atmosphere, leading dialogue or incident. This is the horror writer's equivalent of "Once upon a time." This is where everyone settles down to be frightened. They are counting on you to keep the promise you've made to them—that if they go on this journey with you, you will lead them to victory. In other words, that you will scare them.

Unlike the novelist, you get one shot and one shot only to blow up the Death Star. With your first strafing run, you must convince your readers that they'd better look around for cover from the monsters of your id. Whereas readers may give a book a few pages or chapters to "get going," if your readers aren't scrambling by the first few paragraphs, they aren't going to care about your characters, your structure, your atmosphere or your clever ending. Unless you grab them, and grab hard, they won't go with you to the pitch-black jungle or the smoky, narrow cave. They'll just read another story in the magazine or anthology.

Sometimes newer writers start their stories too soon in the plot. Unnecessary journeys, errands, conversations, etc., should be trimmed. Slice with your bayonet as close to the bone of the main action as you can. If your story is about a murder, begin with the murder, the discovery of the murder, the repercussions of the murder. Generally, short stories concern themselves with *one* main action, told over a short time period. So you wouldn't have the space to cover the perpetrator's decision to commit the murder, the preparations for the murder, a subplot concerning the murderer's lover, and so on. That is the novelist's purview.

Staying lean and mean plot-wise can also help you with your ending. In our murder example, the ending should refer absolutely and solely to the single main action—the telltale heart of the story.

An exaggerated example of the antithesis of a lean and mean ending would be something like this: The murderer commits the murder, goes to his girlfriend to confess, and finds out that she stole some diamonds from the victim. The police come to arrest the girlfriend, she escapes, and they get so distracted trying to find her that the murderer escapes.

Leaner would be that when the police come to arrest the girlfriend, the reader learns that the murderer planted evidence that incriminates her. By a lucky chance, her avarice has provided a motive to the crime, and she is also arrested for the murder.

Stand-up comedy has been called a hostile and covertly violent form of entertainment. Comedians "knock 'em dead," "kill 'em," "slay 'em." They do this by "building a base" in which they tell a series of jokes that have some sort of link. The first joke sets up the premise. The second makes the bridge. The third provides the conclusion that gets the big laugh.

This is analogous to the horror short story writer's wise use of the beginning, the middle and the end. At each point, we're out to build a base of tension and fear. The beginning sets up the premise: *There are monsters in our midst.* The middle builds the bridge: *There are monsters in our midst, and we must kill them or be killed.* The ending provides the climax and denouement: *There are monsters in our midst; we have killed some of them; some of them have killed some of us. Now it's do or die, and we're going to survive . . . This time.*

Fight Dirty

The sixth rule of combat is to remember that this is guerrilla warfare. The American colonists beat the British because they broke the established rules of civilized confrontation. They didn't line up in nice, straight lines wearing fashionable uniforms, holding fifes and drums. They hid in trees, used camouflage and elevated the surprise attack to a high art form. The British were outraged. The Americans won.

As long as you win, it doesn't matter how you do it. If you light your reader's spinal column and make his head explode with fear, you can count coup. If someone has a sleepless night on account of something you've written, carve a notch on your word processor. Find your weapon of choice, make your run, and let 'em have it.

Edward Young said, "War's glorious art, and gives immortal fame." I'm sure Edgar Allan Poe, Shirley Jackson, Henry James, Stephen King, Charles L. Grant and the other great generals of horrific guerrilla literature—the horror short story—would agree.

The Horror, The Horror, The Horror
Plotting the Horror Novel

Alan Rodgers

Would I start an awful row if I said that I can never get any of the obvious advice to work for me? In books like this one, in lectures, in discussion on the Internet with other writers: Almost all the advice I hear is stuff I've tried and found dysfunctional.

When folks say "plot," I'm not even certain *what* they're talking about. When they make pronouncements about what a horror plot ought to be, I think of the old pulp magazines, which, legend has it, really did look for formula plots.

The pulp magazines haven't been a force in publishing since the late 1950s. Nostrums that may well have worked for breaking into pulps don't particularly apply today. Mass-market paperback publishing, the one facet of the modern market with a deep historical link to the pulps, has metamorphosed over the years and continues to change. Today's mass-market paperback business looks an awful lot more like the market for trade books (hardcovers and high-end paperbacks) than it resembles the pulps.

What does this have to do with horror plots? A lot. If there ever was a horror formula you could point at and teach, it's gone now; and it may never have existed.

There is no process theme for writing horror.

If you're going to understand plotting horror novels, you're going to have to understand a whole suite of interlocking ideas.

Defining Plot

When we say *plot* do we mean "sequence of events" or "proposal suitable for submission to an editor" or "essence of the story, less character development and theme" (as if we could really pare those things from one another and leave the work remotely recognizable)?

When we talk about plots for horror novels, we compound the

problem: What *is* a horror novel? Is it a book about frightful events in an old dark house, preferably involving three werewolves, two zombies and a vampire? I guess that'd be a horror novel; it's hard to imagine it as anything *but* a horror novel.

But I'm not sure we're going to write a book anyone's going to want to read by the simple expedient of piling tropes; perhaps more to the point, I've noticed that some of my favorite horror novels use no horror tropes at all.

Let's borrow a quick working definition from T.E.D. Klein, the editor who hired me to work at *Twilight Zone* Magazine. For the annual *TZ* writing contest, Klein wanted "stories about ordinary people in extraordinary circumstances."

We call it *horror*, but in a way the scariness is a side effect, not the main event: *Of course* stories about ordinary people caught up in extraordinary circumstances are unsettling. How could they be otherwise?

Let's use that working definition of horror to build a working definition of horror plot: A horror plot is what you get when you put an ordinary person in an extraordinary circumstance and let him cope with, be victimized by, and, eventually (we hope!), transcend that circumstance.

A woman and her children trapped in a broken-down car, held at bay by a rabid dog: *Cujo*. An idiot finds a woman brutalized and bleeding on the street, and rushes to her aid—only to get her blood on his hands and appear to be the one who's nearly killed her: Sturgeon's "Bright Segment." A dozen ordinary people caught up in the events foretold in the Book of Revelation: *The Stand*, *Swan Song*, my own *Fire*.

Add to this a caveat. When a reader comes to a horror novel—when he comes to just about any novel, in fact—he's looking for something that touches his own life. Editors usually call that *scope*, because the most obvious ways to do it involves telling a story that describes events that shake the world, or a big part of it. (Think: Blow up the world, and remember that it's best to do that after an enormous drum roll.)

You can also get scope by telling a story that's so true, so real, so evocative—a story that touches us fundamentally, thereby helping us understand ourselves more clearly. Every story should try to do that, I think, but it's a plain fact that there are only so many personal epiphanies folks are going to get out of novels; darned few people are going to make good livings writing stories that touch us that clearly and that truly.

All of which is to say that transcendent scope is nifty, a brass ring we should all reach for; but just the same, it's best to hedge the bet with a good measure of the more straightforward sort of scope.

Another caveat: There are people who understand horror novels by counting tropes. "Have we got an old dark house, a werewolf, two vampires and a zombie? Well then," they say, "of course we have a horror novel."

Some of these people are editors. It does not pay to argue with an editor about the definition of a form. If you want to sell a novel as a horror novel, you'll do well to use at least a handful of horror tropes. Think of them as signposts that direct the reader toward the story he's looking for, and try not to let them dictate what you write; you don't want to confuse the map with the territory.

Outlining

As I mentioned before, one of the things people mean when they say *plot* is "the sketch of a work in progress suitable for presenting to an editor." That kind of plot is really a sketch, which needs discussion here, too.

It's darned hard to find sources for sketches. They generally don't see print, and many writers are reluctant to show them around—sometimes with good cause. Because novel sketches don't circulate, every writer very nearly has to invent the form himself. No small task.

People sometimes use the word "outline" to describe the form. Misleading, that; the last thing you want a novel sketch to be is one of those Roman-numeral things you learned in junior high.

What you want is something a whole lot more like a story than an outline. You want a thumbnail of the book, complete with the flavor and the feel of the finished whole. Don't be afraid to drift into scenes or "scenelets"; try to tell the story in ten or twenty pages that suggest the scope and breadth of the whole. Use the amount of detail that's right for you.

A few years ago, I would have said differently. My teacher was big on detailed outlines, and when I started writing, I liked to have a good sense of where I was headed. Then a couple of years ago, sitting in a bar at a horror writers' function, Peter Straub told me that he tried as best he could not to outline at all. He tried, in fact, not to know where he was headed from one word to the next.

That sounded crazy to me. But it wasn't a crazy person talking. It was Peter Straub, who'd written half of my favorite horror novels. And because it was Peter Straub, I tried writing blindly like that for myself.

I've done some of my best work that way.

It doesn't work for every story, but when I'm reaching for a depth of theme beyond my ordinary reach, I use that trick and it works very well indeed. I'm not sure it would have worked as well when I was younger, before I'd spent enough time at the keyboard to have an intuitive feel for the form.

There are many things about the craft that every writer does a little differently, and some writers do very differently. You're going to need to try those things and more to see where you get results, what sort of results you get and whether they make up a work habit you can live with.

Be Engaged and Engaging

All the good advice in the world isn't going to turn anyone into a writer, and worse, listening to too much of it can royally screw you up. It may seem pretty silly, but it's true. Writing is really a tough craft to master; most of the working writers I know spent a good dozen years honing their craft before they managed to get anywhere. Most of them spent so much time and energy learning their craft that they lost sight of the rest of the world.

Which is exactly the problem.

Young writers really do need to embrace their craft so deeply and so thoroughly that they lose sight of every other thing in the world—but they need to embrace the world itself just as vigorously and with the same abiding passion. It isn't sufficient to do one and not the other; and it does not matter that there is no way to embrace the world to the exclusion of the craft while embracing the craft to the exclusion of all else.

The writers we admire do both. You can observe it any moment you take to read their work.

Think about that. Think about the writers whose work you admire most, people like Heinlein, Hemingway, Fitzgerald, Sturgeon, Steinbeck and Twain. Aren't they the folks who spent their entire lives arguing with the world? Generally it was about a single subject, but sometimes about a cluster of related subjects. Aren't they the folks so caught up in the world that we can't think of them without thinking about their subject matter? That kind of involvement in the world around us runs at right angles to concentration on craft.

In so many ways, the important thing about writing isn't writing, craft or anything of the sort; the important thing is the world. We need to be engaged and engaging. The point is what we have to say, not how we say it or to whom we say it. Craft is important, but it's only a starting point. What is really important is having something to say, and building a case that's large enough to consume your entire life.

I don't care whether the case a writer builds is one I agree or disagree with. I care that he's making it honestly (that people really do behave that way) and that he builds it insightfully. I want to be engaged;

I want a persuasive case, but I'm not looking to be persuaded and I may well disagree. I disagree with a lot of what the great writers had to say, but I appreciate the true things they told about the world as they built their arguments.

The ideas in a book are important, neat and wonderful. Even when I disagree with them, they enrich me. They enrich all of us.

Maybe what I'm trying to tell you is that the story is big, and important, and large enough to consume you; it's big enough to set the world alight because the story *is* the world, and if we tell it truly no one will be able to peel away the layers that bind those things together: The world. The story. The things we have to say. Maybe, even though we're telling stories about things that never did and never could take place, maybe we are writing things too true to ignore.

When we do things right.

This is not a great way to make a living. It's big, it's neat, it consumes me—but I can't say I recommend it to young people looking to make their way in the world.

Which is not to warn anybody off. I ended up as a horror writer because horror is what I do well. Folks respond to my work when I sell it as horror; I'm more pleased with my work when I'm writing horror. If it comes naturally to you—if horror writing is your strength—let me encourage you to write it.

Writing horror is big, important and kind of scary, in its way.

I wouldn't miss it for the world.

No Shield of Disbelief

Dominick Cancilla

Before a reader can believe in any vampire, tome of unpronounceable evil or arcane relic with preternatural powers, the story itself must believe in them. The "unbelievable elements" in your work must feel as natural as the people and places with which they share paper.

That prompts a stressful, serious moment of decision: How much unreality do you think you can get away with?

It is usually a good idea to keep a fictional universe as close to reality as possible. A short story should differ from accepted reality in a *single way*: vampires exist; time travel has been invented and, despite governmental regulations, it is actually practical; there's a nationwide conspiracy of flesh-wearing maniacs. Too much deviation from our accepted "world as we know it" will strain the reader's credulity or demand too much explanation. The latter will likely produce stone-dead exposition or utterly contrived dialogue, both as static as a tombstone.

Once you decide how reality will be twisted, you must stick with that decision and keep it in mind for the duration of the work. That means not changing the rules midstream or introducing additional unbelievables in the last sentence to create a "surprise" ending.

Consistency is the core of believability. Think through all the possibilities and implications of your fiction. If uttering the monster's name causes it to appear, then it should always do so—even when the name is spoken in conversation or explanation. The telekinetic who can push aside a speeding truck at the beginning of the story shouldn't be unable to avoid a falling piano at the end. The beam of unholy light that kills on contact through most of the story shouldn't merely wound your protagonist.

Mistakes such as these are usually easy to avoid *if* the limits of unreality are carefully defined. We are talking about reasonably narrow limits, since a reader either will find no tension in a world where everything is apparently possible or will wonder why fantastic things are so little used.

If the repulsive witch lives in squalor, we need to know why she doesn't use her witchy powers to conjure up fabulous wealth. And if those powers couldn't bring her beauty, might not her magically adjusted and enhanced bank balance buy her serious cosmetic surgery?

Many pegs from which horrors are hung are so familiar that it is easy to take them for granted, not giving them a second thought before plunging into narrative. This is almost always a mistake. Just as much thought must go into writing about the "old standards" as goes into a completely original horror (if there is such a thing/thought/whatever).

Let's use vampires as our example. The story premise: A group of vampires wants to capture a small town and use its inhabitants as cattle. (Well, not cattle, but you get the metaphor.)

Question: What is a vampire? Is it a supernatural creature or one that is more scientifically plausible?

At first, you consider making your vampires an ancient race, evil, powerful but *explainable* by science. But in that case, why wouldn't they appear in mirrors? How would they change shape without losing their clothes?

Ah, traditionalist that you are, you want to maintain *certain* classic vampire elements. Vampires are supernatural.

But to what extent are these traditional vampires affected by crosses? Would a pair of crossed chopsticks do? How about a crucifix made of wood from the One True Cross? How about a symbol from a non-Christian religion?

And doesn't that story climax rely on vampires not being able to cross running water? What are the limits of this weakness? Are these vampires stopped dead (stopped *undead*?) only by something the size of the Mississippi or would a swollen gutter hold them back as well? Similar questions must be asked about their vulnerabilities (Any wooden object? Anything through the heart? Only a stake through the heart?), origins (Where have they been? Why haven't we heard more about them? Do they need a better PR guy?), powers (Can they hypnotize people? What animals can they turn into?), etc.

Onward.

The vampires will have to overcome a number of obstacles—credible obstacles dealt with in a credible fashion. Before they can do anything, the vampires must locate an appropriate town, travel to it and isolate it from any source of help. They need a way to keep the populace under control and avoid being overwhelmed by superior numbers. And if three bites will turn a victim into One of the Undead, the vampires will have to take steps to prevent their cattle from joining the ranks of the thirsty.

This might seem like a lot more thought than is necessary for what on the surface appears to be a simple tale, but in the long run it's worth it. There are few things more tragic than endless hours of hard work culminating in a rejection slip on which is written something along the lines of, "Why don't the villagers just wait for daylight and then leave?"

With the level and nature of unreality set, a fictive world must be populated with characters who might realistically exist in it. For a horror writer, the most important consideration might well be: *How do characters react when confronted by the unusual?* A reader must be kept thinking, *Jamie left the dagger behind because the demon that's slowly usurping her will desired it*, instead of, *Jamie left the dagger behind because the author needed her to leave it behind . . .*

Though the unusual exists in your fictive universe, the inhabitants, your characters, don't necessarily know it. A real-world police detective who suggests that a recent string of murders are the work of a werewolf would be laughed off the force. Perhaps in your world werewolves *do* exist, but even so a person who believes in them will likely be ridiculed unless the creatures' existence is common knowledge.

The way a character reacts to the unexpected should be shaped as much by the character's religious, cultural and experiential makeup as by narrative necessity.

In a credible tale, a reanimated mummy will elicit more than an "Eeek!" from those who see it. A skeptic will think it more likely that the creature is a person in monstrous makeup than a shambling corpse and will act accordingly. A devout monotheist would not likely believe that the thing was brought to life by the power of an Egyptian god. A voodoo practitioner might treat a mummy like just another zombie. A child will react differently than an adult, an educated person differently than an uneducated person, a loner differently than someone on whom others are depending.

If something is supposed to be horrifying to the reader, then it must be horrifying to the story's characters. A person seeing a loved one sucked through the space under a door with considerable crunching of bone and not unimpressive spraying of blood is not going to stand and wonder what's going on.

He's going to run!

He's going to scream hysterically!

Or . . .

No matter his style of freaking out, he will most definitely FREAK OUT!

A realistic character will learn from experience and tend to avoid people and places associated with horror. Someone attacked by ghouls in a graveyard will probably not accept a night watchman job there a year later, despite the decent dental care benefits. If a story requires characters to keep themselves in peril, then you need to have a compelling reason for them to do so or the reader may think them fools who deserve what they get—and maybe more besides.

The more unbelievable something is, the more deeply the characters will be affected. If the women of a small, quiet town in the midwestern United States awake one morning to discover that all the men have been decapitated in their beds, that fact would dominate the thoughts and actions of everyone involved for, let's say, "quite a while." You don't forget a house with bleeding walls because six weeks have passed and you've had a vacation in Aruba. The man whose beloved wife is swallowed whole before his eyes by a gibbering protoplasm should be recovering from the experience for, oh, several months at least.

None of this is to say that you can't have characters of extraordinary willpower and determination, but they must be presented as such. The ability to withstand repeated horrors and assaults upon accepted reality should not be taken for granted—because the reader will not take it for granted.

The only time characters' reactions should differ greatly from the reader's is when the characters have a skewed perception of what is normal. The inhabitants of a haunted castle may take their ghost for granted. They might even consider it a member of the family. A town in which the populace gathers every Good Friday to crucify a stranger they've captured should not be horrified by their own actions. A schizophrenic man who sees and talks to illusory demons would not be surprised by the appearance of a real one and would, no doubt, enjoy the conversation.

If a story believes in the unreality it is presenting, if character reactions are what they should be, if the story world's logic is consistent, and if there are well-defined limits for man, nature and monster, then a tale will not be overburdened by the unbelievable. The reader, then, will be denied the shield of disbelief, and the horrors you present will strike at unprotected flesh.

A Hand on the Shoulder

Joe R. Lansdale

In writing, if you're truly connected to a region, sense of place is like a friendly hand on your shoulder.

Recently I was on vacation in Aruba, an island off the coast of Venezuela, and I was working on a story in my head.

I was sitting on a hotel patio in the sunshine listening to the roar of the ocean, feeling the cool blasting winds that constantly pummel Aruba, watching palm trees sway, and I was thinking about a hot, humid, pine-tree littered, sandy soil, clay road region back in Texas.

East Texas to be exact.

I was born and have lived in East Texas most all my life. (People from this region generally spell East with a capital instead of a small letter. It's almost like a separate state.) I haven't always written about East Texas, but mostly. And without a doubt, my best work has taken place there.

First off, it is so unlike most of Texas. More Southern in background, with tall trees, creeks and rivers. It's a little like Louisiana in appearance, maybe not so swampy. There's something unique about it, mysterious even.

It's a land of people, black and white and brown—mixed cultures. East Texas, though Southern in nature with a strong influence of black culture and a way of talking more akin to Louisiana and Tennessee than Dallas or West Texas, is also strongly influenced by Mexican culture, remnants of American Indian culture, Old Spain and Cajun culture from across the Louisiana border. It's the home of country music and country boogie.

Hot country, where in the dead of summer the heat falls down on your head like a wool sweater drenched in sweat and rests on your shoulders like an anvil. And when you walk, it's like wading through molasses wearing concrete boots. Air conditioners hum in homes and stores constantly, and East Texans air-condition with a vengeance. In an instant you can go from feeling as if you're frying in lard to feeling like you're inside a meat locker.

It seeps into your writing. A land like this, thick in contrast, mixed with so many fine cultural wines and a strong sense of good ol' Texas individualism, produces a unique character for both region and individual. A land like this, a culture like this, can brighten or darken your writerly vision from one moment to the next.

East Texas is a place where hyperbole, wild metaphors and bouncing similes spurt forth from the mouths of locals like the nasty matter than runs through a goose after it's had its dinner.

This is my region. A region the rest of our state refers to as being "behind the pine curtain."

Good and bad, East Texas has influenced the way I write.

My point is, I didn't know this until about ten years ago, and as I said, I've lived here all my life. Writers, most of us, really don't recognize the gold mine when we're in it. We stand there with our pick and shovel, we look about, and though the walls glow brightly with strains of gold, we squint our eyes against the light, reach down and pick up iron pyrites instead of gold.

Finding a Unique Voice

So many beginning writers ignore their background and region and try to write about places far away. Places that sound exotic. Places often written about, filmed and glamorized.

I tried this myself. But what I soon realized was that while there's no crime in writing about places you don't know—I've done it and will probably do it again—there certainly is much to be gained by writing about what you *do* know.

When I sit down to write about East Texas, I'm comfortable that the language I use is correct. It's my language. It's unique to my region.

My descriptions reflect what I see every day. I don't need a research book to see what pine trees look like. Or mocking birds on barbed-wire fences. My themes reflect what I feel every day, good and bad, and my writing glows with a brighter intensity than if I'm trying to write about people in New York or Los Angeles or Ohio, who talk differently than I do, have different daily experiences and, for the most part, are culturally different.

I'm not trying to express division between regions, but I am trying to express the fact that whichever region you live in, there is your background, there is your voice and, I truly believe, there is your style: that one thing so elusive to most writers. It is my belief that the majority of writers really never find their voice, or their style. It's the rare ones who do.

Writers like Ray Bradbury. Pete Hamill. Elmore Leonard. Harry

Crews. They have voices unique to not only their regions, but to themselves.

All writers are regional writers. We all come from some region. But not all writers recognize this. It might also be said that even those writers who do recognize this are not always able to open their eyes and ears and profit by it.

Think about it. Voice is found in your experiences, where you live and how you live. You've got to get in touch with that. And when you do, the language leaps, the characters breathe, and themes run beneath the floor of your story like underground rivers.

If the land you live on is rolling hills, it affects the way you walk. If the weather is hot, making it necessary to move slowly, this affects how you walk *and* how you talk. There is evidence that linguistics affect how a person *thinks* because a word picture may not be the same to a Southerner as it is to an Easterner or a Northerner, even if the words used to create that picture are the same. The way words are spoken or employed changes the speaker's perceptions.

If the roads you drive down are bordered by tall dark trees or by huge concrete structures and shoulder-to-shoulder sidewalk traffic, this affects how you view the world, and how you see yourself in that world.

Books as Characters

When you write, who you are invariably finds its way to the page—not necessarily reflected in the nature of the characters, though that can certainly be true as well, but reflected instead in the character of the writing. Writers who are able to tap into their environment, their cultural roots, are generally those writers who actually turn the book itself into a kind of character.

Giving important fine examples of how place affects style and description is James Lee Burke. When you read his books about Louisiana, you can taste the gumbo and the dirty rice, hear the rivers run, and smell the stink of dead fish, putrid swamp mud and the scent of sweet flowers on the wind.

Even if the plot fades, you remember the characters, and I believe, even above that, you remember the character of the novel itself. Rank and ripe, sweet and sour.

Other examples: Neal Barrett, Jr. and his small communities and neighborhoods. Even when Barrett writes about cities, he has a small-town vision of those cities: a rubber-necker from the sticks who may not be as sophisticated as some, but, like Flannery O'Conner, still knows *weird* when he sees it.

And of course, Flannery O'Conner, Faulkner, all the Southern writers I'm fond of. You may well remember the characters in the works of all these writers, because they are all masters of character, but each has something special and rare. They are masters at presenting the book as a character.

This particular trait comes out of a writer who is in touch with his or her environment. The land. The people. The weather. I suppose you might say, unlike so many books and stories, these writings don't have pages that stink of the library with the obvious feeling of research from afar.

In this respect, all great writers, no matter what region they write about, are the same. They write about what they know. Where they live, or where they have been.

They bring to their books personal visions designed by different backgrounds. And consequently, due to this ability, their books become characters.

Telling the Truth

Let me mention another environment: the one inside your head. The one that's full of your life's experiences, your passions, your base instincts. That ol' primitive brain. Getting in touch with your internal environment, letting the delights and the disappointments of your life seep their way into your writing, personalizes it.

You don't necessarily have to tell the truth. As fiction writers, we're all liars. Tell the truth as you see it. Cut open the emotional apple and find the core, not the skin. It's not the events, it's how you *feel* about the events. If you can do this, you can interject these feelings into the work, even if the scenes you're writing have nothing to do with the actual incidents of your life.

This way, you're writing a lie, but you're telling a greater truth.

A truth nonfiction can't tell.

What I'm suggesting here is environment as writing teacher. Internal and external environment. Herein lies the secret to fiction that's chewable, inhalable (and not even illegal), in 3-D and Touchathon. Words that glow. Sentences that writhe with excitement. Paragraphs that shine like the sun.

Think about it, and realize that your own region, as well as the region inside your head, is a wealth of ideas. The source for your voice, your individuality.

Write what you truly know.

Keep It Moving, Maniacs
Writing Action Scenes in Horror Fiction

Jay R. Bonansinga

The action scene is a rabid animal, the pit bull in horror's backyard. It's the mongrel tearing at the cyclone fence, straining the envelope of taste and time-tested technique. It is the hyperbolic amphetamine rush of Rex Miller's *SLOB*, the jagged word-jazz in the final chapters of Thomas Harris's *The Silence of the Lambs*, or the psychedelic dream-chase of Clive Barker's brilliantly demented novelette "The Body Politic."

The bottom line: Action is the engine inside much of our finest postmodern horror.

Literary action arises from a strange intersection of events, the moment where terror coalesces into movement. Action beats (moments of pure kinetic suspense) keep the pages turning, and often—as is the case in a book like Stephen King's *The Shining*, with its psychic battle-fronts and ghostly archetypes—they complicate and deepen both the text and the subtext.

But what's the secret to writing a killer action scene?

What's it like to be inside the skin of the horror writer as they commit their feverish fantasies to parchment? Well . . .

Sometimes the "act" imitates the "art."

For instance . . .

Chapter One

Something ominous was brewing. The horror writer had been sensing it for weeks. An imminent change in the weather. A dark, foreboding cold front rolling across the lonely spaces of his daily routine.

Then, late one night, alone in his cluttered little garret, he decided to let it happen.

He felt a weird certainty deep down in his marrow as he poured the first few fingers of the evening's espresso and lit his first Camel straight. He welcomed the feeling as he settled into his leather swivel and switched on his IBM Selectric. He knew what the feeling meant.

It meant great things were in store for his horror story.

He began typing.

At first, the synapses sputtered weakly. The ideas came slowly. The characters seemed stuck in their prosaic world, their behavior mired in a kind of cut-and-paste progression of events. The plot points were there, certainly, but the action seemed dull and listless. The story was frightening, sure, but it wasn't gripping. It wasn't riveting. It seemed to plod lifelessly along, merely following the prepared outline.

Then the music started.

At first, it was nothing more than a subtle, metronomic beat in his head, a rhythmic ticking that began to build as he wrote the next suspense sequence. He began to hear a sort of internal percussion, complete with cymbal crashes, tempo changes, drum solos and a constant beat underscoring it all, that became the literary glue holding the sequence together, and soon there were characters fleeing monsters, and floors collapsing, and fireworks erupting, and the action began to flow like furious river-rapids, flowing, FLOWING, furiously, carrying the reader away in its currents, and the storm raged in the writer's mind, and the thunder rumbled, lightning strikes searing the sky at odd intervals, floorboards beginning to QUAKE-QUAKE-QUAKE, seams in the wallpaper separating, plaster crumbling, dust and debris beginning to sift down from the ceiling—

The typewriter erupted.

Flames leapt up from the keyboard, singeing his eyebrows, flash-burning his face, tossing him backward, his swivel chair sliding out from under him. He went down hard on his posterior, the breath knocked out of him, and he gasped for a moment, completely dazed, flailing at the air. His fingertips were still smoldering, tiny, thin tendrils of smoke coming off them where they had contacted the molten hot typewriter keys. He finally managed to catch his breath.

He stood up and looked down at the page still crimped in the typewriter carriage.

The perfect action sequence.

Not bad.

Let's look at the layers. On one level, this sequence exaggerates the perfect *modus operandi* of an action writer, the way the writer gets inside the sequence and almost channels it on a visceral level. But on a deeper level, the actual *style* in which this sequence is written illustrates some of the basic tricks of the action trade, which are as follows . . .

Establishing a Rhythm

Great suspense literally sings off the page. If you don't believe me, check out the basement sequence toward the end of Harris's *Silence of the Lambs*. Clarice Starling is plunged into darkness, alone with a mad killer and a six-shot service revolver, and the prose turns into a literary version of Charlie Parker wailing a sax solo ("He cocked the Python as he brought it up *snick snick* and the figure blurred, bloomed bloomed green in his vision . . .") The key is to find the rhythm of the drama itself, the internal "beat" of the scene, and then let it drive the prose as a percussionist would drive a band.

Consider our little barn-burner with the mythical horror writer as an example. Notice the way in which the rhythm develops dynamically from the terse, tick-tock sentences of the early moments—

> Something ominous was brewing. The horror writer had been sensing it for weeks. An imminent change in the weather.

—to the increasingly free-form, rocket-sled run-on sentences of the latter paragraphs, moving rhythmically in a manner emulating the actual thought patterns of the character—

> . . . the action began to flow like furious river-rapids, flowing, FLOWING, furiously, carrying the reader away in its currents, and the storm raged in the writer's mind, and the thunder rumbled . . .

There are myriad other devices—technical tricks—you might choose to employ within the action scene in order to juice up the "psychological edge." Both Rex Miller and Stephen King are masters of this particular manner. You might abruptly insert a word in all-caps ("flowing, FLOWING") to suggest a sort of frenzied chaos, a rush of activity or thought, or you might utilize alliteration at the right rhythmic point ("flow like furious river-rapids, flowing") in order to drive home the unstoppable aspect of your juggernaut. You might even adopt an intermittent sing-song style ("floorboards beginning to QUAKE-QUAKE-QUAKE") in order to further drive home the inexorable rhythm.

Finally, like the crash of a cymbal, the rhythm of a scene is broken by cutting (via our old friend the dash) to a new single phrase paragraph:

> QUAKE-QUAKE, seams in the wallpaper separating, plaster crumbling, dust and debris beginning to sift down from the ceiling—
> The typewriter erupted.

When you abruptly cut to this new paragraph, it works best when it represents a single snippet of action (or a single thought) which punctuates the sequence . . . preferably something pivotal that happens within the context of the overall flow.

Like a typewriter erupting.

Getting Inside the Point-of-View Character

Clive Barker writes action scenes like a mind-vampire, assimilating the point-of-view of the protagonist, literally getting inside the character's sensory perceptions of what's happening. Look at the second act of his incredible story "Dread," when the hero falls to the floor-grating of a sinister prison and then passes out. *("When he woke up he was unaware of his consciousness. There was darkness everywhere, on all sides.")* It's a tour de force of subjective action, and it illustrates the axiom that suspense looks boring from a distance, like ants in an ant farm. But when viewed up close, seen through the living lens of the human being caught up in the suspense, things really start to get dramatic.

Let's turn again to our mythical writer.

As he starts to cook, really cook, the idea is to get inside his head. Get the reader to feel his energy. Taste the coffee, smell the cigarette smoke, hear the rising clackety-clack of the typewriter, and ultimately experience the action as the protagonist experiences it. In this particular scene, we hear what's in his head:

> At first, it was nothing more than a subtle, metronomic beat in his head, a rhythmic ticking that began to build as he wrote the next suspense sequence. He began to hear a sort of internal percussion, complete with cymbal crashes, tempo changes, drum solos and a constant beat underscoring it all . . .

When the real action kicks in, the scene should always be perceived—whenever possible—from the inside character. When gunshots are fired, don't merely describe how they sound to the characters; describe how they feel. When someone is hurt, don't merely describe the blood and guts; describe the mind, what the pain and the fear feels like, the colors and textures. When the characters are in motion, the landscape rushes past them. With apologies to Galileo, in action scenes, the universe revolves around the central characters.

In fact, true action can only be generated through *character*. Period. We must know his quirks; we must know he's got an adjustable-rate mortgage going through the roof and his kid just got back from the orthodontist with a mouth full of metal. And then, and only then, do we care about the outcome. In other words, only then do we feel as our character feels.

And remember, action is a virus. It's radioactive, and it spreads from the main character's mind to the minds of others. A shift from one point of view to another is like a ratchet tightening suspense, intensifying the action, pumping up the energy about a million foot-pounds per square inch.

Engaging the Environment

There's a thin membrane between horror and pure slapstick comedy—especially within the body of an action sequence.

One of the great tenets of slapstick is to engage the surrounding environment. The Keystone Kops. The block-long engine comes screaming around a curve, the cops hanging off the ladder, holding on for dear life—what happens? The ladder slams into a stack of melons, and melons go flying. The cops go catapulting off into various pie shops, pies erupting everywhere, hitting faces, cops scurrying every which way. It's a recipe for laughs—and *screams* as well.

The Keystone Kops routine underlies all great action sequences.

Let's return to the basement in *The Silence of the Lambs*. In Jonathan Demme's brilliant film adaptation, we find the hero—FBI Agent Clarice Starling (played by Jodie Foster)—alone in the serial killer's cellar. Starling has just discovered the grisly remains of several victims, and she now knows that the killer is hiding somewhere in the basement, waiting for her. Suddenly, the lights go out, and now we see Starling stumbling around in the dark, banging into things, touching hot furnace pipes and tripping over her own feet. Add a laugh track and you've got a sparkling little screwball comedy. But watch the poor woman through the infrared green of a killer's gaze, and the comedy curdles into a nightmare that's twice as frightening.

The key is to find artifacts in the environment—the hot furnace pipes, the pie shops—and integrate them into the action. Just as our old friend the mythical horror writer sees "the wallpaper separating, plaster crumbling, dust and debris beginning to sift down from the ceiling," you can build your scene by logically asking yourself what parts of landscape would be impacted by this chase or fight or gunplay or attack. Not only does it reinforce the authenticity of an action scene (this kind of stuff would naturally occur in the real world), but it also intensifies the experience for a reader.

Which is the object of all literary technique, right? Which brings us to . . .

Seasoning Your Scenes With Detail

Horror fiction (perhaps more than any other genre) depends on a suspension of disbelief. Harlan Ellison knows this perhaps better than anybody in the game. Ellison's flights of fancy are driven by copious detail—animal, vegetable, mineral *and emotional*—which gives them incredible verisimilitude. This allows Mister "E" to take us any damned place he wants to take us; and believe me, it's always worth the price of admission.

In his strangely poignant, Lovecraftian short story "On the Slab," for example, Ellison gives us a classic case of details motoring an action scene. Late in the story, the protagonist, Frank Kneller, has accepted the Herculean task of protecting a modern-day Prometheus who happens to be locked up in a museum; it seems a giant carrion bird has arrived from the netherworld and has crashed through the skylight and is now bearing down on the ancient man. The hero, Frank Kneller, immediately springs into action, ripping a fire extinguisher from its brackets on the wall and . . .

> . . . the virulent Halon 1301 mixture sprayed in a white stream over the bird's head. The mixture of fluorine, bromine, iodine, and chlorine washed the vulture, spurted into its eyes, filled its mouth.

Amid the feverish action, Ellison projects this weird litany of chemical minutiae. Why? Because Ellison has one of the best "eyes" in the business. Because he draws us in through detail, through seeing and smelling and tasting the terror, through dreamlike reportage. In real life, during violent events, we do indeed fixate on such minute details, we see these little odd textures. Ellison is merely translating the raw experience onto the page.

And this, gentle writers, is the foundation of good, visceral action.

Funneling Time

Ultimately, good literary action should feel like (if not look like) an inverted funnel.

In other words, as a scene progresses, time should compress in on itself.

Take our old friend the mythical writer, for example. Early on, in the initial few paragraphs, we are covering large stretches of elapsed time. First, weeks. Then, days. Then, hours:

> The horror writer had been sensing it for weeks. An imminent change in the weather. . . .
> Then, late one night, alone in his cluttered little garret, he decided to let it happen.
> He felt a weird certainty deep down in his marrow as he poured the first few fingers of the evening's espresso and lit his first Camel straight. . . .

As he prepares to write his scene, the passing of time becomes more and more compressed. The tension mounts. Then, as the words start flowing, the passage of time is tightened down to a moment-by-moment roller coaster:

> At first, it was nothing more than a subtle, metronomic beat in his head . . . He began to hear a sort of internal percussion . . .

Then, as the action progresses, the passage of time is compressed so tightly that each moment seems to stretch into a surrealistic tableau.

> . . . and the action began to flow like furious river-rapids, flowing, FLOWING, furiously, carrying the reader away in its currents . . .

Finally, the ultimate time compression flattens the event down to a series of vivid, gut-wrenching images.

The Final Blow

Think of literary action as a car accident. You, the writer, are in the driver's seat. You are feeling everything; you are sensing that time is slowing down and all you can do is watch the horrifying movie in your mind. Think of that feeling—the way movement seems to blur and get all bogged down like a taffy pull. That's the moment just before impact. Find the literary equivalent and you'll be holding your reader rapt.

More than anything else, however, the key to writing excellent action is perception. The rhythm, the point of view, the environment, the detail—it's all filtered through the human perspective.

That's what action is.

A human being in peril—forced to *perceive*.

Dark Light Focus
Roger Corman

Elizabeth Engstrom

When I was five, my physical illnesses baffled the doctors. In a last-ditch effort to save my life, my family took me from cold, snowy, smelly, dreary Chicago to the Gulf of Mexico for two weeks of sun. They hoped that a change of diet, air and scenery would provide a change of spirit. While there, the family went to the movies. We saw *Attack of the Crab Monsters.*

The movie was about a tropical island bombarded with radiation, whose resident crabs grew to giant size, ate the researchers, absorbed their intelligence, and then spoke in their voices, luring their scientist friends to a similar fate.

It was a pivotal experience for my absorbent young psyche.

I lay awake all that night, praying that the crab claw I saw silhouetted in the motel draperies wouldn't hear my thoughts, because I didn't want it to eat me and call out in my voice to my parents.

I came home from Alabama mysteriously cured.

My family called it a miracle.

I call it Roger Corman.

I'd heard the call of the imaginative, the scary, the weird.

It was my calling.

When I was a budding teenager, the cool thing to do was to go to a horror movie with your boyfriend, pretend to be scared, and get him to put a comforting arm around you. (I bet all you guys thought that taking your date to a scary movie was your idea, right?) Friday night at the movies gave way to *Shock Theater* at home on TV in the rec room after the parents went to bed.

I say Roger Corman did more for our generation than give us a few scares in our childhood. He was right there with us, supervising our puberty.

How's this for a list of memorable films? *Monster From the Ocean Floor*; *The Day the World Ended*; *The Beast with 1,000,000 Eyes*; *It Conquered the World*; *Not of This Earth*; *The Wasp Woman*; *X—The Man With the X-Ray Eyes*; *Prehistoric World*; *Little Shop of Horrors*; *A Bucket of Blood*; *Creature from the Haunted Sea*; *The Pit and the Pendulum*; *Fall of the House of Usher*; *The Raven* . . .

And on and on. Corman directed over 50 low-budget independent motion pictures and either produced or distributed another 250.

Roger Corman started out first writing and selling scripts, then producing and directing the films others wrote from his outlines. His childhood passion for science fiction clearly shows in his films. He's been called the King of "B" Movies and the Pope of Pop Cinema, but regardless of what anyone might say about him or his filmmaking style, he filled a niche in my youth, and he made a fine living doing it.

He evolved with the times, as well. Eventually he left the low-budget horror films and went on to produce films with larger budgets and more clearly defined headaches. Corman kick-started the careers of many of today's stars, including Jack Nicholson, Peter Fonda, Robert DeNiro, James Cameron, Robert Towne, Jonathan Demme, Francis Ford Coppola, Mike Connors and Charles Bronson, to barely scratch the surface. These were the young, the uninitiated, hired by Corman because they were willing to wear more than one hat, to give him what he needed: a job well done, on time and under budget. And if an actor had to carry a camera or a director had to hold a light, well, that's how it was done on the Corman set.

The Corman legacy has spawned a few subindustries of its own. *Attack of the Crab Monsters* original movie posters now sell to collectors for $450 or more. There is an active market in video rentals and sales. The soundtracks are available on CD. Magazines dedicated to tracking video prints flourish. There's no way to estimate his influence on two generations of writers. I don't need to poll my horror-writing colleagues to know that most of them have seen Corman's movies, just as we all read the pulp horror magazines. Many of my friends have an entire Corman section in their video collections.

"I feel that Corman deserves more credit than he has received for elevating the general tone of horror and science fiction cinema in the 1950s and 1960s," said Tim Lucas, author of *Throat Sprockets* and editor of *Video Watchdog Magazine*. "No matter how wacky the titles of his films might be, their stories usually contained some subversive element—a general approach or ironic denouement that questioned the government, the establishment or (in the case of *A Bucket of Blood*) the counterculture, as personified by the beats. He played no favorites, and his films encouraged young audiences to take everyone at face value and, in X-Files parlance, to trust no one. More than a few of his films portray enlightenment as a two-edged sword; one can point to any number of Corman heroes (Roderick in *Fall of the House of Usher*, Dr. Xavier in *X—The Man With the X-Ray Eyes*, Verden in *The Tomb of Ligeia*, Peter Fonda's character in *The Trip*) who are bombarded to morbid extremes by their sensitivity to the world around them, whether it's induced by drugs or simple introspection.

"If Roger Corman's body of work has taught me anything as a novelist and critic specializing in the fantastic," Lucas continued, "it is that anyone working in the genre is shortchanging themselves (and their audiences) when they have no greater ambition than to startle or frighten. To work in the realm of fantasy, his films suggest, is an opportunity to expose a greater range of truths—it's like being allowed to color with a sixty-four-count box of Crayola crayons (with sharpener) instead of the no-frills, eight-count set available to any child—a chance to extend one's palette and language, to tell truths about the world we live in, that could not be easily faced without the sugarcoating of fantasy. It is not important that audiences recognize the message one intends, but that the message is received and filed away for later processing."

Author and book reviewer Edward Bryant also sees the mark of Roger Corman on today's media. "A phenomenon Roger Corman always fostered has slipped into the brave new world of commercial publishing," Bryant said. "I'd call it John Sayles Syndrome. When Sayles wrote stuff like *Piranha*, *Alligator*, and *Battle Beyond the Stars* for Corman, he always made the scripts smart. He played the game, he worked within the requirements of the job, yet also managed to let his talent tinge the result and make it far more memorable than it had any right to be. No problem for Corman so long as the box office grosses held up. And they did. I'd like to believe there are equally talented writers in gaming and media-related and shared-world fiction who are both coloring within the commercial lines and still pushing the envelope when they can. Roger Corman has for three and a half decades shown us how to do that."

Every time I go to the video store and see young teens hanging around the horror section, it brings back memories. I find comfort in knowing that these kids, who were weaned on the flash of Industrial Light and Magic and/or the weak gore of teenage slasher movies, can still find intrigue and imagination in low-budget effects and papier-mâché crabs. I envy their discovery of Roger Corman, and I trust that in them, we will find the new generation of writers on the edge.

"He Said?" She Asked
Some Thoughts About Dialogue

David Morrell

The principles of writing effective dialogue in horror fiction are basically the same as those for writing dialogue in any other type of fiction, with the exception that some horror writers need to make a more rigorous effort to avoid tilting their dialogue into melodrama. How to create first-rate dialogue is not something that can be taught, but the reverse applies when it comes to showing someone how to avoid the common mistakes that lead to dialogue that isn't acceptable.

So many errors come to mind that I'm going to choose one arbitrarily: the use of names in dialogue.

"Jane, I'm going downtown to the library," Dick said.
"Okay, Dick, I'll see you later," Jane said.

The needlessness of the repetition should be obvious, and yet I see writers repeating names all the time. Because the speech tags indicate which character is speaking, it isn't necessary, within the dialogue, to include the name of the person being addressed. Perhaps someone might object that names need to be included in dialogue for the sake of verisimilitude, to imitate the way we speak in life. The problem is that, for the most part, we do not in fact speak this way. Try an experiment. Listen to conversations with no other purpose than that of noting how often people say each other's names. It seldom happens.

Good Dialogue Imitates Life

As near as I can guess, many writers throw names into dialogue whenever they can because they're not imitating dialogue in life; they're imitating dialogue in the movies. On the screen, names have to be said often—at least a couple of times in each sequence—in order to identify the characters. But fiction writing isn't movie writing. As a discipline, to unlearn the unfortunate habits the movies have taught us, I recommend eliminating names from dialogue completely. When this avoidance becomes second nature, slowly introduce names in dialogue but only when absolutely necessary. You'll find that it feels right to use names in dialogue when those names are included for unavoidable reasons—when people are being introduced to each other, when people are identifying themselves at the start of a telephone conversation or during a dark scene in a cellar, in short when there is no other way for a character to find out the identity of the person to whom that character is speaking. Or when there is no other way for the reader to find out a name.

Let's go back to the initial example. This time, the dialogue (and the use of names within it) are more acceptable.

> "Jane, I'm going downtown to the library."
> "Okay, Dick, I'll see you later."

This exchange isn't exactly true to life. I'm still not sure that Dick and Jane would go to the trouble of addressing each other. They know who they are, after all. Better to eliminate the names completely and use another identifying device. But because the clumsiness and wordiness of the initial example have been eliminated, the dialogue at least doesn't draw attention to itself.

Real Men (And Women) Don't Rumble

What has made the difference, of course, is that the speech tags have been cut out. Not a bad idea, it seems to me, for speech tags are an especially troublesome device, as you'll see in the following example.

> "I'll track you down and kill you!" Jane hissed.

Apparently Dick failed to return from the library. Big mistake. So is the one in the dialogue, which should be obvious. You can't hiss if you don't use sibilants, and there aren't any in this speech. How about "Jane growled"? It won't work. In this speech, only "down" has the lower register sound that we associate with a growl. "Jane spat"? Have you ever seen anyone spit while they speak? And anyway, "spat" doesn't really communicate the sense of what the writer is trying to say. Similarly, characters shouldn't bark, rasp or rumble their dialogue. At best, these expressions are inaccurate. At worst, they are clichés. In either case, they draw attention to themselves, and as was the case when names were used within dialogue, drawing unwanted attention is exactly what you don't want to do.

To eliminate the problem, restrict the verbs used in speech tags to "said" and "asked." In extreme cases, "demanded" or "insisted" may be used, and "shouted" or "screamed"—although isn't that why exclamation marks were invented, to indicate that someone is shouting or screaming? But let's include the latter two anyhow. And maybe "whispered" or "murmured." Not many.

Dialogue Without Tags

If you limit your speech tags accordingly, you'll discover some interesting consequences. One is that your tone will be less likely to be melodramatic. Another is that any weakness in your dialogue will become more obvious once the crutch of an overwritten speech tag has been eliminated. Yet another benefit is that you will start to question the need for any speech tags at *all*.

Let's look at speech tags even more closely.

"I'll track you down and kill you!" Jane said.

After the exclamation mark, "said" seems an understatement.

"I'll track you down and kill you!" Jane shouted.

"Shouted" is redundant. So what is the proper verb? Do we surrender and say that speech tags are inherently problematic, a necessary evil? Or do we look for a better way? After all, what is the purpose of a speech tag? Only one—to identify the speaker. But suppose what comes after Jane isn't a verb of speech. Why can't it be one of action or description?

"I'll track you down and kill you." Jane's cheeks were as scarlet as her hair.

Now that added sentence isn't going to win anyone a Nobel prize, but on the basis of economy, of getting bang for the buck, it does a good job. First, it provides a dramatization of Jane's anger (without the triteness of actually using the word "anger"). Second, it adds a physical detail that makes Jane more vivid to us.

That last point deserves elaboration. Unfortunately, description is almost always used in uneventful moments, when someone strolls into a room, for example. We feel description coming on, and we go to sleep. Why not include description a little at a time—where there would normally be fill-in-the-blank speech tags?

"I'll stab you in your sleep." Jane's eyes meant every word.

The "Jane said" has been eliminated, but we don't miss it. We know who the speaker is. We intuit how the dialogue was said. There aren't any empty words. Of course, you can change the dialogue and decide that you want another detail besides Jane's eyes. But as the passage now stands, on its own terms, it has reached a perfect reduction. I especially like the notion that Jane's eyes aren't described—the reader does the work for the writer.

I don't want to give the impression that I'm against speech tags entirely. When carefully placed, their fill-in-the-blank quality can create interesting effects—subtle pauses, for example.

"I know he doesn't believe I'll come after him," Jane said. "His mistake."

Take out "Jane said," and the progression of the dialogue isn't as dramatic. Sometimes "Jane said" can be a version of "Jane hesitated" or "Jane thought about it." Conversely, "Jane hesitated" is sometimes more effective than "Jane said." Every speech tag is a challenge. Sometimes, for variety, writers invert a speech tag: "said Jane." I do not recommend this approach. It is not idiomatic and distracts the reader from what is being said.

Adverbs

While we consider speech tags, the topic of adverbs can't be ignored.

"I gave that jerk the best three days of my life," Jane said bitterly.

It shouldn't come as a surprise that "bitterly" is redundant, and yet we often come across redundancy of this sort. Does the speech tag look so lonely with its meager function of identification that some writers can't resist giving the verb a companion? The temptation needs to be resisted. If the dialogue communicates what it is supposed to, the adverb in the speech tag isn't necessary, and if the dialogue fails to communicate what it is supposed to, the adverb merely points out that the dialogue hasn't been successful.

One of the few cases in which a speech tag's adverb would be acceptable involves dialogue that is meant to be spoken in contradiction to its apparent sense.

"I gave that jerk the best three days of my life," Jane said proudly.

Here the adverb contributes something. The better way, though, would have been to cut "Jane said proudly" and add a narrative sentence in which Jane does something in a proud manner—but without the use of the word "proud."

"I gave that jerk the best three days of my life." Jane stood straighter.

When Gertrude Stein and Ezra Pound were teaching Hemingway, they told him to eliminate adverbs entirely until he learned to use them judiciously. If that advice was good enough for Hemingway . . .

Punctuation

And then there are the problems associated with punctuation in dialogue, specifically the exclamation mark. Horror writers are especially inclined to overuse it. Page for page, are there more exclamation marks in horror-fiction dialogue than in any other class of narrative? Do some horror writers believe that, by adding a lot of exclamation marks when characters verbally react to terrifying situations, the situation is going to be even more terrifying than it would be with a plain old simple period? If so, they are wrong. By its nature, the exclamation mark is an attention-getting device. It upstages. It draws attention to itself. When overused, it can even push the reader away, distancing rather than engaging.

To get in the habit of not overusing the exclamation mark . . . Well, by now, you probably have anticipated my recommendation. Don't use exclamation marks at all. After several hundred pages of purity, you can then slowly reintroduce them, one at a time, in special situations, after soul-searching justification. Some of you might object that it's impossible to avoid exclamation marks. I disagree.

Note the following:

"You son of a bitch, I hate your guts!" Jane shouted.

Poor Jane has finally found Dick, but she still has her problems, and so does her dialogue. The speech tag is redundant. So is the exclamation mark, which is implied by "You son of a bitch." The whole business feels stagy, hysterical and off-putting. But let's try it this way.

"You son of a bitch, I hate your guts." Jane's gaze never left his.

The intensity has been retained, but the staginess has been eliminated. By cutting the speech tag and exclamation mark, the writer has been forced to find a better way to present the dialogue.

No one is going to complain that "Look out, she's got a knife!" involves an unnecessary use of the exclamation mark, but suppose "My God" is substituted for "Look out." "My God, she's got a knife!" is a much stronger statement, perhaps too strong if you've got fifteen exclamation marks on the same page. "My God" implies an exclamation. It probably doesn't need enhancement. "My God, she's got a knife." I don't miss the exclamation mark.

This sort of bartering should become a deliberate exercise. Add and subtract to avoid stabbing the reader in the eye with too many !!!!.

Another punctuation problem that intrigues me is how to add emphasis to a question.

"What am I going to do?" Jane exclaimed.

Well, for starters, Jane, you should stop exclaiming. But "shouted" doesn't do the job, nor does "shrieked." "Wailed"? Maybe, but it's still melodramatic. Using an exclamation mark after a question mark as in "What am I going to do?!" is an abomination. Let's try this.

Jane could barely get the words out. "What am I going to do?"

Again, finding a substitute for a speech tag has led to a solution.

"*What am I going to do?*" Jane stared at every face in the library.

Here, the italics serve the same function as an exclamation mark. When used in moderation, they are an acceptable way to enliven questions and sometimes to improve the drab look of a page. But remember—if the question has some form of cursing, the italics become redundant just as an exclamation mark is redundant after a statement that contains cursing.

One further category: colloquialisms. A certain amount of "well," "yeah," "you know," "okay," and the like are necessary to create the illusions of verisimilitude, but unless Jane is a Valley Girl and vapid expressions are a method of characterizing her, this sort of filler should be used in extreme moderation. The words don't say anything, after all. They are blank spots on the page and impede the flow of the story. Slang, too, is a form of colloquialism. It's necessary to enliven dialogue, but unfortunately current slang quickly becomes dated.

"That's cool. Give me a high five."

Unless your character is a parody, there's no reason to inflict these trite expressions on both your character and your reader. To avoid the problem, invent your own slang.

What about spelling words the way someone sloppy with diction would pronounce them?

"Dinja know he wuz gonna gitcha?"

I've never been fond of the technique because it upstages the dialogue. My immediate reaction is to note the unusual spelling. I slow my reading to try to understand what the character is actually saying. By then, the impetus of the narrative has been stalled. Sometimes, of course, a character is so illiterate that unusual spelling has to be employed. But must there be so much of it?

"Didn't you know he was gonna get you?"

For my taste, the single misspelling adequately dramatizes the character's illiteracy—without the expense of obstructing the narrative.

The techniques of writing dialogue are too numerous to exhaust here. I'll close by emphasizing: Don't let yourself be contaminated by dialogue from the movies, the radio or the stage, i.e., dialogue that is spoken out loud. Years ago, when I was a literature professor at the University of Iowa, I had a student who had been a news announcer. He was assigned to read a report to the class and did so brilliantly, his voice getting every nuance out of every word. But my suspicions were aroused, and when I asked to see the text of the report, I wasn't surprised to find that on the page the text was flat and cliched. The student had been relying on a tone that he imposed. Someone once told me, "I've discovered how to write dialogue. I talk into a tape recorder and pretend I'm various characters speaking to one another. Then I transcribe the results." A variation is to read dialogue out loud after it's written—to see how natural it sounds. *All* are bad ideas—they tempt a writer to add inflection, to supply a tone and a drive that are perhaps not in fact on the page. In fiction, dialogue is an act of silent communication. You can't rely on a reader to imagine that your characters speak with the inflection you intend. Rather, you have to invent visual cues that will force the reader to imagine the tone you require.

Which writers impress me with their dialogue? Elmore Leonard comes immediately to mind—because he invents his own vivid slang and uses sprung rhythm to make his dialogue appear colloquial. Even more, I'm impressed by Hemingway's lean approach in "A Clean Well-Lighted Place" and James M. Cain's in *The Postman Always Rings Twice.* For each of these writers, every word of dialogue is carefully considered and never wasted. The more I read them, the more I learn from them. If you adopt their discipline and build on it, you'll have an advantage. But having learned from them, forget them. Don't try to imitate them. Your task is to be as fresh as they are—in your own way. Ultimately, no matter how much you avoid the technical problems I've discussed, there is only one method of creating brilliant dialogue, and that is by concentrating on the essence of dialogue, by giving characters something interesting to say.

Darkening the Mood

Gregory Nicoll

Creating a mysterious, menacing atmosphere is important for a memorable horror story, but many writers overlook this while rushing to set their plots in motion. There are, however, some simple and effective ways to "dim the lights" quickly in your fiction and to get your readers' flesh crawling even before the real creepshow begins. These tricks include the artful use of similes, metaphors, sensory images, brand names and other carefully selected details.

Sinister Similes and Murderous Metaphors

As we all know from fifth grade language arts class, a simile is a comparison using the words "like" or "as." Almost everyone uses similes as a common means of describing things, but a well-chosen simile can serve as an immediate mood-setter.

My short story "Close to the Earth" (from the anthology *Cold Shocks*) begins:

> The early evening cold sliced at Tacker's neck like a frozen knifeblade.

The simile is "like a frozen knifeblade," and it's the first of many moody clues I plant to suggest the theme of this story, which concerns modern industry turning against the common people who depend upon it. Note also how my verb "sliced" works in support of the simile.

Unlike the simile, a metaphor is a comparison using "is" (instead of "like" or "as") and it has a considerably stronger effect. Because of this, metaphors should be used more sparingly than similes. In my story "Dead Air," from the anthology *Ripper!*, the first line of dialogue begins with a spoken metaphor:

> This place is a tomb, Mary thought. Feels like I'm buried alive.

It's a heavy metaphor and, yes, it does foretell the finale of the story (which doesn't happen until about 7,000 words later), but notice that I immediately soften it with a simile inserted in the next sentence. In context this passage follows a brief view of the broadcasting studio in which Mary, a radio disc jockey, is working. It's a room I describe as "long and narrow like a coffin." Yes, my "tomb" metaphor is flanked by similes on both sides!

Several cautions, if you please: Metaphors and similes—any form of figurative language—*must* be used sparingly and only to make an idea clearer than you might with literal language. Never attempt to adorn, poeticize or fancify your writing.

You see, going overboard with figurative language puts you in danger of creating florid overwriting, the dread "purple prose" syndrome to which horror writers might be more prone than workers in other genres. If a reader pays too much attention to how something is said—i.e., ultra-creative metaphors, similes, hyperboles, etc.—he is probably not devoting enough attention to what is said.

A Slithery Sense of Smell and Touch

Movies and TV present us with only two senses: sight and sound. But prose also wields the power to evoke smell and touch. A good writer will give his tale a sense of reality by bringing in one or both of these, usually within the first 300 words of the manuscript. Smell and touch are particularly helpful in setting a creepy, menacing mood for horror stories. Examine this passage from the second page of "Close to the Earth":

> The [interior of the] car smelled of cold plastic and frosted vinyl. The once-inviting aroma of coffee was gone now, another victim of the freezing air.

Notice how I even mention a smell that's no longer present, which actually gives this descriptive passage some narrative progression. The coffee aroma is gone, of course, because it succumbed to the evening chill; it, like one of my characters, has become "another victim."

Though the spooky applications of smell are somewhat obvious, many writers draw a blank when challenged to evoke a sense of touch. The easiest way I've found to suggest the tactile sense is to describe the temperature of the scene. Look back again at the first sentence of "Close to the Earth":

> The early evening cold sliced at Tacker's neck like a frozen knifeblade.

By the fourth word of this story, I've already established the temperature; and by the end of the first sentence I've made a tactile stroke—

right across my main character's neck, in fact. But there's more to the sense of touch than just degrees on a thermometer. Look at another passage from "Close to the Earth":

> He fell against the restaurant's metal door handle and, with a tremendous rush of relief, felt it swing inward on its hinges. An instant later he stood inside, sweet warm air as soothing around him as a heavy blanket.

I could have merely stated, "He went inside, where it was warm." But instead I chose my words to suggest the feel, the texture of this action.

Beastly Brand Names

Some writers dislike the use of actual product brand names in fiction, claiming it's as distracting as the commercials on television. But brand names are distracting only if the writer lets them become distracting. If one of your characters arrives on the scene in a Buick and the other in a Plymouth, there may not be much of a point in listing the makes of their vehicles; the words "cars" or "sedans" could suffice. But if one character arrives in a Volkswagen Beetle and the other in a Rolls-Royce Silver Cloud, *those* brand names make a statement.

I tend to give my characters an automobile with a name implying something. Roman, the girl-chasing stud in my story "Romulus and Rema" (from the anthology *Sex Macabre*), drives an Alfa-Romeo. Not only is that just the sort of sporty little Italian roadster a playboy named Roman would be likely to own, but also the name of that car contains the word "Romeo," which carries some heavy literary and cultural associations.

Cigarettes offer many moody possibilities. All cigarettes are basically the same—shredded tobacco rolled inside white paper—but cigarette manufacturers spend huge amounts of money cultivating an "image" for each brand in advertising. Writers can use these as a short cut in characterization, simply by giving characters the appropriate smoke. Marlboro is the most obvious, a brand consistently associated with images of range-riding, cattle-roping westerners.

Deadly Little Details

Carefully orchestrating even the most tiny details, especially in the first few pages of a story, can be a great way to build atmosphere. These details may take the form of an object in the background of the scene, a symbolic image, or even an artfully chosen adjective.

In both "Dead Air" and "Romulus and Rema," the first page of my text includes a reference to a poster on the wall of the room in which the scene takes place. In the former, a radio broadcasting booth is decorated with a poster advertising the heavy metal band Motley Crue's album *Shout at the Devil*. At the time I wrote the story, another popular poster commonly seen in such a setting was for Van Halen's album *Diver Down*; but it's obvious why I made the selection I did . . .

That's right! It darkened the mood! In "Romulus and Rema," the protagonist first spots the girl of his dreams as she stands "underneath a gilt-framed poster of Marlene Dietrich in *The Devil is a Woman*." This is a pretty broad hint that his dream girl is gonna become a problem.

Symbolic imagery is another useful tool in devising details that set a mood. "Dead Air" is, in part, about the threat of rape and the vulnerability of a broadcaster working alone on an overnight shift. As Mary sits by herself in the radio studio, I describe her puffing Marlboros and blowing smoke rings around the microphone. This sexually potent image prefigures a forthcoming attack.

Choosing just the right modifier can also make huge difference in setting a mood. I describe Mary's Marlboro as "her fifth since she'd started her airshift." In one draft this cigarette was her seventh, but later I decided to give the character a drinking problem. And since a "fifth" is also a common unit of measure used in over-the-counter liquor sales, I scaled her back from seven cigarettes to five, just so I could sneak the word "fifth" in there. Similarly, in "Close to the Earth," I was working hard to convey a sense of the coldness of the scene. Thus the car radio which "hissed static" at Tacker in one draft became a radio which "sprayed snowy static" during the final revision. The new text made the scene colder.

Edgar Allan Poe's "Unity of Effect"

It's crucial that all your similes, metaphors, sensory images, brand names and other details work together toward precisely the same mood-setting goal. Edgar Allan Poe called this the "Unity of Effect," a convergence of all the various supporting elements for a common accomplishment.

My story "Romulus and Rema" offers a serviceable example. The tale concerns a young man on the hunt for sexual adventure. He encounters a mysterious foreign female of ambiguous background and sexuality, who is ultimately revealed to be a werewolf. My protagonist also has an obsession with women's breasts. I wanted the first two paragraphs of the story to suggest the romance of meeting people from faraway places, with a hint of unusual new sexual possibilities they may present. I also wanted strong breast imagery and some tiny hint of the lyncanthropic transformation which figures in the story's finale.

Here's what I wrote:

> He spotted her across a crowded room at one of Bear's legendary "international" parties, where the big stereo pumped spritely salsa music and the shortwave in the rear hall captured the faraway violins of Radio Rumania; where the tables were laid with bowls of ripe mangoes, curious fruits, and fragrant seafood spreads; where melons bobbed in the two matching crystal punchbowls which Bear splashed full of potent white wine sangria; and where the women were as exotic as they were plentiful.
>
> Roman watched her eagerly as she stood there against the far wall, underneath a gilt-framed poster of Marlene Dietrich in *The Devil is a Woman* that Bear had brought back from London. . . .

Note my choice of the name "Bear" for an important character, and the phrase "from London" which I'd hoped would hint at the titles of the movies (and Warren Zevon's hit song) about werewolves from that city. Also, note my use of sexually charged words such as "pumped," "laid," "fruits," "spreads," and "melons"—all included in a seemingly innocent context. Perhaps I pushed the limit when I described the white wine anointing the two matching punch bowls, but the image does portend a key sex scene which occurs later in the story.

A final word of warning: You can get carried away with these techniques and make an embarrassing mistake. It's best to exercise restraint and remember that sometimes you can have too much of a good thing. In fact, I blush to admit that there's a real howler of a goof in one of my own little "masterpieces."

Yes, in my effort to intensify the frosty cold imagery of my story "Close to the Earth," I changed the brand name of a snack food from a Moon Pie (an oversized cookie coated with chocolate) to an Eskimo Pie (ice cream coated with chocolate). Whatever I may have gained by sneaking the word "Eskimo" into those early pages, I surely must lose it whenever very careful readers note this absurdity: My protagonist, who is nearly freezing to death, selects a frozen dairy treat as his late-night snack!

Dr. Frankenstein's Secrets of Style

Norman Partridge

I'm sure you're familiar with our old buddy Dr. Frankenstein. You've read Mary Wollstonecraft Shelley's classic novel, maybe a few anthologies chock full of Frankensteinian stories, and you've seen those old movies, too.

There's a scene in most of those movies. One that I love. Where the good doctor's son, or grandson, or granddaughter, or (better yet) some conniving interloper invades the doc's dusty old castle and finds a big thick book entitled *Dr. Victor Frankenstein's Secrets of Life and Death*, which naturally spares the prospective mad scientist a whole bunch of hair-tearing, grief and anguish when it comes to the fine art of monster-making.

When it comes to developing a writing style, we may borrow from the good doctor.

If I gave you six or seven horror novels—novels by the likes of Stephen King, Dean Koontz, Anne Rice or Peter Straub—with the covers ripped off and the titles and authors blacked out, I'll bet a big wad of green money that you could tell me who wrote them after just a chapter or two.

You want to know why? King, Koontz, Rice and Straub all have discernible styles, that's why.

Of course, it's likely the aforementioned quartet of best-selling authors have been at this game a little longer than you have. They developed their respective styles through countless hours of hard work.

Work on short stories and novels, that is. Telling story after story, getting each one down on paper, typing "The End" time and time again. Learning what works and what doesn't by trial and error. Even learning *unconsciously*. Because, let's face it, no beginning writer sits down at the good old word processor or typewriter and says, "Forget all that story and plot junk . . . today I'm going to develop a *style*."

Well, maybe someone *has* tried that. Actually, I wouldn't doubt it. But I'm still holding that green money, and I'll bet that any misguided boob who attempted such an endeavor failed miserably.

Because your writing style comes from within. In fact, you've probably already got it, or at least a good chunk of it. You just don't know about it yet. But maybe I can help you find it . . . or at least show you where to look.

All you'll need is a shovel and a stout heart.

Now, follow me to the cemetery . . .

Digging up the Parts

Here we are. Cool fog raising gooseflesh on your arms. The full moon shining up above. Gnarled branches scratching the night sky. A forest of marble monuments and granite headstones looming before you.

You recognize the scene, don't you? Sure you do. Any horror writer worth his salt recognizes Dr. Frankenstein's favorite bone garden. Just as you remember why the good doctor invariably makes the cemetery his first stop.

It's the mad scientist's very first rule: *If you're gonna make a monster, you're gonna need parts.*

Creating a writing style isn't much different. Just as Frankenstein's monster is a crazy quilt of dear departed humanity, your writing style is an amalgam of influences. Which is why you must read—and read widely—if you want to write.

Mad scientists open graves.

Writers open books.

I knew this from the start, long before I ever became serious about publishing my fiction. I worked for several years in the local public library, during which time I read the very best the horror genre had to offer. From Poe to Bradbury, from Matheson to King, and on through Lansdale and Schow, I absorbed the lessons of those who labored in Dr. Frankenstein's cemetery long before I ever picked up my shovel.

But I also learned a great deal from writers in completely unrelated genres. For me, crime writers were a big influence in developing every element of my work. I learned a great deal about mood from writers who specialize in *crime noir.* And when it comes to pace and plot, I found my best teachers in writers such as Elmore Leonard, John D. MacDonald and Dan J. Marlowe.

I didn't confine my reading to novels, either. I found anthologies especially valuable. In the space of a single anthology, I'd invariably be exposed to as many styles as there were stories. Not all of them were successful or effective, of course. But sometimes it's just as important to learn what *doesn't* work as what does work . . . and why.

The Sincerest Form of Flattery

Now, please don't get the impression that I'm telling you to imitate other writers, especially when it comes to style. I certainly wouldn't advise you to do that.

But I'd be less than honest if I didn't tell you that a certain amount of imitation is unavoidable, especially for a writer who is just starting out. H.P. Lovecraft's early work strongly echoes Poe. Other Lovecraft stories recall the tales of Lord Dunsany. Robert Bloch began his career as a student of H.P. Lovecraft, only to evolve into one of the finest psychological suspense writers of his generation. Ramsey Campbell also followed in Lovecraft's footsteps, publishing Cthulhu-mythos-inspired fiction as a teenager. But Campbell didn't stop there. He continued to grow and evolve, and today he is thought of as one of the most original stylists in horror fiction. While Campbell is still more than capable of putting a twist on Lovecraftian themes, his style of writing is now thoroughly his own. In fact, these days more than a few young writers have begun their careers by imitating Ramsey Campbell.

Consciously or unconsciously, every beginning writer imitates. Including me. But the truth is that some of those imitative stories actually do work out. Compiling my recent short-story collection, *Bad Intentions*, I was surprised to rediscover early tales written while I was obviously under the sway of writers as disparate as Dennis Etchison and Joe R. Lansdale. But reading those stories today is kind of like looking at a ten-year-old photograph of yourself. Sure, you recognize the guy in the picture, but the clothes you're wearing may surprise you!

So while a certain amount of imitation is necessary, in the final analysis it's just another way of developing your own creative filter, of learning what works and what doesn't. But it's certainly not the end of the process.

Too Much of a Good Thing

Okay. You're stitching your monster together, working every day. You're reading. You're writing. You're putting in the time.

But you don't want to overdo it. Especially when it comes to style. You're walking a fine line. A dash too much mood, an extra dollop of flowery description, and your horror stories will read like parodies. They'll invoke laughter rather than fright.

It's the "Hey, Ma, look at me write" syndrome, and it's usually the result of over-polishing your prose.

One of the hardest things to learn as a writer is when to quit. Some beginners become so obsessed with making each story "perfect," each line of prose "deathless," that they sabotage their own fiction by revising it to death. And sabotage is not too strong a word. Because overblown description, multiple metaphors, and overused similes can wreak explosive destruction upon your tales of terror.

Too much of a good thing is indeed too much of a good thing. Remember that.

It's (Not) Alive!

But also remember that even Dr. Frankenstein had his failures. That nasty bit of business with Igor and the abnormal brain, for example. But the good doc wasn't a quitter. When things didn't work out the way he'd planned, Victor Frankenstein always got out his shovel and headed back to the cemetery.

So don't give up. Put in the time. Write those stories. Read those books. Stitch that monster together.

One day he'll be stretched out on that slab before you, just like in the movies. You put him together—an experiment here, an influence there—but I think you'll find that he doesn't quite look like any of those things you made him from. No sum total of his parts, this guy. He's an original.

And just as you're about to throw the switch and juice him with electricity, he'll probably surprise you by sitting up and stalking off completely on his own. See, you've already done that. All the work you put in, that was the juice your monster needed. Your creative spark gave him life.

Just look at him.

You can even holler "It's alive! It's alive!" if you want to.

Because this monster's lookin' good, isn't he?

That's because he's got *style*.

HORROR

GENRE AND SUBGENRE

More Simply Human

Tracy Knight

Horror fiction deals in aberrations: aberrations of nature and circumstance, of fate and destiny, of the cosmic and the exquisitely human. Of these facets, the most memorable and compelling are the human beings who populate the writer's fictional world. Through their eyes the reader is able to behold existence from a unique and unexpected perspective. With those characters the reader is able to live another human's endeavor to understand, able to avoid or defeat an unimaginable reality, a loathsome monster or a mind-bending situation.

Creating believable characters who invite a reader's identification and investment is the hallmark of effective writing of every genre. In horror fiction this can be particularly challenging since in so many ways the writer is asking us to accept and embrace the unreal. For this reason, characterization in horror writing is central to a story's success.

Characters who embody the struggles, tragedies and terrors of mental disorders—from eccentricities of personality to psychoses—are widespread in horror fiction, whether they are the protagonist or, as is the case all too often, the malevolent horror itself. When they are effectively developed, nurtured into completeness, these characters become the centerpieces of unforgettable short stories or novels.

Consider Norman Bates in Robert Bloch's *Psycho*; Hannibal Lecter in Thomas Harris's *The Silence of the Lambs*; the characters' interlocking pathologies in Ed Gorman's political thriller *The Marilyn Tapes*; the stark, chilling, and sometimes comedic psychopaths in J.N. Williamson's *The Book of Websters*; and the almost alien derangement of George Smith in Theodore Sturgeon's *Some of Your Blood*.

As a clinical psychologist, I am interested in how writers portray personality types and mental disorders. However, with alarming frequency authors make basic errors that interfere with the enjoyment of their fiction. Perhaps because we all possess our own personal psychology, we tend to assume that we know how human difficulties and insanity manifest themselves, and how they are expressed in thought, perception and behavior. Couple this with the strange and inaccurate portrayals of psychological difficulties in media of all ilk and you have a recipe for a myriad of fictional missteps.

Yet, in order to create compelling characters who accurately portray human personality types and mental disorders, a writer need not pursue an advanced degree in psychology. The necessary references are literally at one's fingertips. Adding these psych resources to your existing ability to create characters will sharpen your proficiency to integrate human aberrations into your horror fiction, thus fashioning characters who not only are beyond the norm of most readers' experience, but believable as well.

I hasten to add I am not sounding a call to create characters with mental disorders merely to add color and strangeness to your stories. Rather, these characters are used so frequently, I'm only interested in its being done accurately—and, ultimately, more humanely.

In the past six months, I've read works of horror fiction in which: (1) A schizophrenic switches personalities helplessly, from priest to murderer to three-year-old child; (2) A severely depressed law enforcement officer engages in car chases, leaps from building rooftops and participates in frenzied pursuits of suspects, all with incredible energy; (3) A psychotic killer methodically plans a series of murders with clarity and an extraordinary lack of emotion; (4) A psychologist laments that she cannot treat mental illness since psychologists are only trained to work with family relationships, then later injects a patient with medication as part of his treatment.

What do all of these examples have in common? They are *wrong*. They rest on foundations of inaccurate information, thus splintering the seamless dream the writer is attempting to create.

To quickly address each of the above-mentioned errors:

Schizophrenia and Multiple Personality Disorder (now termed Dissociative Identity Disorder) are distinct clinical entities. Please write this down in large block letters in your notebook. If I accomplish nothing else in this chapter other than to reduce the grotesque number of times this error is made, I will consider my existence on this planet well spent.

Schizophrenia is a devastating mental illness which may manifest as hallucinations, delusions, disorganized speech and behavior, social withdrawal and dulling of emotional responses. While the term "schizophrenia" is derived from Greek words meaning "split mind" (which may be where the confusion originally arose), a more accurate definition is "shattered mind." The split is not between personalities; it is between Self and World. The boundaries blur, or even vanish. Thus an internal image becomes an external phenomenon; an idea becomes a worldly truth.

What has been known as Multiple Personality Disorder is marked by the presence of two or more distinct personalities which repeatedly take control of an individual's behavior, often with the activities of one personality remaining virtually unknown to another. Even more interesting is the debate in psychology and psychiatry on the prevalence and actual existence of this syndrome as a pure disorder; some in the field believe that this disorder can be inadvertently created or encouraged in psychotherapy.

A severely depressed man would not likely have the physical energy necessary to engage in James Bondian adventures. Cardinal signs of a major depression include loss of interest and motivation, difficulty concentrating, diminished energy and feelings of worthlessness; none of which is particularly conducive to the spirited pursuit of a quarry.

A psychotic killer and a psychopathic killer are not synonymous. A psychotic person has experienced a break with reality, likely including delusions and hallucinations (and generally *less likely* to be dangerous than the rest of us!), whereas the common use of the term "psychopathic" refers to an irredeemably antisocial individual who is impulsive, deceitful and aggressive, with little to no conscience or empathy.

A psychologist treats mental illness. Although most psychologists have doctorate degrees (e.g., Ph.D., Psy.D., or Ed.D.), they are not medical doctors and don't prescribe or administer medication. However, their central function in a clinical setting *is* the diagnosis and treatment of mental disorders through assessment and psychotherapy. Of all the media portrayals of mental health professionals, Bob Newhart's sitcom character was perhaps the most accurate—which says much about the media's accuracy.

A psychiatrist is someone who has earned a medical doctor (M.D.) degree, then goes on to specialize in the treatment of mental illness. It is the psychiatrist who prescribes and monitors the use of psychotropic medications.

Getting it Right

These inaccuracies represent common errors writers make when including psychological terms in their fiction. However, as is the case in the whole of life, it is much easier to point out errors and mistakes than it is to chart a positive course. As I often tell my clients, "If blame cured anyone, we'd all be perfect by now." In the remainder of this chapter, therefore, I will offer horror writers suggestions on how to more successfully integrate human abberations into their fiction.

Invest in a copy of the American Psychiatric Association's Diagnostic and Statistical Manual of Mental Disorders *(currently in its fourth edition and often referred to as the* DSM-IV*).* It is the standard diagnostic reference for psychiatry and psychology. Used by researchers, clinicians and insurance companies to approach some consensus about the definitions and signs of various mental disorders and to facilitate communication among professionals, the later editions of this manual offer clear and concise listings of the symptoms and characteristics of everything from childhood disorders to organic brain syndromes, from psychotic disorders to anxiety disorders, from sexual disorders to personality disorders. This book is a treasure for the writer seeking to portray human psychological difficulties accurately; it contains not only basic descriptions of currently recognized mental disorders, but also enhances these descriptions with information on the prevalence, course and associated features of the difficulties.

It is important to recognize that psychiatric diagnoses undergo constant change as new evidence emerges to help shape our understanding of the human condition. Did you know, for example, that "homosexuality" is no longer a psychiatric diagnosis, or that "neurosis" as a concept has nearly disappeared from current diagnostic formulations? If you are writing a story set in a time other than the present, it will prove valuable to research the psychiatric diagnoses which exsisted at the time of the story. For example, Ed Gorman's *The Marilyn Tapes*, Marilyn Monroe's psychiatrist diagnoses her as evidencing "cyclothymic personality," a diagnosis which no longer exsists but *did* when the story took place.

After using the *DSM-IV* for basic research, a writer can then bolster his or her understanding of a disorder by using the countless books and journal articles available on each disorder, or even by perusing a standard college textbook on abnormal psychology.

Recognize that most modern psychotherapy is not Freudian psychoanalysis. Writers have a tendency, when including psychotherapy in their stories, to include a couch, free association, dream analysis, endless discussions of childhood, and those ubiquitous Rorschach inkblots. These are all facets of classic psychoanalysis which, while it still exists, is not currently practiced by many psychotherapists. There are over 350 distinct and definable systems of psychotherapy. I recommend that you avail yourself of Raymond Corsini's series *Current Psychotherapies*. Each edition of this work includes succinct and clear coverage of a number of psychotherapeutic approaches, including a brief statement of the underlying theory, the basic concepts of the system, its history, its current status, its applications and even a case example.

Resources such as these will not only strengthen the factual foundation of your fiction, but likely spark a legion of creative ideas.

Caveat. The *DSM-IV* poses the same danger as any other research resource: It can inadvertently encourage a writer to create a caricature rather than a living, breathing human character. Therefore, I offer here some further insights on human functioning, with hopes that these simple ideas will help you to create characters in your horror fiction who not only display all the color and uniqueness you hope to invoke, but also the internal consistency that a reader expects from any fictional character.

What is personality? Human personality is the characteristic and enduring way that each of us perceives and interprets the world; the beliefs and assumptions we make about ourselves, the world, and other people; and the patterns of behavior we are likely to show regularly. These patterns range from the smallest (the way a man plays with his mustache) to the most general (reacting with rage whenever one's judgment is questioned). In short, personality is the map we use in order to navigate our lives.

It is as if each of us wears a pair of colored eyeglasses with its unique hue. Everything we experience is filtered through those glasses and thus each of us has an individual take on the life we're living and the world in which we live.

When someone has a personality disorder (distinct from a clinical syndrome or illness), he or she has a limited, predictable and inflexible way of perceiving, interpreting and acting in the world. Thus, a paranoid personality will interpret a comment, no matter how benign, as demeaning or threatening; an avoidant personality will perceive remarks from others as indicating potential rejection or humiliation; a schizoid personality will show little interest in relationships with others and will be unaffected by comments, good or bad. Because inflexibility is so much a part of a personality disorder—indeed of most mental disorders—many clinicians, myself included, believe the word "disorder" to be a misnomer. If anything, most of the clients we see are *too ordered*, too predictable and limited in their perceptions and responses, and a goal of psychotherapy is to help them become less predictable.

Too often, unbalanced or psychotic characters in horror fiction deviate from this insight. Apparently the writer assumes that since he or she created a "crazy character," that character can do virtually anything in the story, that the label of mental illness is a license to act totally unpredictably and irrationally. This is not true. Which leads me to my next point:

Every behavior has a goal. When I was an intern psychologist, I was called in to see my first floridly psychotic patient. She was a pleasant and polite woman, but she insisted God was talking to her, even as we conversed, and she was afraid her husband would cause her to lose the child she was carrying—the result of God impregnating her. At first, being the wide-eyed intern, I made feeble attempts to somehow reel her in and encourage her to share the world I was inhabiting. Suddenly an insight struck me: If I had God talking in one of my ears, and a young psychologist in the other, who would *I* listen to? Having recognized that, I proceeded to immerse myself in her world and, to my surprise, found not that her behavior was horribly disorganized or random, but rather that every single behavior had a goal. Of *course* she walked backward with her hands on her stomach because God had told her he would strike her dead if she didn't protect their child. It all made sense.

You can understand, then, that you must know not only what your character's "symptoms" are, but how your character views the world *from the inside.* To truly captivate your reader, that world must be coherent and consistent, no matter how bizarre it may seem on its face.

Everyone is doing his or her best. Upon first glance, this may sound ludicrous, but it's true. With the world they perceive, the concepts they have of themselves and the options they see, people in general make the best choices they can at any moment. Remember this.

Everyone is more than a collection of symptoms. Although the *DSM-IV* is a wonderful way to provide some structure to your aberrant characters, to give them a cohesive and accurate form, it is crucial to understand that not one person is contained in any diagnostic description. The diagnostic system, like all systems, was created to *simplify* the world; therefore, the search was not for Ultimate Truth but for patterns, characteristics that tend to appear together. No one perfectly exemplifies any diagnostic pattern and no diagnostic pattern captures a human being. Not even close.

There is a philosophical concept known as the "A/Not A Absurdity," which states that when one draws a line between any two constructs—whether those constructs are mentally ill/mentally healthy, diabetic/nondiabetic, even dead/alive—and then one approaches that line from either direction, *the line disappears.* There is relatively little difference between people who are considered mentally ill and those who are not. Psychiatrist Harry Stack Sullivan said it best: "We are all more simply human than otherwise."

And perhaps that's the secret of creating believable characters who portray any type of human aberration. It's not that they are radically different from the rest of us; it's that we share so much with them. We share their irrational fears, their unacceptable desires. We have our moments when we feel out of control, or when our ruthlessness rushes to the fore.

That is why the most effective characters in horror fiction who display some mental or personality disorder prove so chilling. After all, even cold-blooded killer Hannibal Lecter voiced the romantic notion that he and Clarice were looking up at the same stars. Even Norman Bates quietly mourned his mother.

We are all more simply human than otherwise.

Archetypes and Fearful Allure
Writing Erotic Horror

Nancy Kilpatrick

Erotic horror. Either alone or as a couple, these two words evoke a strong reaction in most people. The spectrum ranges from revulsion to titillation, with a myriad of emotions caught in between.

Both separately or combined, these words have never been politically correct. If being a politically correct writer is your goal, you'd better not attempt writing erotica, horror or erotic horror. Despite the fact that some cultures during some eras have been more liberal than others, those are exceptions in human history.

But, of course, if you weren't interested in writing erotic horror, you wouldn't be reading this, would you?

Because erotica and horror have always been outside the mainstream, they hold a strong appeal. Forbidden fruit is the tastiest, and readers are drawn to these genres, although usually surreptitiously. Which means there is and always will be a market.

At this point, it might feel like a cold shower, but starting with a dictionary will help clarify just what I'm talking about when I use the words erotic and horror—and link them.

The Random House Dictionary of the English Language, Second Edition Unabridged, defines horror this way (emphasis mine):

> An overwhelming and painful feeling caused by something frightfully shocking, *terrifying, or revolting*; a shuddering fear . . . Anything that causes such a feeling . . . *A strong aversion; abhorrence.*

About the word *erotic*, the same dictionary says (emphasis mine):

> Arousing or satisfying sexual desire . . . *Subject to or marked by strong sexual desire.*"

On the surface, these two words form an oxymoron and should have little in common. Horror we move away from; the erotic we move toward. Or do we?

The Complexity That Is Man

Human beings are complicated creatures. For example, we have been responsible for more atrocities on this planet than all other life forms and natural forces combined. Yet in fiction there exists a popular category called "horror," which focuses on atrocities, committed by humans, by natural forces, by supernatural forces, on humans who are the victims of these horrors, either individually or collectively. In real life, people are drawn to the scene of an accident. If you'll excuse the pun, the category of horror is not dead. Readers go out of their way to unearth horror books, despite too-frequent poor promotion of titles by publishing houses and the "creative placement" of the volumes in bookstores.

So the dictionary is right. And the dictionary is wrong. Horror is an emotion, extreme and shocking. While we might abhor and have an aversion to horror, we are also attracted. We want to read about horrors, and some of us want to write horror.

When it comes to the erotic, well, Freud said it all. As much as most people have a desire to move into the sexual arena, human beings also have quite a bit of resistance to actualizing their erotic fantasies. This is compounded by serious health concerns of our time—like AIDS. Some have said that the surge of cyber sex—and who doesn't know somebody having an online affair?—and the proliferation of erotic writing seeing print is a direct result of our struggling to satisfy carnal desires in a safe way.

If you put "horror" and "erotic" together you end up with one of the most intriguing and fastest growing subgenres in fiction: erotic horror.

As with any other creative pursuit, the erotic horror writer has a wide range of expression to choose from. Horror can be about real-life serial killers, or supernatural beings like werewolves. It can be soft, psychological, reality based, hard-edged or what used to be termed splatter—graphic, in-your-pretty-face writing. Erotica, likewise, can be soft and gentle, sensual, romantic writing reminiscent of nudes photographed in artistic poses through a gauze-covered lens, all the way to what is deemed pornographic—blatant descriptions of "the act" in all its permutations, using graphic language. Erotic horror, blending both worlds, creates a complex mosaic of styles and angles on the fire-and-ice subject matter of this subgenre.

Of course, one person's dreadful horror is another's lengthy yawn. And what's erotic to you might leave a reader, shall we say, "nonplused." In other words, your idea of erotic horror may not be a reader's idea of erotic horror. Which begs the question, how do you write erotic horror that will leave readers shivering with conflicting feelings?

The answer: You work with archetypes.

The Monster With 1,000 Faces

I'm going back to the dictionary one more time before I close it. The word *archetype* is in vogue and consequently is frequently misused. Clarity is everything in writing, so here's a definition (emphasis mine):

> The *original* pattern or model *from which all things of the same type are copied or on which they are based*; a model or first form. Prototype.

To encourage even more precision, here's how the word is used in Jungian terms, since this is specifically how I'll be using it: "A collectively inherited unconscious idea, pattern of thought, image, etc., universally present in individual psyches."

To understand *archetype*, let's work with the familiar image of much erotic horror: The vampire. What is the *archetypal* vampire? If you could persuade all the vampires that have ever existed in fact, fiction and mythology, in artwork, film and print, to congregate in the same mausoleum; and if you could convince each to let you superimpose them on each other, the elements that they all have in common would comprise the archetypal vampire.

Certainly vampires have changed from century to century and from culture to culture. The first vampire who ever saw print was in the Epic of Gilgamesh, circa 2,500 B.C.: the Death-Bringer. Ancient Chinese vampires are not Baltic vampires. The vampires of the Middle East are not the same as those appearing in South American cultures. But whether the vampire is a disembodied spirit or corporeal being, whether the Nosferatu sucks blood or brains or air or souls—I wrote one in *Freak Show* that sucks dreams!—there are elements that they all share. They may prey on strangers or family members, or be thwarted by the symbols of any and all religions or be utterly unthwartable; they may or may not be allergic to sunlight and garlic or repelled by crosses and sunlight. They can be romantic seducers—aka Good Guys with Fangs—or repulsive grab-'em-and-suck-'em reanimated corpses.

Bottom line: vampires are out to *take* something from *us*. All vampires are predators; they are parasites that live off humanity.

Here, then a definition of erotic horror as it pertains *specifically* to vampires from *The Kilpatrick House Dictionary of the English Language, First Edition, Unabridged, Uncensored*: "A predatory being that preys on human beings in a sexually arousing or satisfying and/or sexually repulsive way."

Voila! Vampire: the erotic horror archetype. Coming soon to a bookstore near you!

Archetypes are not just important in terms of writing erotic horror; they are the crucial raw energy on which all powerful writing is based.

Inside Us All

According to Carl Jung, archetypes dwell in both our personal psyche and within the collective psyche. We know that these powerful energies have come to the fore, meaning our consciousness, when we feel an emotional "charge." Likewise, when we get charged by a piece of writing, it is because the archetype is affecting us. What we read on the page mirrors a universal energy each of us carries within.

It's easy to see with the image of the vampire that the fictional tropes employed vary from era to era, culture to culture and writer to writer. Some recent titles illustrate this. Sonja Blue, the female vamp in Nancy Collins's books *Sunglasses After Dark* and *In the Blood*, is a different being from Deirdre in Karen E. Taylor's series *Blood Secrets; Bitter Blood;* and *Blood Ties*. The former writer's works present a hard and cold vampiress, but that is exactly what makes her alluring. The latter's work involves a romantic figure, close to a Harlequin heroine. Both *femme fatales* live on blood, prey on men and fit the definition of erotic vampire.

On the male undead side of things, Chelsea Quinn Yarbro's vampire Count St. Germain still retains a high level of empathy for the human females he seduces and upon whom he preys. In my own grittier novels *Child of the Night* and *Near Death*, André and David have different styles when approaching blood-stocked women, ranging from aggressive to tender, but always highly sensual. More extreme versions of an erotic vampire can be found in Poppy Z. Brite's gay vampire novel *Lost Souls*, and also in a pansexual pastiche I penned under the *nom de plume* Amarantha Knight, *The Darker Passions: Dracula*, a retelling of Bram Stoker's classic. In my scenes behind the scenes, where Victorian skirts are lifted, the Prince of Wallachia, Dracula himself, becomes a full-blown sexual being with no inhibitions. Didn't we always know he had it in him?

You'll notice that all the examples given are by female writers. In the last twenty years, women have excelled at writing erotic horror. And while you may be very familiar with the men who write in this subgenre, I thought you might enjoy hearing about some female horror eroticists who illustrate some of the new ground women writers have broken.

What is important about all of the above vampire examples, and what they all have in common, is that they employ the essence of the archetypal vampire. None are stereotypes. *Stereotypes* are *dead* archetypes. The power of an archetype is fresh, and it is universal, because it spans time and culture. This means that the energy embedded in the image resonates with all readers.

This does not mean all readers will love every one of these books. Nobody can guarantee that. Reaching some of the readers some of the time is as good as it gets. The reader might be excited or repelled, horrified or aroused, by any or all of these archetypal vampires. Or she may be bored. But provided the writing itself isn't doggerel, if a bored reader is honest with him- or herself, the realization *might* dawn that what seemingly is not of interest is actually unsettling in some way, provoking feelings and responses the reader would rather not know about. You can't control readers by forcing them to face what they cannot or will not face. But you can write the most powerful story or novel you can write, finding the archetypal energy and working with it through imagery.

When you work with an archetype, it's important to figure out what the past holds, as well as the parameters of current cultural images. That way, you don't repeat what's been done and you can get a grip on the next step in the archetype's evolution.

Weaving Erotica and Horror

Another important point about writing erotic horror is that any piece of writing in this subgenre must work as both a piece of erotica and a piece of horror. Lucy Taylor has an intriguing story in *Flesh Fantastic* called "Love in the Age of Ice." In this story, a porn star is cryonically frozen and brought back by her loving husband. You can see the thrust, as it were, of both the erotic and the horrific elements, and I won't spoil the story by giving away the climax. Most of Lucy's stories can be read in either light, which is why they are so effective. Another writer of well-crafted erotic horror is Nancy Holder. Check out her "Blood Gothic" story in *Shadows 8*. She takes the vampire victim to an extreme here, where we see a woman wasting away with erotic fantasy. Elizabeth Massie's amazing story "Abed" in *Book of the Dead 2—Still Dead* is a ghastly portrayal of how a southern matriarch deals with a zombie in the family. One more writer who, I might add, pulls off an incredible feat is Dawn Dunn. "Death's Hot Embrace," which she wrote for *Sex Macabre*, does what I have never seen another story do. Dawn's hot protagonist wants to get it on with a ghoul, one of the most repulsive supernatural beings ever created. Amazingly, she makes it work by careful weaving of the two elements, erotica and horror.

To ensure that your story succeeds on two levels, try this: Forget the horror element for a moment. Read the piece as if it were strictly erotica. The simple question: Does the writing turn you on? Do all the parts fit, as it were? Now, reread the story as if it were in the horror-only section, shelved next to the latest Anne Rice or Stephen King. Does it creep you out? Does the plot hang together strictly as a good horror read? If you must answer "No" to *either* of these sets of questions, you have not written an effective erotic horror story. You will need to go back and strengthen weak elements so that the story can stand alone as either erotica or horror. The story needs to perform on both levels equally.

Erotic horror is a fine line. If you can tap into the archetypal power of your images, if you can balance the erotic and the horrific, you will be giving the readers what they want, whether you're aiming for a soft line that gently touches the reader or the deep razor's edge cut.

Dark Light Focus
EC Horror Comics

D.G. Chichester

In the 1950s, a virus was unleashed upon the unsuspecting populace of America. It was transmitted through the retinas of direct-contact victims, causing them to see reality in a whole new way. Some claimed it warped the minds of the young and unraveled the fabric of society. Measures were taken to prevent its spread.

The "virus" was Entertaining Comics, a short-lived but highly influential collection of publications founded by William Gaines. Illustrated in loving, gruesome detail, the hugely popular EC line was fueled by tales of satisfying revenge and O'Henry-from-Hell comeuppance, all executed (ahem) with style. Gaines and his crew put out titles like *The Haunt of Fear* and *Shock Suspenstories*, the success of which spawned truly horrible hack-and-slash gutter-level ripoffs and gave the McCarthy Era censorship hounds more ammo. As a result, the Comics Code was born, which ended the ripoffs—and EC comics, as well.

Fortunately, the virus had been loosed. Although it lay dormant for awhile, microbes with names like Gaines, Craig, Ingels and Feldstein did not completely vanish. The next generation came across the germ in garage sales and paperback collection reprints, and they too suffered similar effects from the Entertaining Comics disease.

EC's viral seed grew the dark garden of the mind that is the contemporary horror field.

I'm not talking the "Tales From the Crypt" aisle at Toys "R" Us! Casual, HBO-approved public acceptance is not the issue. Let the sheep think it's safe pasture. We are the wolves—rabid with the EC viral strain, you betcha—empowered by that legacy in our own explorations in horror, both what we enjoy and what we create.

That's not to say the many approaches to penning a scary story have been supplanted by the "EC formula" or should feature blood in the same wholesale quantities. What Gaines & Co. said—and, I believe, has inspired in each of us dark fiction disciples—was that it was cool to bring terror out of the shadows. EC proved that in the right set of hands (not necessarily still attached at the wrist), well-done horror still held its unsettling power.

Don't mistake that achievement as the cheap thrill brought on by morbid graphics. Comics can't depend on the visual shock that a movie can get away with. You can flip ahead or back to any comic panel and dwell on every line to your heart's content. If EC had been built solely on violent imagery, like so many of their cheap mimics, they'd have been gobbled up by the years along with those useless copycats. Their survival—if not as a publisher, then as an icon—after the better part of half a century is due to a foundation of well-crafted horror. These guys knew how to unravel (okay—shred!) society's safety net. Their brand of rock-'em-sock-'em-robot kidney punches were just not the order of the day, when the suggestion of menace was still the popular, polite tack for sailing the midnight sea. The first "law" of horror remains that what's behind the closed door is the greatest apprehension. But like some sinister therapist, EC whispered to us, "It's okay to throw open that door and shove people through . . . *And* lock it back up behind 'em. It's a good thing. A very good thing."

If you've been exposed, chances are you've made the connection, even if not consciously. If you've never had the pleasure, don't think you're immune. Horror writer, horror reader, trace back your favorites, if you will, your influences, and I'll guarantee not that far along the way one has been touched and has transmitted the condition to you.

In the best tradition of pop culture, EC distilled fear and passed that on to its readers with brazen, garish impact while having a ball doing it. You can feel EC's resonance in the hard-hitting horror that followed, horror that put down a footing of established dread but was no longer afraid to go that grisly step farther to frightening effect.

In the lingo of the comics that overran the EC empire, it might be called a super-power. Given the nature of our beast, I'd recommend thinking of it as your secret weapon.

The EC infection is clearly a battle cry. Sharpen your pencils, fire up your word processors, and go get 'em. Send the sheep bolting from the pasture.

And spread the virus to tomorrow's pack of wolves.

Editor's Note: Gemstone Publishing currently publishes reprints of EC comics. Titles include *Tales From the Crypt*, *Weird Science* and *Shock Suspenstories*. Not only can you see the effect EC stories had on today's horror crafters, you'll discover artists who, unlike many of today's comic bookers, knew a heck of a lot about anatomy—and proved it on the page. Gemstone Publishing, P.O. Box 469, West Plains, MO 65775.

Breaking All Codes
Horror Comics

David Quinn

When it comes to creating on the dark side for that fevered, pulpy, wonderful field *I've* plowed the most—comic—books, these are a few of my favorite things:

Madness and its genius: I don't think I have lived enough to fully dramatize madness in all its horror, or the primal mind in all its genius. But that hasn't stopped me from chewing at the edges of insanity in *everything* I've written.

The scenes I describe, the language I provide as their counterpoint, work toward a glimpse of the madness. As the devil father-figure "M" says to Faustian John in the comic series I'm best known for, *Faust: Love of the Damned*:

> Dare to see through these eyes but the price of this wager is ignorance—something you no longer have to offer. So you make insanity your bid.

Going beyond good and evil: Characters who make an art of brilliantly defying the clutter of conventional ideas and the mire of easily defined morals intrigue me. The transgressors and border-crossers are the true antiheroes. They fall only when they fail their own sense of what is true.

Nowhere is this more true than comic books. This most American, this cheapest, dirtiest, most directly accessible of bastard art forms has been deadlocked, in a cultural context, in the pigeonhole of "Cautionary Moral Fables for Children, Humor Optional." I'm sorry, but Art Spiegelman's deceptively simple, subtly brilliant *Maus* remains the prize-winning, rule-proving exception.

Now this is *not* a good thing to those of us who like to be pricked a little by what we read. As D.G. Chichester says in the previous Dark Light Focus, William Gaines set us free—but the Comics Code Authority, weakened though it is, still seems to throw a sour-faced Ozzie Nelson injunction on thoughtful, philosophical, detailed comic books, comics that, without pretension, strive to be Art.

It gets to me and gets me thinking when *all* codes, written and unwritten, are broken. I hope the same can be said for my reader. Hence my conscious choice, with *Faust* illustrator and co-creator Tim Vigil, to show and tell all sexual and violent aspects of our little black-and-white spectacle on paper in clear, dead-on direct focus.

Some critics responded to *Faust* by saying that they could not "relate" to characters who were not "redeemable." But *Faust's* protagonist, John Jaspers, searches for a moral code when he castrates a rapist, murders a murderer, threatens to kill his love if she abandons him, and dares to buy back his once-sold soul. He is a psycho, sure. But he attempts to define for himself *right* and *wrong*. He wears on the outside the dilemmas we all know are stewing in Batman's soul.

You'll find the "naughty words" and the "naughty bits" in *Faust*. We've got devil worship and disembowelment, savage instant rhinoplasty performed by a sort of super non-hero with long sharp claws, and some cross-gender stuff you aren't likely to see on Oprah.

But I still don't think I've really shredded the envelope.

What do I mean by this? Well, it's one thing to push the buttons in explicit X-rated terms, but that limits my subversive effect. I could keep pouring on/out the blood, but I want to deliver some "musings" on Eros/Thanatos in terms that *all* audiences can get.

To do that, I'll have to continue to *let it rock*. I became the kind of writer I am through my experience performing as a roaming actor and post-punk rock musician. Those experiences have carried over, you see: To those who can feel the beat, I've been told, *Faust* is the Ramones of comics. Music helped me get primal, shake the walls; and when I feel I'm behaving myself, I take a break, dance and scream.

If I had never dared to rock out, to jump and scream and generally be willing to be stupid or brilliant in pursuit of expression, I would be your kid brother's English professor, quoting a bit of Yeats or Milton or Dante adequately, but never going deeper into my own abyss.

But I dared, and now I am stoking my ideas for the next comics I write—what some will call horror comics—with this feeling: *Characters may not get what they want, but what they need will rip their face.*

Writing For the New Pulps
Horror Theme Anthologies

John Maclay

During the first half of the twentieth century, pulp magazines such as *Weird Tales* provided a ready market for horror, occult and supernatural short fiction. H.P. Lovecraft himself contributed to these periodicals, and such writers as Ray Bradbury and Robert Bloch got their start in their pages. But with the advent of television, the quantity of magazine fiction in all genres fell off drastically. Indeed, one often hears the comment that the commercial short story is dead.

Those who would say so are simply not looking in the right place. They need to go beyond the periodical racks of their favorite full-service bookstore and study the paperback section instead. There, they'll find dozens of anthologies, printed on rough stock and (usually) bearing sensationalistic covers. Here are the new pulps—and not even in disguise!

What do you have to do to sell stories to those books that fall into the horror genre? As is true of all writing of commercial fiction, you must be inclined to be prolific, to shrug off rejection and submit again, and to hone your craft to the market's needs. In short, you must be professional, not a prima donna. Many horror anthologies have specific themes, too, so you're obviously not going to place a vampire story in a werewolf volume. You might also join the Horror Writers Association, whose newsletter includes an up-to-date market report, and attend the annual World Horror Convention, where you'll meet helpful professionals in the field.

What can you expect when you *do* sell a story? Payment varies from three to ten cents per word, typically as an advance against royalties. And there can well *be* significant royalties. Anthologies such as *Stalkers* have sold so well that they have returned more than $2,000 to each contributor. Stories from these books have been nominated for awards and included in subsequent "year's best" volumes, so that your efforts will have been highly worthwhile.

Advice From the Pros

Let's hear from some other writers, editors and publishers of horror anthologies. In recent years, the genre has also seen, among others, the *Whispers* series, edited by Stuart David Schiff, the *Shadows* series of Charles L. Grant, the *Night Visions* series from Dark Harvest, and many theme volumes originated by Martin H. Greenberg and various co-editors. The following, therefore, are just a representative few.

J.N. Williamson

J.N. Williamson says, "My approach to editing the quartet (so far) of *Masques* anthologies was primarily twofold: to try to get stories by several writers whose appearances tend to sell copies for the publisher, and also earn reviews—that was the first. The other part of my approach was to find several underrated or even unpublished writers of talent-coming-to-fruition, introduce and give them a boost.

"And in all instances," Williamson says, "I sought to accept work that was original, well constructed with a minimum of grammatical and logical problems, and genuine stories—*not* vignettes. I expected a beginning, middle and satisfying ending and can recall just one piece, nominated for a few awards, that violated these principles but got in. (No, it was not written by a so-called 'household name.')

"When the first *Masques* anthology was published in 1984, I was primarily a novelist and had placed just 29 short stories. Since then, operating on the same (but opposite) premise, I have written and sold 125 more works of short fiction, 62 of them directly to anthologies. The other factors they have in common is that (1) they obeyed the editorial guidelines, and (2) began with some sort of 'grabber,' something that makes people want to know more. These are the secrets I have used for getting into anthologies so I suppose I recommend them."

Williamson touches on another feature of horror anthologies that appeals to me: one's ability to appear among famous names. For example, my own stories have been published in volumes that have included work by Stephen King, Dean Koontz, Joyce Carol Oates and John Cheever. It's also been my pleasure as an editor and publisher to work with a multitude of writers, veteran and new.

Richard T. Chizmar

"Editing an anthology is essentially a juggling act," says Richard T. Chizmar, whose entries include *Cold Blood, Thrillers, The Earth Strikes Back* and *Screamplays*. (Chizmar is also the editor/publisher of *Cemetery Dance*, the leading magazine in the horror field, and an author in his own right.) "First, you have to find a balance with your contributor list—a successful mixture of well-known, commercial authors (whose name value will help sell the book) and newer, lesser-known (but certainly not less talented) writers who can carry their weight. Then there's the actual editing . . .

"A few stories arrive in perfect shape and your job is easy. You simply file the story and write and mail the check. Most stories, however, need a little fine-tuning; some punctuation changes, a few deletions or additions to help pacing or flow; nothing too intrusive. And, of course, a few stories need more significant work, such as major changes in structure or plot or characterization. These tales go back to the author for rewrites. Finally (and unfortunately) there are usually a few stories which are just dead-wrong for the anthology, and in that case you have no choice but to return them to the author with your regrets.

"As I said, it's a juggling act," Chizmar says. "You have to balance your publisher's needs with your own editorial tastes with the author's personal feelings and ego. Hard work, but fun."

I might add that it's the writer's job to make the editor's task less difficult; as the saying goes, hard writing makes easy reading.

Jeff Gelb

"Don't expect to get rich writing for anthologies," says Jeff Gelb, co-editor of the *Hot Blood* series and editor of the *Shock Rock* series and *Fear Itself*. "It is true that you can ride the coattails of established writers like Stephen King to antho royalties. But contributions by the likes of King are rare indeed. The *Hot Blood* books are all earning royalties, based on healthy additional printings, book club and foreign sales. Generally, though, no one writes short fiction for anthologies for the money; they do it for the love of writing and the love of the subject matter. If you've always wanted to write an erotic horror story, or a rockin' horror story, or a story based on your greatest fear, anthos offer you what may be your only chance to do so—and to reach an enthusiastic worldwide audience.

"If you're a young writer," Gelb says, "anthos offer you the opportunity to share the stage with the pros, and to bask in their glory and help establish yourself with their fans.

"It's a great way to get noticed. And these days, with the dwindling short-story market, it's one of the best ways to escape the ghetto of small press magazines (as good as they may be) and hit the bookstore shelves. And hey, it looks great on your writing resume!"

"But," says Gelb, "it is a tough, competitive market. Great ideas don't always sell to publishers, and great stories don't always equate to great sales. Your job is hardly over when your story or book is done. Be ready to publicize your work as writer in whatever ways you can to keep it from falling by the publishing wayside. Fliers, bookmarks, signings, articles—anything you can do to make the public aware of your work—is bound to pay off.

"Know your marketplace. I can't tell you how many stories we've gotten for the *Hot Blood* series, well known as an erotic horror antho series, that are not in the least erotic! It's downright rude of a writer not to do his or her homework before submitting. If you're contributing to an ongoing series, take the time to buy and read a book in that series before sitting down to write a story—or worse yet, before dusting off an old, unsold story that's been in your files for some time.

"Have *fun*!" Gelb says. "Anthos are about doing something you love, and having a great time doing it!"

Michael Garrett

Michael Garrett, co-editor of the *Hot Blood* series, offers additional practical insight. "Prospective anthology authors must keep in mind that publishing is a business," he says. "As business people, publishers intend to make a profit on every published collection. This in turn places the anthology editor in the 'middleman' position of simultaneously meeting the needs of both the publisher and the anthology's intended audience.

"Restrictions imposed by the above condition prevent me as an anthology editor from simply selecting the submissions I personally prefer most, or from accepting the first twenty or so reasonably good submissions. In order to please the publisher I must secure a large percentage of stories from known authors whose recognizable names will help sell the book. This places me in the unfortunate position of occasionally rejecting a better story from a lesser known author in order to accept something by a name author. This equates to a business decision, pure and simple. I would obviously prefer to accept the very best stories submitted, regardless of the authors' names, but that simply isn't possible. Space for stories by newcomers is extremely limited.

"Within the above boundaries," Garrett says, "I must also consider the wide interest range of a series's readership. Because of varying tastes of readers, I must sometimes accept stories targeted to a certain audience segment, even when a story doesn't especially interest me. Obviously, it would be impossible to produce an anthology wherein all readers thoroughly enjoyed all stories. Book reviewers consistently vary as to their opinions of which story in a particular collection is best."

"With an ongoing series such as *Hot Blood*, quality is of utmost importance to assure consistency from volume to volume," Garrett says.

"I prefer to work with authors who understand and appreciate the author/editor relationship and are willing to perform requested rewrites to make their stories the best they can be."

Well, there you have it, from some people who've been there. Now, as it should be, the rest is up to you. If you're not a self-starter, you won't sell to horror anthologies—the "new pulps"—or anything else. But if you are, anthologies can be exciting and rewarding markets.

Capturing Kids

Jill M. Morgan

What scared me most when I was a kid were things I couldn't see but could hear in the dark—a shuffling step on the hardwood floor of my room, a fingernail scraping the screen of the open window beside my bed, a breath coming from the pitch-black corner, where even the flickering pilot light of the gas heater couldn't reach. Sounds created images so vivid, my mind filled in dramatic shapes and colors, creating heart-thudding terrors which kept me wide-eyed and watching long into the night.

Capturing kids as readers for young adult (YA) and middle grade (MG) horror novels is recreating those heard-but-not-seen images and shaping them into words that grip as relentlessly as scary sounds hold children in that hour just before sleep overwhelms and carries them *away* from their fears . . . or *to* them.

My career began with writing novels for adults. I sold several. Then, something happened: Writing horror for adults became one vast, dry wasteland without an oasis in sight. The market became so hard to find, you needed binoculars.

Not so for the juvenile market. In quick succession, I sold two YA horror novels, received an eight-book contract for a MG horror/fantasy series, sold a vampire MG novel, and signed a two-book anthology contract for co-editing spooky and mystery stories for eight- to twelve-year old readers. The juvenile horror market was hot, and hottest of all was writing scary books for eight- to twelve-year olds.

Since I was new at writing for kids and teens, I asked lots of questions. I heard advice ranging from, "Never write about witches; the editors won't buy it," to "Never write on-stage violence in books for kids." There is some truth in both these warnings. Some editors *do* shy away from anything that hints of the occult in children's books, including witches. The advice about see-it-here-and-now violence in juvenile novels also has a firm basis in truth. Most editors want you to evoke that scary feeling without drawing a single drop of blood from your characters.

If you pick up a sampling of current horror books for YA and MG, you'll see that none of the rules for children's books applies all the time. There are some excellent books about witches, and books that offer a lot more view of violence than simply a thrilling sense of danger. Are these the norm? No, but that doesn't mean you can't succeed at writing them.

The Middle-Grade Market

MG has become a tremendous market for scary books, thanks to successful series like *Goosebumps*. Young readers are loyal. Once they find an author or series they like, they want to read everything that author writes, or every book in their favorite series. Books for kids have a long shelf life, too. Compare the shelf life of a paperback adult horror novel by a mid-list writer—maybe six weeks—to the shelf life of a similar book for MG—months or even years.

If you've decided to try writing for MG, eight- to twelve-year old readers, here are a few guidelines to keep in mind:

Manuscript length: Typically, 120 pages. Like any other manuscript, this should be double-spaced with one-inch margins.

Point of view (POV): Generally, MG books have a single-character POV. The protagonist won't know what other characters are thinking, but she can observe their actions and expressions and draw conclusions based on that. I have written MG novels with multiple viewpoints, and they work; but a single POV is still the norm.

Length of chapters: Ten pages is about right. In this case, you'd have twelve chapters per book.

Illustrations: Not many. Novels that have illustrations at the beginning of each chapter are called chapter books, meant for younger readers.

Where to begin: Start on a day that is different.

When the first chapter opens, the MG reader wants to step right into the setting and the plot, like moving into an instantly familiar room.

You can accomplish this remarkable feat by beginning with action or dialogue that carries the reader forward into the story. One of my MG books begins with the line:

> In the morning's rays of sunlight, when the Spider's web ladder was sparkling with dew, Mr. Ambrose descended from the now hidden moon, climbed down the lacy rungs of the Web, and stepped onto the sidewalk before the shop, Broadmore's Used Books and Antiquities.

In one sentence, you're there.

It doesn't take a first line as complex as this one. Your first line might be: "I don't want new friends," said Jenny. Look at what you have here—a girl with a problem kids can immediately understand and relate to, and once again, they are there. They know how miserable she's feeling. What kid hasn't been lonely, or afraid to make new friends?

MG readers have shorter attention spans than YA readers. They like their horror fiction fast paced, with all the terrifying highs and heart-stopping lows of the world's greatest roller coaster. This means they want to know what happened, not necessarily why it happened. YA readers enjoy the building tension of what might be lurking in the woods, the suspense heightened with every step deeper into the dark and lonely forest. *MG readers want to see the bear.*

Does this mean that your novel must be shallow, simply racing forward with a spooky plot, with little attention paid to developing multi-layered characters? Absolutely not. MG readers are a discriminating audience who appreciate rich subplots and fully developed characters with a past, present and future. They like to identify with characters in their favorite books, and empathy is one of this age group's strongest traits.

The following is generally true of children's literature:

The main character needs to show growth. This has nothing to do with birthdays, and everything to do with *changing*, or coming to realize. Kids' lives are about learning. They are constantly changing, becoming wiser, stronger. The main character in a MG novel needs to demonstrate that kind of progression by the book's conclusion.

The protagonist needs to solve the problem. Forget last-minute rescues, the police arriving just in the nick of time, somebody else figuring out what's wrong and saving the day. It's all up to the child protagonist.

Show and not tell. Keep the writing active. It's boring to read a chapter in which the main character tells us how scared he was when the flash flood knocked his house off the foundation. But it's thrilling to read the same chapter *showing* the kid falling off the roof of that house, right into the churning water. Be there.

The Young Adult Market

The following are guidelines for YA horror novels:

Manuscript length: YA novels are between 150 and 200 pages.

Point of view: It's common to have more than one POV in a YA novel. Keep the POV shifts in separate chapters, or sections of chapters. Use a dropdown/white space transition or chapter breaks to mark a change in POV.

Length of chapters: 10 to 15 pages is normal.

Setting: The setting in a YA novel is always seen from the teen's perspective. Familiar places include school, friends' houses, their cars, their rooms, the local hamburger or pizza joint and other typical teenage hangouts.

Fear level: In YA horror, the stakes are higher. The roller coaster thrill ride isn't enough. You have to keep upping the odds, starting with a bad situation, making it worse, and worse, until those final scenes are rushing at the reader so fast, it's like fire burning on the page.

Parents: YA protagonists should have parents who are like sturdy trees in the background, around for support but rarely noticed. YA horror novels rarely deal with parents. Consider them on vacation from the plot. Parents play a bigger role in MG novels, since younger characters need parents to drive them places, etc.

Keep it clean: No matter what you've heard teenagers say in real life, on the printed page it's better to keep swearing and four-letter words to a minimum. Beware of using the latest phrases, too. Peppering your dialogue with current slang is sure to make your novel seem dated relatively quickly; "current" doesn't last as long as it used to. Strive for "young but not trendy" dialogue.

Sex: Thinking about the opposite sex *is* the stuff of teen novels. Secret crushes and budding romances make wonderful subplots. The tension for this can build throughout the manuscript with a shared glance, a few well-chosen words, hand holding—and then: *The* romantic kiss and the suggestion of future dating by the book's conclusion. Characters remain chaste.

When you're imagining the age of your readers for MG and YA novels, think of a nine-year-old for MG, and a twelve- or thirteen-year old for YA novels. Realize that many ten- and eleven-year-old readers are sampling YA books. The audience for YA books is getting younger and younger, which is why it's important to temper violent or sexually explicit scenes.

It has only been in the last few years that kids' novels have claimed a real share of the bookstore market. A large percentage of this space is dedicated to paperback originals. At paperback prices, kids are able to choose books they want to read, rather than having a parent buy a hardcover (expensive) novel for them. Kids know what they like to read. And they love chillers.

When you're ready to begin writing for kids, make a point to be around a group of them and listen to their conversations. Are their sentences constructed in the same way that adult conversations are structured? Or do kids speak to each other in a more choppy, abbreviated style?

A good place to pick up current-sounding character names is from recent name-the-baby books. Many of these books list distinctive names by ethnic origin—Irish, Italian, African, etc. Also useful are books that list multinational last names. These reference books suggest power names, old-fashioned names or biblical names, giving you a chance to really consider your character's traits before you name him or her.

Before you begin writing the first chapter of your novel, think about where the real action or excitement begins. Is it where you planned to start? If not, maybe you should rethink the order of your novel. Jump right in and get things moving. Kids want to find "the good parts" as soon as they open the book.

This might be the right time to consider where you're going to sell you story or novel. Does this step seem premature? It isn't. Writing for a specific market will tremendously increase your chances of selling your finished work.

An editor I had worked with in the past on my adult books later became an editor in children's publishing. I called and pitched my MG series concept to her. She gave me valuable insight into what she was looking for, suggesting changes in my original ideas. By the time I presented the series proposal to her, it was a package designed specifically for that particular editor, and I received a contract offer.

You may not have access to an editor, but you do have access to the kinds of novels a particular publishing house seems to prefer. Study your market. Look at what the company is *successful* at publishing. A lot of valuable time can be wasted by sending the wrong kind of proposal to an editor.

Another way to study the market is to pay attention to what *isn't* there. Three of my most successful proposals for children's books came from being able to say to my editor, "There isn't anything else like this on the market." That means a lot in publishing.

To be successful as a children's writer, capturing both editors and kids, you need to know your readers and give them dramatic openings, realistic and likable characters, fast-paced chapters and a steady dose of excitement leading to high-peaked thrills. And always remember to keep it clean. Combine this with studying the market, focusing your writing on the requirements of specific editors or publishing houses, and noticing what isn't out there as well as what's been overdone.

In addition to the joy of becoming published, the fun of writing nail-biting chillers, and a hearty profit for your hard work, there is the bonus of fan mail from kids—the delicious icing on the cake of success. Their letters will make you feel like you're the best writer in the whole world. And you know what? To your enthusiastic readers, you will be!

Capturing kids is a big challenge. If you're ready for it, here's one final piece of advice: Have fun along the way. Kids know if you're really into the game, and writing for kids *is* a kind of complicated game. Enjoy!

Oh, and always look behind your back. You never know what could be lurking in the shadows.

Something to Scare the Kids

Five Do's and a Five-"D" Don't

Richard Lee Byers

1. Do create *believable* youthful characters, with a real kid's hopes, anxieties, concerns and general outlook on life. The author must be able to portray what it's like to ask the prettiest girl in ninth grade for a date and choke on your own shyness. Play a cruel practical joke on the class pariah. Con Dad into giving you some extra money, even though you just brought home a terrible report card. Make the football team.

Or—this being horror, after all—sneak into the old, ruinous Blackwood mansion at midnight to prove you're not chicken.

2. Do get the details right. Check out contemporary youth culture. If, to use an extreme example, the fourteen-year-old hero of your story spends a lot of time playing that state-of-the-art video game *Pong*, or rocking to that cutting-edge band *The Guess Who*, your readers will laugh him off the page. Luckily, you can prevent such gaffes with a little research. Watch MTV. Go to a clothing store and ask the clerks which brands and styles are selling. Stop by an arcade and see which games are popular.

Or spend a day or two at schools, perhaps being the "writer in the classroom"—and the on-location researcher as well.

3. Do remember your hero is youthful, but nonetheless a hero. He should be a nice kid struggling against a menace which isn't nice at all. That doesn't mean he can't have rough edges. He may seem more believable if he does, and his efforts to rise above his flaws will add richness and complexity to your story. Nor does it mean that you must shun any hint of irony, moral ambiguity or iconoclastic social commentary.

But readers expect a rip-roaring clash between a Representative of Good and a Minion of Evil. If you want to explore the inner life of a serial killer, write a hallucinatory tale about a befuddled soul's attempts to cope with the nauseating instability of reality itself, or turn out a nihilistic homage to *noir* master Jim Thompson, use that ambition on your next story for the *adult* market.

4. Do be sure the avatar of evil and his fiendish crimes are *genuinely frightening.* Remember though, you don't have as much freedom to present unsettling ideas and gut-wrenching imagery as you do in adult horror. Our society considers certain kinds of material inappropriate for young readers, and that imposes certain limits.

The limits vary from publisher to publisher and on a case-by-case basis. As a rule of thumb, the younger the target audience, the less violent the story should be. A mummy in a story for teens can strangle the occasional archaeologist, night watchman, and museum curator. In a tale intended for eight-year-olds, it should probably just chase people around.

5. Do present a "wholesome theme," one that reflects acceptable, decent and realistic values. Not that you're going to preach. Your readers want a thrill ride, not a sermon. But if your characters behave badly—which in practice means, if they do something which would cause a parent "grave concern"—they must eventually face the adverse consequences of their actions. For instance, in the YA horror genre, an editor likely will not let you show a kid sneaking a beer from time to time with no harmful effects, even though, in real life, many teens do precisely that. Such a naturalistic, non-judgmental bit of business would be acceptable in a book for adults, but not in a story targeted at a younger audience.

And finally . . .
The Five-"D" *Don't*

1. Don't Dare Deliberately "Dumb it Down." You need not worry too much about talking over your audience's heads. They won't fling the book away in despair if they occasionally encounter a word they don't recognize, any more than you quit reading when the same thing happens to you.

You're more likely to lose them by writing so simplistically that they feel you're talking down to them.

Do the do's, don't do the don't, and your stories will kindle night lights in bedrooms across America.

Pushing the Horror Button
The Art and Business of Interactive Horror

Matthew Costello

Interactive storytelling is about pressing buttons, not much different from the button horror writers like to push in their fiction—except in interactive entertainment the trick is to scare people while giving *them* control. But can we give away control and still hold onto the reins of good storytelling?

Imagine for a moment if I said: *Please*, don't press that button. That button over there . . .

And what is it that you want to do?

Exactly. You want to press that button. The very one you've been told (warned?) not to touch, to not even think about, to get the hell away from.

You want to press it—because you are curious. You just want to see what happens.

No need to apologize for any blatant disregard of my instructions. Such disregard has been going on since the beginning of time, back to the time when a certain fruit of a certain tree was declared verboten.

We, as writers, understand curiosity. The appeal of the forbidden. The excitement of "what-if." But—so far—the multimedia/CD-ROM/interactive business doesn't get it. In the interactive world they tell people: *Press that button, please. And now* this *button, and then* that one *over there*, as if the human mouse-user was the equivalent of a chicken mindlessly pecking and clicking on seeds laid out in a trail.

The multimedia biz just doesn't get it. The human imagination isn't being stimulated. But we know how to do that. We writers live in the imaginative landscape. Multimedia needs us.

In a way, it's like magic tricks. Magic is about illusion and interactive media is, to large extent, about the illusion of interactivity. We think we're making decisions, we think we have an active role . . . but it's an illusory one. Nothing will happen that the designers haven't programmed. The interactivity is all a fantasy. But that's okay because we know people love fantasy. Nobody really wants to face a town of vampires—but we'd love to experience it vicariously.

So it should be with creating an interactive experience. But there's a vast difference between what the interactive revolution promises and what it's delivered. So as part of this mini-seminar, here's a quick look at different levels of interactivity, starting at the bottom of the food chain.

The Seven Pillars of Interaction, or
The Zen of Multimedia:
1. Click on Everything

Most interactive multimedia—especially kids' media—assumes that if you went into a stranger's house you'd automatically walk over to anything and everything, poke it, and wonder, "Gee, I wonder what this darn thing does?"

You'd turn on the blender, open the microwave door, look through their basement . . . touch and poke everything you could see, usually for no reason at all. But the computer's mouse has buttons to click, so click we must!

Some "interactive experiences" consist almost completely of gliding your cursor over 3-D rendered objects and clicking your mouse button. There's something almost Cro-Magnon about all this electronic poking. Yet it's a staple of most multimedia. That shows you how far we have to travel.

A good thing about a horror interactive project is that there are so many gruesome things to click on: the coffin, the cracked skull, the dead rat (which suddenly springs to life).

2. Games

Everything from one hundred-year-old chess problems to variations of carnival shoot-'em-ups can be found in interactive entertainment. In some CD-ROMs, like the Disney Activity Centers or a cute compilation called *Putt Putt's FunPack*, they serve as a modern version of the family toy chest, filled with a bunch of games for a rainy afternoon.

A lot of interactive adventures use games and puzzles as "locks" on the story: Open a lock and get a piece of the tale. And while there's nothing wrong with chess problems or electronic versions of shoot-the-bear, it's pretty obvious that such activities as an entertainment medium are a dead-end. If that's how we define "interaction," the revolution is over before it begins.

3. Aimless Wandering

Prowling a mall is a recognized favorite American pastime. With glazed eyes, we wander past Radio Shack's remote control dinosaurs, grab a Mr. Pretzel, and then score some stone-washed jeans at the Gap.

In the interactive variant, we cut out the middleman of actual physical locomotion. Best of all, we can wander everywhere from a haunted house to the Great Pyramid of Cheops.

As a crowded mall or museum shows, this wandering is something people like. But when yoked to a story, the meandering gains the power to motivate and to fire imaginations. *The 7th Guest's* moody graphics made it a smash, but it needed a story to give you a reason to keep you wandering its haunted halls.

With this level of interactivity we start to attain the potential to actually do something with this new medium. There are a lot of places we haven't been, never will be, or don't really want to be—at least physically. And multimedia has the potential to take us there.

Want to explore the mysterious face of Cydonia on Mars? CD-ROM would be perfect for that. How about a dive to the Titanic to search for John Jacob Astor's knickers? Or maybe a trip inside the human mind? Now we're talking about interactions that have the potential to excite the imaginations of creators.

4. Point of View

Point of view, a staple device of fiction and cinema, is an enticing interactive prospect that hasn't been fully developed. The best-selling game *Doom* delivered a single-person POV as you went monster hunting. Players saw their hands holding the gun, and they went eyeball-to-eyeball with monsters from beyond.

But in *Doom* there is only one POV, and the story never develops past "march and shoot." *The 7th Guest* also had a single POV, using puzzle-based challenges rather than Uzi blasts to progress through the environment.

What I'm talking about is using multiple points of view, as you would in a novel, letting the viewer/player skip from one to the other, never getting the whole story (just like in real life).

Tamara was a play performed in New York and Los Angeles in the late 1980s, and it's an interesting model for something that can be done with interaction. The drama was set in fascist Italy in the 1930s. The audience became guests at a banquet at the Commendatore's mansion.

There were plots and murder weapons, intrigue and assignations, and the audience had to decide who to follow through the mansion. It was great fun but more importantly, Tamara let the audience follow the story thread they wanted, trailing characters, moving on to another character whenever they wanted.

Imagine an interactive *Salem's Lot* with all hell breaking out! There's so much happening, and now *you* have to decide which of the dozen threads to follow. You'd want to come back to see how *X* connects with *Y*.

Or think perhaps of an interactive Agatha Christie's *Ten Little Indians* where you follow one suspect—but there's no way you can watch *all* the reprobates. What fun that would be and also the beginning of a great use of this new medium.

5. Branching Mania

Branching, for those who never cracked a "choose your own adventure" book, is a storytelling device that gives the player the chance to make key decisions for characters; each decision creates a variant stream of a story arc. From a single tree trunk, a maze of story roots runs upward. The player decides how to deal with the aliens, how to escape the hitman or how to get the jewels out of the temple of doom.

The important thing with a branching story is to avoid mundane possibilities. Again, there's only the illusion of choice. The multimedia writer really shapes all the dramatic decisions.

A note: Creating a branching story shouldn't be viewed as threatening. There are always options when writing a story. In traditional fictive forms, authors simply choose one story line to show the reader. But in an interactive medium, the writer can get to show *all* the intriguing possibilities. It's not an abdication of creativity, it's a celebration of creativity.

6. Putting Viewers in the Movie

I don't want to really learn how to fly an F-15. I want to get into that cockpit feeling like I already *know* what to do, and live that movie experience. I want to walk down haunted hallways, but not if there really are ghosts. I want "safe frights."

What would you like to do? Climb the cliffs of K2, already knowing how to use the equipment? Or maybe you'd like to dive to Atlantis . . .

Multimedia can take you places you haven't been before, and it can let you do things that you might never get to do. Multimedia can give you a risk-free adventure with a low learning curve. For the Walter Mitty in all of us, multimedia could be a godsend.

7. Quest for Artificial Intelligence

Some designers feel that the highest form of interactive challenge will be to create a computer-generated world with completely free interactions. They seek the grail of an open world with fully developed characters with unfettered interactions.

One project being developed features King Arthur's court with real and computer-generated personalities and no limit on your interactions with those characters. In a very real sense, your interaction with the artificial characters makes the story.

But that may be the problem here: What about plot, the scope, the theme? How do we keep that compelling material in such a game—assuming that it *could* be created? And the bigger question is whether true characters with their own "intelligence" can be *created*.

The burgeoning online world of multi-player games will be the true arena for free interaction with fully developed characters, with some who are real, and some the product of a writer/designer.

Multimedia as Art

These seven interactions show the possibilities for writers of multimedia. But we are not setting up a new media restaurant, taking one from column A and one from column B. It's important for writers to develop a philosophy of interaction, and that philosophy should be based on the story (or stories) we want the viewer/player to experience.

The reason it's so important is that maybe, just maybe, we have the possibility of creating a new art form out of this hodgepodge of clicking and Quicktime VR. I'm talking about creating real emotional power, and dealing with compelling themes, the art of a great film or a book, a multimedia *Citizen Kane* or *2001*. Such art is possible—but not to judge by what's out there. Most multimedia is far from art and twice as far away from fun. To go to a big electronics show and see new software is to experience a supernova of mediocrity.

But I'd like to suggest that the interactive possibilities of multimedia can be a powerful tool to draw the viewer into a story, into the world, to scare people, to touch people and make them feel. Imagine making players/readers/participants (do we yet have the right word?) too terrified to hit that mouse button, or melt in tears because of something they did.

We're at the nickelodeon stage of what may *become* an art form.

Early films served up gee-whiz effects like the "thrilling" sight of train roaring by, or a man with a bushy whiskers giving a woman in a high-necked collar a kiss. Audiences loved this new toy—and that's what "movies" were—a toy, a novelty.

Not unlike multimedia.

But a few visionaries like D.W. Griffith, F.W. Murnau and Georges Melies saw the possibility of something more, the possibility to match image and story to create emotion, to make people laugh, to make them cry, to scare them.

And film became a popular art form even when it had tremendous technological limitations. It was art well before there was sound and color. In fact, Rudolph Arnheim, in his classic book *Art of Film*, argued that sound wouldn't add much to the true artistic power of film.

Film was art before sound, before color, before wide-screen. And the change that occurred in the medium was not one of technology, but of vision.

And where will that vision come from in this new medium?

The writers will have to push and pull this interactive toy, prod everyone who works with it.

It won't be easy.

But can you get a chance to make this new art form come to life? Read on . . .

Selling Multimedia

With your eyes open and aware of the possibilities and limitations of multimedia, whether online on the web or running off a CD, now you wonder, *How do I get in to play the game?*

First, if you're a published writer, that has great value in the marketplace. In the early years, most software and content companies were, with a few exceptions, writing their own stories, creating their own characters and making up their own game scenarios.

Need I say any more?

But most multimedia makers (sadly, not all!) have awakened to the value a real writer brings to project. And here are some steps that may help you get your foot in the door.

Step 1: Organize your credits and emphasize those most applicable to interactive projects. Horror and science fiction are staples of interactive games. If you have any professional experience with games, highlight it. (Note: All-nighters over a Monopoly board do not count.)

Step 2: Research the field. Do the obvious. Search the net for online games, check out VRML sites offering the latest 3-D experiences, play the current CD-ROMs, especially in the horror field, and then check out the companies. See what kind of titles each company releases, and how many. A company with a dozen releases a year is more likely to need outside writers than one with one title a year.

Step 3: Contact the companies. Most companies will be glad to hear from you. Try to reach a vice president of development or a producer, or even call the company and ask for the name and title of the person who works with outside talent on projects or looks at pitches. That name won't necessarily be the right name but it will point you in the right direction.

Step 4: Write a letter. Send your contact person a brief letter via the U.S. post office (snail mail, it's called). State who you are, what you've done, and your interest in the medium. Say you'd like to set up a meeting about possible projects. And if you've prepared your own project to pitch, you can offer to send an outline.

Step 5: Hit the road. Just as in launching a writing career, contacts are important. Go to game and Web conventions, meet people, hand them your business card. Go to speeches and shmooze with the speakers afterward. Ask people working in the field for help and guidance and suggestions. Work the room and look for opportunities. Even writing the instruction manual is a way to get your foot in the door.

Step 6: Create your own dream. I hate to go all "Tony Roberts" on you, but if you've done your homework, you'll have some cool ideas of your own: your own creative vision. Take that idea, polish it and pitch it to anyone you're fortunate enough to meet. Your dream might prove to be as exciting to others as it is to you, and maybe an original project can be your entry into the House of Horrors known as multimedia writing.

Step 7: Be careful with contracts. More than even in book publishing, multimedia contacts are lined with more heavily armored boilerplate than a T-34 tank. There are entertainment lawyers in New York and Los Angeles who specialize—to some extent—in multimedia. If you get a deal and don't have a multimedia savvy agent, you should use a lawyer. And having a deal in hand will make you more attractive to the few agents in the field who are on top of multimedia and understand it as well as anybody.

Finally, let me recommend two books. Douglas Varchol's *The Multimedia Scriptwriting Workshop* (Sybex) is filled with examples and invaluable hints, as is *Writing for Multimedia*, a comprehensive look at the field from Timothy Garrand (Focal Press). Both books come with CD-ROMs loaded with samples from best-selling games.

Now, armed with a vision and some strategy, get out there and *interact*, kiddo.

The future, you know, won't wait.

Splat Goes the Hero
Visceral Horror

Jack Ketchum

I wrote a book a while back called *The Girl Next Door* which opened with the line, "You think you know about pain?"

Personally, I'm no expert (so far; knock on wood), though as a kid I had my share of broken bones and various other less than delightful body surprises: a cortisone shot into an inflamed tendon; my upper jaw peeled and scraped—did you know that pain can be a *sound?*—and a fall, stark naked, through the branches of a tree that left me looking like something out of *100 Days of Sodom*.

(Curious about that one? Too bad. You'll have to wait for the story.)

But the point is that if you're writing about violence, you're writing about pain. Somebody's pain. Maybe not yours but somebody's. And my preference is to face it squarely. As honestly as possible and very much up close and personal.

I've noted this elsewhere but it bears repeating here: The great director Akira Kurosawa once said that *the role of the artist is to not look away*.

That pretty much defines what I try to do.

There are plenty of ways to look away, and bad writers at some point have found all of them. We'll get to some of the more disastrous ways later but right now let's just stick to violence.

Remember those old Hays-Office-era cowboy movies where everything is completely bloodless, where people get shot with a rifle that would stop a bear for God's sake, and fall down and die as neatly as Baryshnikov executes a *tour j'ete*? Then along came *Bonnie and Clyde* and *The Wild Bunch* and blew all that away forever. A little later, horror movies kicked some dirt over the grave.

The first tentative steps in that direction had come earlier from Hitchcock, with black-and-white blood swirling down the drain in *Psycho's* shower scene, and with Tippi Hedrin pecked nearly to death and the bloody, empty eye-socket in *The Birds*; from Hammer Studios in England; and from that master of gore and total boredom, Herschel Gordon Lewis. Then suddenly things exploded with items like *Night of the Living Dead, The Last House on the Left, Texas Chainsaw Massacre* and the early Cronenberg films.

I just couldn't believe 'em.

I *expected* none of them.

They each dropped me like a steer and collectively changed the way I looked at death-as-popular-entertainment forever. People didn't just die in these movies, they got *gnawed on* right in front of you, before and after death, and by God, you *saw* it! They *wanted* you to see! People got hung on meathooks, got raped and murdered and hacked and chewed in detail so graphic you almost wanted to look away.

Almost. But not quite.

Not Looking Away

I remember seeing each of them sprawled in my seat, feet spread across a popcorn-crusted, Coke-and-let's-not-think-about-what-else-sticky floor, smoking Winstons with complete impunity, at all those old 42nd Street grind-houses in Manhattan. And at some point I realized I wanted to carry this new sensibility I was seeing into writing—drag it popcorn, Winstons, graphic-sex-and-violence and all, screaming into a novel.

Then along came this idea. I went to work, using freelance writing jobs for magazines to support time on the book. A year later I had it. There were instances where what I was imagining made me cringe from my keyboard but I had it.

Texas Chainsaw and *Night of the Living Dead* were my main models. They have obvious things in common. For one thing, both exist in a universe of simulated real time. They begin in the afternoon, run howling and screeching through the night, and end at dawn. Both have *intimate* violence. They seemed to shrink from nothing. From no atrocity. Not even from the very bleakest of endings. That was the innovation I had in mind. I'd never seen it done before, and I'd been reading in the genre. Stephen King got pretty gruesome—but there were things Steve would not show you. He'd use a cutaway. I loved what he and others were doing in the field but it wasn't what I was after.

I wanted to show you everything. I wanted to make you *feel* everything. Every last nasty detail. The knife sinking into your very own flesh while you watched and listened and struggled not to die.

Off Season was an updating of the Sawney Beane story, a true story about a family of seventeenth century highwaymen-turned-cannibals along the rugged cliffs of Scotland. A big family, from kids to ancient crones. I was taking the notion into modern times and posited an equally repulsive *familia ferox* hidden for years off the coast of Maine, forced suddenly onto the mainland to wreak bloody havoc upon a group of vacationing Manhattanites on one gruesome roller-coaster of a night.

The roller-coaster being the third thing *Chainsaw* and *Night* had in common.

I researched and researched and researched. To do this kind of thing you've got to. If you're going in for the really tight close-up you've got to get it right. I talked to doctors, asking basically the same questions all the time. *If I do this and this and this to him, can he still survive? And then what if I do* this? *That one's going to kill him? How* much *will he bleed? Are we talking drops of blood here or gouts of blood or what?*

I studied recipes. I went to the library and read everything I could find about cannibalism. Some of the early shipwreck accounts like *Mrs. Frazier on the Fatal Shore* included delightful hints on humans-as-cuisine. Others details I extrapolated from books like *How to Survive in the Wilderness* and Vardis Fisher's *Mountain Man* made into the movie *Jeremiah Johnson*. I figured that except for the fat-to-muscle quotient, there's not much difference between jerking deer meat and jerking Newt Gingrich.

Make It Real

It should go without saying that realism's the key here, just as it is with a lot of other aspects of fiction. You don't want to jar a reader who may just know about something top-to-bottom, inside out, while you haven't quite done all your homework. You'll block his flow, kill his suspension of disbelief. Every writer makes mistakes but it's important to catch as many as possible.

An example: At the end of *Off Season* I have a character riding in an ambulance. She's been through 108 forms of hell by now and she's practically delirious. She looks up at the figure riding with her and wonders briefly if he's a paramedic or a doctor and hopes that he's a doctor because she knows she's hurt bad. After the book was published I got a letter from a guy who said he loved it—though he had one wee bitty problem with the end. Because he *was* a paramedic, and in a situation like this one, a paramedic's better trained to save her butt than a doctor is. I'd gotten it wrong. I blew it for the guy.

I wrote back and apologized and promised that if I ever had a chance to correct the thing in reprint, I would. When the book came out in England, I did.

You've also got to know your setting inside out. If an attack is coming through a window, you'd better not have said previously that in this space we have a large oak door. And you've got to know your instruments of mayhem. What sort of entrance wound with this kind of gun? What sort of exit wound? Where would I probably have to shoot somebody and how many times in order to stop him? That sort of thing. If you've got a character shooting a .357 magnum without ear protection, especially if he's shooting indoors, he'd better be deaf for a few pages. Maybe a few chapters. A .22 rifle? No problem.

These are mechanical things but they count. Anything short is just laziness and a form of *looking away*.

It's also important—and this goes for realism too—to engage all the senses. Not just sight and sound—those are the easy ones—but smell, taste, touch. Remember, we're dealing with somebody's pain here; we're engaging the reader in somebody's *experience of* pain. And you can't do pain without touch. The reader has to feel what the character feels when the blade touches the body, presses *into* the body, invades the body and then finally roots around in there. In this kind of writing it's every inch of the way or nothing at all.

Rehearsing for Death

The question of course, is, *why the hell do this stuff in the first place?*

I have to go back to my first question.

You think you know about pain?

There is nothing I can think of that is ennobling about pain; emotional or physical. Suffering breaks us down in both body and spirit, isolates us in our misery, cuts us off from one another. It's also something we'll all experience someday in one form or another, whether in a hospital bed or on a dark city street in the wrong part of town. Pain partakes of something primal in us, something all sentient creatures know, not just humans. And we'd sure better have a look at it. At what it does to us, how it changes us, at why and how it grows.

Someone once theorized that horror films and horror writing allow us to rehearse for death. I don't know about that but I do know they rehearse us for worlds of grief and agony. They reflect those worlds, our worlds, through someone else's: the characters in a novel.

There are few things I find hard to watch in movies but inevitably they're the most familiar, the least removed from my experience. There's a scene in *Marathon Man* which roars instantly to mind. You know the one. Larry Olivier going at Dustin Hoffman's teeth with his power-drill. The thing makes me cringe. And as far as I'm concerned the hardest thing to watch in *Chainsaw* is Granddaddy trying over and over again to coldcock Marilyn Burns with his hammer. Ever go to a sloppy dentist? Ever miss that nail and plant one on your finger?

You feel those scenes because you know them.

As Doug Winter says, horror's not a genre, it's an emotion. Likewise, *pain is us.* We've all had it, we'll all have it again. To shrink from pain in any form of art is to shrink from something fundamental about life, from part of the human, animal condition. Not that everybody has to tackle it, but that's not to say we should walk away from it either. It's dishonest.

There's a fine line, though, between honesty and exploitation. I've walked it many times.

Because pain is also fundamentally grotesque.

You don't go to that sloppy dentist every day, thank God. You don't whack yourself with a hammer either. Or get beaten in an alley or hit by a truck or a roller-blader or suffer bone cancer or lose a loved one or, I dare say, get munched by cannibals. The major part of most people's lives is lived without pain. Most days there's fair weather. Pain happens when the normal day breaks down, when something fails in the system, when things go haywire.

It's unusual. And like anything else unusual, as Madison Avenue would say, it's sexy.

Make Us Care

Have a look at your basic daytime talk show. One day they're interviewing teenagers with pierced tongues or women whose husbands have cheated on them with their own mothers, and the next day they're doing a satellite broadcast from prison and we're listening to Diane Downs try to convince us that she didn't *really* murder her kid because her boyfriend preferred her to be childless.

We are curious about anything unusual. Including agony. Including bloody murder.

We want to know what it feels like and I believe that we *should* know what it feels like. That's one thing writing's good for—getting us into dangerous waters while keeping us safe and dry at home. But there's only one way to do that, folks, to get to the actual feeling, and a lot of the writing in the area doesn't try. Still another form of looking away.

You've got to make us give a damn.

About all this grief. About all this suffering. You've got to exercise the compassion muscle.

If we don't care, it's just teenagers with pierced tongues again.

The keys to making it more than that involve character, intent and meaning—intertwined:

First, your characters—real people. Take the time and care to *make* them real, to submit to the truth of your characters, their histories, their hopes and fears, as much truth as you can muster. They'll reflect us only if you let them have their way as people. People can be zany and unpredictable sometimes but they pretty much go by the book. So you don't just waltz your second female lead into a darkened room in a spooky old house with a candle and no weapon saying, *Larry? Larry?* because you figure it's time to off her. You arm her to the teeth and she turns on every damn light in the joint.

Second, your intent. You must want us to *care* for these people one way or another, even if it's only to despise them. Often I contrast one evil with another and let you take your pick. Who's worse? Cannibal or scofflaw dad? Moral choices.

Third, the meaning of their suffering. I'm not talking philosophy here. I suppose some would say suffering doesn't necessarily have any meaning at all but I don't agree—it sure as hell has meaning for the sufferer, even if he can only arrive at the question, *Why me?* But it seems to me that pain always involves the loss of something—not necessarily the loss of life and limb, but sometimes of capability, innocence, personality, the capacity for joy. Loss eddies outward into other lives and it always has meaning for the loser. And the writer's job is to find it, know it—then share it with the rest of us.

Here's an example from my own stuff:

At the beginning of my book *Red* I've got an old man fishing by a stream, his tackle box and his old dog Red—a long-ago birthday present from his now-dead wife—lying beside him. Along come three boys, one with a shotgun. They ask for money. The old man doesn't have any so the kid shoots his dog. Not for any particular reason. Just out of meanness and because he can.

The line is, I think, appropriately nasty:

> And there wasn't even a yelp or a cry because the top of the dog's head wasn't there anymore nor the quick brown eyes nor the cat-scarred nose, all of them blasted into the brush behind the dog like a sudden rain of familiar flesh, the very look of the dog a sudden memory.

So the dog goes splat. The boys just laugh and walk away. Leaving the old man to deal with it.

> He got up and closed and locked his tackle box and set his rig, picked them up along with the cooler and walked back to where the dog lay. He tied the arms of his shirt around the dog's neck

against the seep of blood and picked him up and tucked him under one arm with the rig and the cooler and tackle box all gripped in his other hand and then he started up the path.

The dog grew very heavy.

He had to stop twice to rest but he would not let go of the dog, only sat by the side of the path and put down the cooler and fishing gear and shifted the weight of the dog so that it rested in his lap across his knees, holding him in his arms until he was rested, smelling the familiar scent of his fur and the new smell of his blood.

The second time he stopped he cried at last for the loss of him and for their long fine past together and pounded with his fist at the hardscrabble earth that had brought them here.

And then he went on.

Could be I'm just tooting my own horn, but I think I got it right that time. No goofs like with the ambulance.

At least *I'm* happy with it.

I didn't look away.

INNOVATION IN HORROR

TODAY AND TOMORROW

Innovation in Horror

Jeanne Cavelos

When I teach creative writing and ask my students what they believe their strengths and weaknesses are, almost all of them include creativity as a strength; almost none include it as a weakness.

As a result, few developing writers spend a lot of time and energy on *making* their work creative. They feel, by the very act of typing in words, they already are being "creative." After all, they are creating something new.

But there's the rub: How *new* is it?

Horror is a genre, a type of literature that has certain identifiable characteristics. When people who enjoy horror read your story, they are not reading it in a vacuum. They are reading it as part of a genre, constantly comparing your story to other horror stories they have read. If I have never read Edgar Allan Poe's "The Tell-Tale Heart" and I write a story very much like "The Tell-Tale Heart," readers who know Poe's story may not be as thrilled with my Big! Surprise! Ending! as I had hoped. To them, it's no surprise. They've read it before, and they've read it better (you can't beat Poe).

To be a creative, innovative horror writer, you must read a lot of *everything*, and a lot of that everything must be horror. You may be thinking, *How can I be creative and original with all these other authors' ideas floating around in my head?* But this is critical: The sheer amount of material floating around in your head will prevent your copying from any one author.

Instead you will find a tiny piece of character from this book, a tiny piece of plot from that book, a certain stylistic technique from that other, which you will combine into something totally new. It is the writer who reads only Stephen King who will turn out stories that sound like Stephen King—on a very, very bad day.

If you can accept the need to know the horror writing that has gone before, you might still have difficulty with the idea of extensive reading *outside* the field. Simply by the law of averages, more great writing has been done outside the field of horror than within it. Another law of averages: The more great writing you read, the more will rub off on you. Read works from different periods of history, from different cultures. Read fiction and nonfiction. Many innovations arise from taking ideas outside the genre and bringing them in. Some of our favorite stories even mix genres.

When a story is innovative, it brings fresh ideas and techniques to the genre. It helps enlarge the genre and to renew it. It helps keep the genre exciting and alive for future generations of readers. And it creates one hell of a great story.

Innovate or Imitate?

Why do so many people think John Carpenter's *Halloween* a great movie? (I'm using a movie rather than a novel as an example because I think more of you will be familiar with a particular movie than a particular novel. But my point holds equally true for novels and stories.) If you watch it now, it may seem a rather tame and predictable slasher movie. But when it came out, nothing quite like it had ever been done before. It was intense, tightly plotted (the whole story takes place in one night), concerned itself very little with explanation (we have no idea why the killer goes after Jamie Lee Curtis with such determination), and had an incredible amount of suspense (every scene either had the killer in it or had in it evidence of something the killer had done, like a dead body). It didn't spend half its length building up to killings, as so many movies of the day did. A murder occurs in the first five minutes. Each of these elements was not new, but this combination of them was, and it was very powerful, touching off a whole series of sequels and imitators. *Halloween* expanded and renewed the genre.

Stephen King has had a similar effect. He combined elements in a totally new way. Never before had classic horror archetypes, like the vampire (*Salem's Lot*) or the haunted house (*The Shining*), seemed so possible in our mundane, middle-class world. He brought these horrors down to earth, making them not the province of unstable minds and rarefied atmospheres, but of Anytown, U.S.A., in the plumber's house, the son's room, right under the bed. In the early 1980s, King had a huge impact on the genre, expanding and renewing it and spawning hordes of imitators. Even today his influence is strong on many developing horror writers; there are more than a few who believe that to write horror is to write "Stephen King horror"—since they've never read anything else they've liked.

The question is, do you want to be an innovator or an imitator? It's normal for young writers to be inspired by books or movies and to begin writing by emulating those sources. But horror that simply reflects the source that inspired it is not going to be rich and powerful; it's going to be a pale reflection of its source. A writer must take various sources of inspiration and filter them through his own unique sensibilities.

There are, of course, an infinite number of ways you can make your story innovative. Writing is a layered and complex process, and each story combines multiple elements. In creating new combinations and new patterns, you are innovating.

Innovative Plotting

What will the plot of your story be? What fear will it focus on? Many writers choose a plot by choosing a horror archetype to write about. Maybe you decide to write a vampire story, or a ghost story, or a serial killer story, or a zombie story. That's okay. These archetypes have developed and persisted over the years because they tap into our fears and have a strong, resonant effect on us. But they also present a serious challenge to today's writer: What is *your* vampire story going to do that no other vampire story has done before? (This is quite a question, considering how much material has been written about vampires.) What unique sensibility do you bring to a vampire story? If you don't have a powerful, significant difference to offer in your story, then you probably shouldn't write it.

Maybe you decide to center your plot around a specific fear—one of *your* specific fears. This can be a wonderful technique, because if you are afraid of "it," chances are you can also make the reader afraid of it. But when I ask writers what they are afraid of, they usually come back with answers like "cockroaches." That's a perfectly valid answer, and if you are truly afraid of cockroaches, perhaps that can play a part in a story sometime.

But that's not a very deep-rooted fear. What I want to know is what frightens you at all levels, not only at the surface but at the deepest levels. That way, perhaps cockroaches cannot only be scary and gross, but can symbolize a deeper fear, the fear, perhaps, of chaos, of forces beyond your control. Most of us fear this a lot more than we fear cockroaches. Don't just throw a ton of cockroaches in a story and assume your reader will be horrified (how many cockroaches are in a ton, anyway?). The cockroaches need to tie into a deeper fear: *Why* do they scare you so much? Becoming aware of the unique way that you see things and writing a story that reflects your unique sensibility is the key to writing innovative horror.

Once you have a basic concept for your story, you need to develop it into a plot. Now, the great thing about the horror genre is that, unlike other genres, it allows infinite possibilities. The horror genre has only one requirement for membership: The story must make the reader feel . . . *horrified.* Many writers don't realize how revolutionary this is. In other genres, a fairly strict plot is imposed. In a mystery, a crime must occur—usually a murder—which must then be solved by the end of the story. In a romance, two people must meet and fall in love. But the plot of a horror story can be anything, as long as it makes the reader feel horror. So why is it that the plot of so many horror novels can be summarized like this:

Prologue: Evil creature is awakened and kills one or more victims in spectacularly gruesome fashion.

Chapter 1: Introduction of thirty-something family man (often a writer) who's carrying around a problem from his past.

Chapters 2-15: Evil creature creeps into life of family man, killing numerous other victims on its way (in spectacularly gruesome fashion) and threatening members of the family man's family. The family's pet usually gets it at this point. Family man continues to suffer over problem from his past.

Chapters 16-19: Family man recognizes the threat of the evil creature, fights evil creature, figures out the secret to killing it, and triumphs, killing the creature in spectacularly gruesome fashion and simultaneously resolving his problem from the past.

Chapter 20: Family man and his family (minus pet) live happily ever after. Creature is dead (or is it . . . ?).

If horror, as I said, puts no constraints on plot, why does this darned thing sound so familiar? As an editor, I have read this plot more times than I can count, and many more than I want to remember. These days, any horror manuscript with a prologue makes an editor sigh in despair. Reading a lot in the field will help these old, tired patterns become more apparent to you. Then as a writer you can decide to avoid them, or you can play off them, beginning your novel in a way that makes us think we know exactly what is going to happen and then surprising us by taking the plot in a totally different direction.

Innovative Style

So one important method of innovating comes from choosing and developing your plot, in deciding *what you are going to say.* The other method arises from deciding *how you are going to say it.* Your writing style, or your voice, reflects your personality, your beliefs, your concerns. In writing, you are commenting on life, the human condition. What do you believe? What do you want to say?

Just as each person has a distinctive speaking voice, a distinctive tone and timbre, a distinctive way of putting words together, and certain preferred words, so do we each have a distinctive writing voice. This is often more difficult to develop. Beginning writers tend to write like the authors they have read. One of my students told me she would write like Stephen King when she was reading King, like Harlan Ellison when she was reading Ellison, and on and on. She had no style or voice of her own. And truth to tell, she wasn't really writing in King's style one week and Ellison's style the next (a writer could have worse problems). She was writing in a style that was a pale, inferior reflection of King's style, or Ellison's style, or . . . She could never write King's style as well as King, because King's style reflects who he is, how he thinks, and how he expresses himself. Your style, if it is to be *your* style, must do the same for you.

How you say something is just as important as *what* you say. Critics today bemoan the elevation of style over substance, but style is critically important in powerful and innovative writing. In fact, much of the innovation in horror in recent years has come in the area of style. While Stephen King introduced a style that was immediate, concrete, accessible and down to earth, post-King authors are introducing literary, postmodern, experimental styles.

Perhaps you don't understand what I mean when I say style. In the following two passages, the plot is the same, but the style is very different. In other words, *what* is said remains the same, but *how* it is said changes drastically. Here's an example of a very familiar, overused style of horror writing:

Colin stared at the razor, shiny and sharp, that Robert held above him. *OH MY GOD*, Colin thought. *HE'S GOING TO KILL ME!* The hairs on the back of his neck prickled.

Robert prodded the knife into his neck. "I will kill you. I will leave no one alive to talk about me after I'm gone."

Colin's brain sent an urgent message—*Push Robert out of the way! Scream! Do something!* But shock had frozen him still.

Robert laughed, his breath an execrable stench hanging in the air like a cloud of corruption. He fixed Colin in his hypnotic gaze, the twin black orbs holding him immobile.

Colin realized sickeningly that he was helpless. *I'm going to die (oh God please help me God). I'm going to die! And when they're finished with me they'll kill my beloved Mary!*

With a snarl of rage, his lips drawn back from his teeth, Robert brought the razor down across Colin's throat. He let out a demonic yell.

Colin's world went black.

I'm afraid I don't have the space here to tell you all that's weak and derivative and clichéd in the above example, which I wrote myself, but if you've read a fair amount of horror, this probably sounds about as familiar to you as the plot outline I gave earlier. If something sounds quite familiar, then you know it's not innovative. Many developing writers, having grown up on the horror of the 1980s, think that this is the *only* way horror can be written.

Let me give you another example, this one by the fine author Ian McEwan:

> Mary was watching the object Robert clasped in his hand. Suddenly it was twice its length, and she saw it clearly, and though every muscle in her body tightened, only the fingers of her right hand clenched softly. She shouted, and shouted again, and all that left her was a whispering exhalation.
>
> "I'll do whatever you want," Colin said, the level tone all lost now at the sound, his voice rising in panic. "But please get a doctor for Mary."
>
> "Very well," Robert said and reached for Colin's arm, and turned his palm upward. "See how easy it is," he said, perhaps to himself, as he drew the razor lightly, almost playfully, across Colin's wrist, opening wide the artery. His arm jerked forward, and the rope he cast, orange in this light, fell short of Mary's lap by several inches.
>
> Mary's eyes closed. When she opened them, Colin was sitting on the floor, against the wall, his legs splayed before him. Curiously, his canvas beach shoes were soaked, stained scarlet. His head swayed upon his shoulders, but his eyes were steady and pure, and blazed at her across the room in disbelief. "Mary?" he said anxiously, like someone calling in a dark room.
>
> "Mary? Mary?"
>
> "I'm coming," Mary said. "I'm over here."
>
> THE COMFORT OF STRANGERS

The main difference here, for the purposes of our discussion, is that the first author is trying to emulate the voices of other authors she has read; the second author is trying to reproduce his vision of life—and has developed his own voice to do so.

To get a better idea of the possibilities for innovation in horror, read these genre-stretching works: Patrick McCabe's *The Butcher's Boy*, Jennifer Lynch's *The Secret Diary of Laura Palmer*, Ian McEwan's *The Comfort of Strangers*, or Tim Lucas's *Throat Sprockets*.

Innovation is a critical component in any strong work of horror, and it does not come easily or automatically to us "creative" souls who write. Strive for innovation in your writing and never give up. If you can express what concerns you in a way that reflects your own unique sensibility, then you are being truly innovative, and the horror you create will be truly special.

No More Silver Mirrors
The Monster in Our Times

Karen E. Taylor

Everything old is new again. Or so it certainly seems these days. There is a proliferation of the classic stories; everyone seems to be taking Bram Stoker's *this* or Mary Wollstonecraft Shelley's *that* and putting a different, modern (usually) spin on the story, twisting the original details and events to fit individual perspectives. From novels to anthologies to movies, we are being regaled with portraits of traditional and familiar monsters from new points of view. Some may see this as a bastardization, others, as a natural evolution of the genre.

The purpose of this chapter, though, is not to pass judgment on current horror trends, but to attempt to show you (at least from this author's viewpoint) how oft-told legends and venerable (OK, *old*!) monsters can be brought into contemporary times.

A basic truth: People love monsters. Whether these monsters are vampires, ghosts, werewolves, demons or shapeless blobs that devour everything in their paths makes little or no difference.

Today's readers, like yesterday's, pick up a horror novel to be scared, to be entertained, to be drawn away from the conflicts of their own life into the conflicts of the supernatural. They want larger-than-life struggles, heroic efforts facing almost insurmountable odds.

But modern readers are more sophisticated than their parents and grandparents. Today's readers also require credible premises and explanations; they want things to be scientifically possible. They want reality in their non-reality. Very few people truly believe in the old monsters, and in order to produce an effective novel or story the writer must foster a belief strong enough to carry the reader throughout. Talk about insurmountable odds!

But there are ways around the nonbelievers. And ways to drag those old-fashioned monsters kicking and screaming and dump them full-grown and growling into the "here and now," right where readers live. "I am here," you want your monster to say, "and I exist in your world. Deal with me, if you can!"

Know the Rules

So where do you start? First, approach your monster scientifically. Sedate him if necessary, lay him out on the examination table, and take him apart piece by piece. What is it that makes him what he is? What are the rules of his existence? Exactly what makes a vampire a vampire? These rules are extremely important to your monster's believability. The writer must know them intimately—because the readers do. They know emphatically that a vampire feeds on the blood of humans, that he must shun the daylight, that he sleeps in a coffin and is repelled by holy water and crucifixes. They know this not from first-hand experience, but because other writers have told them so.

Before beginning your project, research as much as you can, read as much as you can and catalog the rules for your particular monster, from the most basic to the most trivial and ridiculous. Gain an understanding of the perspective from which these rules have come.

There must always be inner rules for each monster that are "true" if he is to be recognizable to the reader. Decide within the context of your story which rules are basic to your creature, and stick with them throughout. Consistency might be "the hobgoblin of little minds," but it is the spine of an "old monster made new" story.

If your vampire feeds on souls instead of blood, you can't have him vary his diet halfway through. If your werewolf must see the full moon to effect his transformation, you can't have him growing hairy in a windowless room. The readers will cry "foul," and rightly so.

Once you have delineated the essentials of your monster, you can (should, in this writer's opinion) *break* some of the other rules. *Stretch* the limits . . .

But be prepared to defend your actions. Your vampire has a reflection in the mirror? Perhaps it's because mirrors today are made with mercury and not a holy/mystical metal like silver. He doesn't sleep in a coffin? Well, maybe he never knew he was *supposed* to, and therefore adapted to other methods of rest. Or maybe your particular vampire is just plain claustrophobic and would rather chance facing the sun than being trapped inside close wooden walls. Don't be afraid to play with the rules, to twist them to your purposes, to update the ancient myths to reflect modern sensibilities.

This is your story. This is your monster.

Characterizing Your Monster

After rules have been made, and after some have been broken, you must deal with the character of the monster. He has to have a strong enough presence to balance out microwaves, satellite dishes and neon lights, to stand up to a society that says "There's no such thing as *you!*" Remember that he should remain larger-than-life in today's world while still seeming real. Give him a purpose in life (*un*life, in the case of Mr. Vampire), a goal to his actions.

Is he interested in world domination, creating and unleashing legions of his own kind on an unsuspecting human population? Or is he hungry for revenge, searching for a lost love, or just struggling to survive in a world that has left his kind behind? Give him a job, glamorous or mundane.

Just as in mainstream fiction, or the bleakest, most minimally plotted "slice of life" story, the monster character must have human traits with which readers can identify: lust, love, anger, hate, pain. And, like all of us, he has weaknesses as well as powers; there is nothing more dissatisfying in fright fiction than an invincible creature—who must be "defeated in the end" by totally implausible means.

Now take your monster by the claw and help him, even force him if necessary, to face modern-day situations. Regardless of the type of being he is, he needs to learn to deal with ordinary day-to-day events. So have him ride the subway, take a cab, order a meal from a hot dog vendor, meet a mugger in a dark alley. How he reacts to "outside stimuli" goes a long way to bringing this creature to life. If he can strike a familiar chord, if he can evoke a response of "I would have done that, too," then you have succeeded in making him a viable character.

Believability of characters is integral in any story, horror or not. Creating human characters that seem real is an important and difficult job; the task is doubly difficult when you are working with a creature readers know does not exist. There are no chemical formulas for giving your creation life in fiction, no special laboratory equipment, no convenient lightning storms. Instead you must rely on your skills as a writer.

Point of view is essential in making your unreal characters real. Get inside the creature's head as much as possible; show the reader what he is thinking, what motivates him, the senses that drive his instinctual behaviors. Is your vampire's hunger nothing more than a pang, akin to something as trivial as a human missing a meal? Or is it a soul-devouring, conscience-overcoming rage? Is the transformation of your werewolf a painful process? When the hair grows in, does it tickle? Hurt? Itch? Give your reader the benefit of the monster's experience; guide the reader on a trip deep inside the monster's psyche. It is not necessarily important or even always desirable to garner sympathy for the creature (some monsters are evil and meant to stay that way), but try to provide an understanding of the internal as well as the external processes that make this particular being possible.

Know the Reader

Finally, you should attempt to understand the audience you are trying to reach. Horror fiction contains many subgenres and readers who are voracious for one type (vampire fiction, for example) may not read another. So it is important to realize that your readers may hold certain expectations about what a "traditional" monster should be.

Vampires are portrayed today as sexual and ultraseductive creatures, deadly but ultimately attractive (as well as closely related) to humankind. From our human perspective, they appear sophisticated and desirable; often they are pictured as misunderstood heroes. Yet this does not mean that they cannot also be the repulsive, ugly and blood-thirsty creatures of the original legends. Hold true to *your* image, your view of *your* monster.

Yes, writers have an audience, and therefore an obligation to fulfill *some* audience (reader) expectations. If you meet the audience halfway, then you are safe in grafting your new vision onto the established one that is in the reader's mind. The guideline: Your monster is indeed *yours*, grown out of legend but belonging to your world and your times.

Make rules, break rules, and provide your character with traits and skills enabling him to make his way in our modern era, while still remaining true to that which makes him what he is.

The Prime Rule of Modern Monster-Making: *Know Your Monster!*

He is your creation, your responsibility and your child, misbegotten or not, loved or hated, hero or villain.

Dark Light Focus
Forrest J. Ackerman

Owl Goingback

In August 1968, at age nine, I received a weekly allowance for the very first time. A whopping fifty cents. I persuaded my mother to drive me into town to do a little shopping. I grew up in rural Missouri, and there weren't many places to spend money. But our tiny town did have a drug store with a magazine rack, a place I loved to visit whenever I could. I had originally planned to spend my allowance on comic books and candy, the staples of my childhood, but my eyes were drawn to a magazine on the newsstand's bottom shelf—a magazine with a cover adorned with the frightful images of werewolves. Even the magazine's name, *Famous Monsters of Filmland*, brought goosebumps, conjuring up images of the things dear to my heart: *scary* things.

With trembling hands, I lifted the 51st issue of *Famous Monsters* from the shelf and opened it, gazing in awe at page after page of monster photos. They were all there, all my favorites: Frankenstein, Dracula, the Wolf Man, even the Creature From the Black Lagoon. Not only were the monsters there, but the actors who played them on the silver screen were also featured. Karloff, Lugosi, Chaney, the gods of fear marched past my eyes in an endless parade. It was a young horror lover's dream come true, an experience so monumental that it changed my life forever and turned me into the warped writer of dark fantasy and horror fiction that I am today.

At the front of the magazine, I found the name of the man responsible for making my dreams come true. That man was Editor-in-Chief Forrest J. Ackerman. Known affectionately as "Uncle Forry," Mr. Ackerman personally assured his thousands of readers that it was quite all right to love monsters, horror movies and things that go bump in the night—despite what our teachers and parents might say to the contrary. In each issue he took us by the hand, leading us into the universe of scary things, allowing us to spend quality time with the men, women and movies we loved. Many top horror writers, including Stephen King, will tell you that Forrest J. Ackerman and *Famous Monsters of Filmland* had a positive and profound influence on their lives.

The first issue of *Famous Monsters of Filmland* hit the newsstands on February 27, 1958. Originally planned to be a one-shot, it was the first magazine ever dedicated to the Hollywood horror scene. The response was overwhelming, greatly exceeding Forry's and publisher Jim Warren's wildest expectations. In only a matter of weeks, the dynamic duo were swamped with over three thousand fan letters.

Famous Monsters was a hit. A new era in horror had been born.

And why shouldn't it be a hit? Each issue of *Famous Monsters* treated its readers to in-depth articles on classic and new horror movies and the people who starred in them. Uncle Forry took us behind the scenes, to places no one had ever been before. We learned about the lives, the happiness and the tragedy of those who gave so much of themselves for the horror genre. Along with the articles, the pages were filled with rare photos and movie stills, many of them from Forry's personal collection. Were it not for *Famous Monsters* and Forrest J. Ackerman, many of the classic movies might have been forgotten, along with the names of the greats who starred in them. He kept them alive in the pages of his magazine.

But it wasn't enough for Forry just to write about horror movies; he wanted us to experience the world of the scary up close and personal. He helped to establish and run *Famous Monsters Conventions*, bringing the lovers of the genre together in a festive air of celebration. He also opened the "Ackermansion" to the public. Located in Hollywood, California, the eighteen-room mansion is packed with over 300,000 items of horror movie memorabilia, including King Kong and Ray Harryhausen animation models, Lon Chaney Sr.'s makeup kit, and Bela Lugosi's *Plan Nine From Outer Space* Dracula cape.

In addition to being the Editor-in-Chief of *Famous Monsters* and the guardian of rare treasures, Uncle Forry has also had cameo roles in over forty films—and has had the star spotlight on him in *My Lovely Monster*. He also created the comic book character Vampirella, a young lady with fangs and much healthy-looking skin, whose story will soon be presented in a full-length movie.

At the 1992 World Science Fiction Convention in Orlando, Florida, I was scheduled to do an autographing session alongside Forrest J. Ackerman. Since his line was considerably longer than mine, several minutes elapsed before I had a chance to talk with the man who so influenced my life. Grasping Mr. Ackerman firmly by the hand, I introduced myself. Then I told him what was a key truth in my life: He had raised me.

Uncle Forry has raised a lot of us. And for me, it's been a very good life.

Werewolves
Bending the Legend

Gary Brandner

Because of a book I wrote a while back I have been gifted with a middle name that never occurred to my parents. When I am introduced to a group or referred to in print, by way of identification I become Gary "The Howling" Brandner. Never mind that I have written a couple dozen other books, a hundred or so short stories and a handful of screenplays; thanks to *The Howling*, I am forever associated with werewolves. Does this disturb me? Hey, did it disturb Disney to be associated with a mouse? Not that I am in Uncle Walt's neighborhood, but wolves have been very good to me over the years, and I am honored to join the pack. What does annoy me a little is that in recent years my furry friends have taken a neglected backseat to vampires.

I'll grant you that vampires are sexy. Dracula was, let's be honest, something of a babe magnet. And who is hotter these days than Tom Cruise and Brad Pitt, fey bloodsuckers in *Interview With the Vampire*? The 1990s have been a vampire decade. Go count the books at your local Barnes and Noble. Vampires are hot. They provide good bloody book covers and movie posters. Vampires can even be cute. Check out Count Chocula. In some circles vampires are homoerotic. Hi there, Anne Rice. Vampires, it seems, have something for everybody.

With all this hoopla for Nosferatu, where does that leave the werewolf? Sucking hind tit, that's where. He's simply not a "now" creature. Or so the stake-and-crucifix crowd would have us believe. He is relegated to old black-and-white movies and used-book stores. Much of the blame for the current neglect can be placed at the door of the man who revived them half a century ago—Curt Siodmak.

And who, some of you are asking, is Curt Siodmak? Simply the man responsible for most of the things we believe about werewolves today. Curt Siodmak wrote the screenplay for *The Wolf Man*, the definitive lycanthropic movie. In so doing he established rules for shapechangers that fit the plot needs of his 1941 movie, but put heavy limitations on those who would follow.

There had been film versions of the werewolf legend before that one. In 1913 Universal made *The Werewolf*, in which a Navaho named Watuma turns himself into an actual wolf, the better to chew up white folks. That theme inspired no sequels or knockoffs, and cinematically the beast languished until *Werewolf of London* in 1935. In this one Henry Hull is bitten by the villainous Warner Oland while in Tibet seeking a rare flower that blooms in the moonlight. Coincidentally, a prick of its thorn can also cure lycanthropy. Too late for Oland, who is killed by Hull, and for Hull himself, shot dead by Scotland Yard. This movie proposed the concept that "the werewolf instinctively seeks to kill the thing it loves best," a notion that has largely been abandoned. We all know that werewolves kill anybody who wanders into their path. It is noteworthy that in *Werewolf of London* the beast was brought down by standard lead bullets, and the moon was used only peripherally in connection with the Tibetan flower.

Although Hull's makeup foreshadowed that used on Lon Chaney Jr., he lacked the physical bulk to make a scary werewolf, and in human form he was simply not very likable. So the cinematic werewolf took another sabbatical until 1941 when Universal revived him in the person of Lon Chaney Jr. in *The Wolf Man*. It is from this movie, Curt Siodmak's creation, that we get such wolf dogma as the silver bullet, the pentagram in the palm, and the full-moon-only attacks. This one is a classic, and deservedly so. It is often shown on television and readily available in video stores. The hulking Chaney was a sympathetic Lawrence Talbot and had the size and outstanding makeup by Jack Pierce to scare audiences out of their socks. The stop-motion transformation scenes were amazing in their day and are still impressive in good old black and white.

By the time I began writing my werewolf novel, *The Howling*, in 1977, the werewolf canon was universally (excuse the pun) accepted. Full moon, silver bullets, infectious bite, pentagram had become gospel. And the marvelous couplet delivered by old Gypsy Maria Ouspenskaya had the authority of a psalm:

> Even a man who is pure of
> heart and says his prayers at night,
> Can become a wolf
> when the wolfbane blooms
> and the moon is full and bright.

Great stuff, all of it, but downright constricting for a contemporary novel. I did not want to tell the *Wolf Man* story all over again, so what did I do? I changed the legend. Forgive me, Curt Siodmak, but if they can rewrite King James, I guess I can make some revisions to Universal.

I opened with a prologue tracing a legend of my own invention. No need to recount it here, but it involved the Arda forest between Greece and Bulgaria, the village of Dradja, a shepherd named Kyust, his wife Anna and their daughter. None of these existed before *The Howling*, but so what? I needed them to lay a foundation for the modern story I was going to tell, so I created them. There are times a fiction writer feels worthless as dirt, but once in a while he gets to play God.

Werewolf stories until that time fell generally into two categories: (1) the tormented innocent who can't stop biting people (see Lawrence Talbot), and (2) the puzzled villagers searching for the werewolf among them (see Stephen King). The first change I made to the legend was to fashion a town where everyone was a werewolf. My heroine would realize this only gradually, and her struggle to escape would make the story.

Next, the full-moon business had to go. My research into werewolf lore of the Middle Ages turned up no reference limiting the transformation to moon phases. Good news for a novelist, who does not want to write four weeks of nothing happening between bursts of action. So I dumped the moon.

Then there was the anguish of the people bitten and infected. There was not a fictional beast I could find who did not suffer a hell of guilt and remorse between moonlight maraudings. However, the ancient tales gave another slant. People *wanted* to become wolves. They sought out the devil or a local witch who could give them the power of transformation. Being a peasant back in those days was no picnic, so loping through the forest devouring unwary travelers and generally having your way with the populace was a pretty attractive lifestyle. And did not the ultimate shapechanger, Dr. Henry Jekyll, have a pretty good time as his alter ego, Mr. Hyde? With this in mind, I made my modern vulpine villagers a group generally happy with their lot. There were exceptions, of course; there had to be for plot purposes. Still, there was no Lawrence Talbot figure bemoaning his fate in *The Howling*.

Now then, the silver bullet. Siodmak had but one way to kill a werewolf—the silver bullet. Or in the case of Lawrence Talbot, a silver-headed cane wielded by Claude Rains. The silver angle was too good to lose, but I took a closer look. The cane was effective in the movie, but using it is chancy. Clubbing down a werewolf is not like pounding a tree stump. He can bob and weave like Ali in his prime, and you have to be damn good with your stick to smite him a lethal blow. A silver knife blade would do the job, but again you have to get close to a ravening beast to use it effectively. Which leaves us the traditional silver bullet. Fine for the Lone Ranger, but where does the modern werewolf hunter go to get such ammunition? To find out, I visited a gunsmith in Hollywood and asked him. The exchange that followed went almost verbatim into chapter 25.

Finally, I gave the werewolf . . . sex. Whereas Siodmak's creature had no recreational activities beyond ripping up the villagers, I couldn't square that with the desire to become a wolf. Wolves, after all, are not celibate, else where would little wolves come from? Mix the animal instinct with human lust and inventiveness, and you are looking at some pretty spectacular hanky-panky. With this in mind I created the delectable female werewolf Marcia, embodying male fantasies of all species, and joined her with Roy, the newly bitten husband of my heroine. The result has been called the greatest werewolf sex scene in literature. The fact that it may be the only such scene need not concern us.

My remarks to this point refer to my book, not to the movie released in 1981. There are, not surprisingly, major differences. Joe Dante, the director, took my thesis of the village of werewolves, and he took my aforementioned sex scene and made a fine movie. He also took full credit for everything short of the Salk vaccine, consigning the book author and the screenwriter, John Sayles, to the distant background. In fact, much credit for the movie's success should go to the special makeup effects of Rob Bottin. His werewolf transformation set the standard and created the wet, just-born look that is common for movie monsters today. But let director Dante attach his own name to the title; that is what directors do. I bear no ill will. *The Howling* and its lesser sequels have made it possible for me to live in luxury all the rest of my days. OK, that's an exaggeration, but as I said earlier, wolves have been good to me.

Having brought up the subject of sequels, I should explain a little about what happened here. I did write two subsequent novels— *Howling II* and *Howling III*—that were more or less connected to the original. The second focused on Marcia, the sexy werewolf, for whom I have special feelings. It was necessary to bring her back to life after I had killed her off in the finale of the original, but in fiction all things are possible. In the third book, in my opinion the best-written of the trilogy, I followed a young boy and related the werewolf transformation to the torments of puberty. These stories bear no resemblance to the movies of the same Roman numeral.

I give all due credit to the talented Curt Siodmak and Montague Summers, whose exhaustive recounting of lycanthropy through the ages, *The Werewolf*, shows that there is room for bending the legend when it will make a good story. I've bent it more than a little, but there's still plenty of room in this pack for all.

The Green Mile
A Conversation with Stephen King

Where did you get the idea for The Green Mile?

SK: Ideas tend to come, for me, in waves, and each one builds a little more on the previous one. I started with an idea about a guy in prison who was going to escape by learning magic. And his last trick, after he'd made all these coins and oranges and apples disappear, was, before he was executed, to make himself disappear.

The funny thing is, *The Green Mile* is not an escape story, *per se*, it's a prison story. It's a story that's set on death row. But it's not really about escape the way that, say, "Rita Hayworth and Shawshank Redemption" is about escape. Little by little, the story just evolved and changed. It stopped being a story about escape and became a story about death and execution instead. I think I got interested in death row as a subject when I was a teenager. I'd read a book called *20 Thousand Years at Sing Sing*, by Warden Lewis Laws. And I thought, from that point on, I've got to write a story about the electric chair.

How did you react to the suggestion that you write The Green Mile *as serial novel?*

SK: I leapt at the idea. Because I saw a chance to really put myself in harness. I knew that if I had to deliver one of these a month, I would get the story done. I really wanted to make the story happen, and so far, it has. But, as we're talking now, the story is still not done.

Do you know what the ending is going to be?

SK: Well, I do, but I've done this long enough to know that that doesn't make any difference. Because what I think the ending is going to be almost never is what the ending will be. I know there's a bridge overpass somewhere in Alabama. I see that very clearly. It's like being a cheap, sleazy, two-bit medium. I get images that I know are very powerful images if I use them the right way. So, in a sense, what I'm doing with *The Green Mile* is what I do with every story. I look into my magic eight-ball—I don't consider myself high-rent enough to have a crystal ball; I just have a magic eight-ball—and it says, "Cannot see clearly now, consult me again later," or, in this case, it gives me the image that I need—the bridge overpass.

You're in the middle of writing The Green Mile *as a serial novel. How would you describe the experience?*

SK: Right now, I would say that writing the serial novel has been one of the most interesting challenges of my life. A novel is this funny kind of expandable box, whereas with the serial novel, we said in advance there were going to be six segments. And I know approximately how long each segment is supposed to be. So the result is that these parts have to be balanced pretty neatly. The only analogy I can think of is, it's like frosting a cake. You've got the frosting in a bowl, and you've got the cake on a plate, and you're saying to yourself: I hope that I have enough to frost the last side, and I hope I don't have so much left over that I have to make cupcakes and frost them. Because I don't think the readers of *The Green Mile* are going to want any cupcakes. It's not a cupcake type of story.

How is writing a serial novel different from writing a novel in one volume?

SK: The work is a lot different. You know, it's like the song says, the fundamental things apply as time goes by. People still want to have characters that they care about, or at least I do. People still want to have a story that involves them. But with the serial novel, I find myself trying to build a sort of self-containment into each part. Because I am what I am. I mean, my idea is to scare people, to discomfit people, to make them stay up late. So, as each of the segments ends, hopefully people will spend a month saying, "I can't wait to see what happens next."

What are your daily work habits?

SK: I work every day. I like to keep it hot. When it's going good, I like to stay on a roll, and if it's not going good, my theory is the gamblers' theory in Vegas: *If I lost today, I better come back early tomorrow and get back what I lost plus twice as much again.*" So my general work habit, particularly when I'm working on the first draft and it's coming right from my head out onto the page, is to work every day. I like to sit down, if I can, around eight o'clock in the morning and work until maybe noon, maybe one o'clock.

Has the process of writing gotten easier over the years?

SK: It's changed, but I don't think I could describe how it's changed. The big trick, as the years go by, is to try to close the door, close out the readers and the critics and people's expectations, and try to stick with what makes me happy—going on the theory that, over the years, what's made me happy has made the readers happy.

Do you ever think about retiring?

SK: I think about it. I don't think about lining my pockets with cash and running off to some South Seas island. What I would like to do is quit while people are still having a good time with what I write, and while I'm still having a good time with what I write. I don't want to still be around thirty years from now having descended into self-parody.

I love to write. I still can't believe people pay me for it. And I think I'd probably go on even if I weren't publishing. The act doesn't actually need publication to complete it for me. But if it's not going to be good, I would like to quit. I just hope I have sense enough to know when that time comes.

Do you scare easily?

SK: I don't think that I do, and I'll tell you why. I think that, over the years, I've had so many shocks in movie theaters and in books that I've read and written both, that I've become a bit inured. So, for instance, if I hit a patch of black ice on the turnpike, and the car does a 360, the thought that goes through my mind is not, *I'm going to die*; it's *This is interesting. This is just like in a movie.*

Do you think electronic publishing will ever supplant the book?

SK: No. Books have their own kind of sweet reality that can't be matched by a disk or a floppy or a screen. To me, a book says, "I'm finished, I'm for the ages." And a floppy says, "I'm just waiting for the first electromagnetic pulse to wipe me just as clean as a whistle." I'm very old-fashioned about that. I've been dragged kicking and screaming into the computer age. But I still like to walk up to people and say, "Do you want to see my word processor?" And then I pull out a pencil and point to the tip and say, "This is *Insert*." And then I show them the eraser and say, "This is my *Delete* function."

What has been your most satisfying experience as a novelist?

SK: I was living in a trailer with a wife and two kids. The phone company had taken the phone out because we hadn't paid the bill for a couple of months. I was teaching school and making $6,400 a year. And I got a telegram that said, "Congratulations—*Carrie* officially a Doubleday book, $2,500 advance, the future lies ahead." What I remember best was that line: "The future lies ahead."

So that was it. My first was still my best. A guy never forgets his first, you know.

Editor's Note: This interview with Stephen King appeared in the Halloween 1996 issue of *M.A.I.N. Magazine,* a trade publication focusing on comic books and collector cards, and is reprinted with the kind permission of that periodical and its editor, Rusty Gilligan.

Contemporary Lip Synching to Horror's Gothic Tune

Robert W. Walker

Even Maestro Shakespeare had to scavenge for material and re-fashion from scratch and research (and what a rich vein he struck and utilized to such great advantage). Writers in general, and horror writers in particular, have been told countless times that there is "nothing new under the sun," that in fact all we can do is put a new "spin" on old themes; there are limited and few plots, all of which have been covered in the Bible.

This reality might dampen some spirits but it hasn't stopped invention. So, like the ubiquitous gargoyle, the old question raises its ugly head here again: *How can the old be made new in horror writing?*

Contemporary horror can be about insomnia or any number of diseases, plagues, curses, TV newscasts, wars to end wars, the latest killer virus, giant crocs, lizard-like aliens, a man-eating shark, bear or were-wolf, or it can be an invasion of ancient creature-cousins of the cock-roach, but no matter the menace, readers today demand some sem-blance of logical progression as to how the monster came to be. My work has been compared to the popular *X-Files*, and although I was writing my *Instinct* series long before the show premiered, there is an edgy *X-Files* form of logic required of me by my readers. Inquiring minds do want to know *how* the alien or the creature or the human killing machine came into existence.

This "need to know" was not the case in early works of horror about haunted houses, spirits, stone gargoyles coming to life; two words sufficed to explain away all such elements: *Supernatural* and *Magic*.

In today's horror, a supernatural explanation, even an alien inva-sion explanation, for all that goes on in the story, is felt to be a cop-out, and magic alone does not suffice or fulfill intelligent readers.

Of course, today, just like yesterday, we are "stuck with the old"—because we have only so many stories to tell, and only so many forms that the telling can take—just like the western or the science-fiction tale. The film *Independence Day* is a retelling of an old, old story. It's the presentation, the execution, the special effects that lure us into suspending the disbelief system, and so, we are taken in and come to see *ID4* as something unique.

The forms vary in a long work such as a novel, but every story takes a form, a shape, and these shapes are *fixed*: the "Journey" story, the "Slice of Life" story, the "Bear at the Door" story, and one of Stephen King's favorites: the "Disruption of Perfection and Peace" story. I use them all in a long work, whereas a short story might use only one. These forms are described in detail in Jerome Stern's remarkable *Making Shapely Fiction* in which we're ever reminded that a story is only as good as the effect it has on a reader.

Horror for Today

As horror writers, we have to take new ground just as Michael Crichton and Dean Koontz have been doing for years. We have to stretch out into the mainstream to make such elements as the "Journey" story fresh and new. This means we have to explore characters more deeply, layer them, creating complexities within our lead and minor characters.

And thus we also need to layer the plot. We are obliged to explore unique plotting devices, more intricate and exotic settings—or transform a less than exotic setting into the exotic. It means that every line, every paragraph, every scene, every chapter must be *compelling* (a word branded on my forehead as I write), feeding the dynamo of the story.

It may also mean we should explore "modern magic" and "modern supernormal" sciences, to mine the gold of fresh perspectives on the supernormal and the magical elements of life around us. In my novels, for example, I've explored such divergent "magic(s)" as forensic medicine, handwriting analysis, blood chemistry, cannibalism, psychism, computer religion, obsessions and madness.

Yet there are those readers and writers who fear that horror cannot survive being "mainstreamed" and stripped of its Gothic considerations and sensibilities. After all, horror has long been heralded as the last bastion of the Gothic and the arcane.

That argument ignores that horror has held within its "Gothic" sphere a classic modus operandi (opera of good vs. evil) from its inception. And classical methods and themes abound: The haunted house immediately comes to mind, but there's an entire list of props, elements and settings necessary to creating the classic horror tale from Edgar Allan Poe to present.

While these elements have always been with us, fact is, all of these and more, often thinly disguised, *remain* with us, just as a certain amount of Plutarch remains in Shakespeare's creations. These elements figure heavily in modern horror, in setting, in characterization, in plot. All must be familiar up to a point, *then* they must change course and become fresh and unique, all at once.

Setting: The Gothic haunted house becomes the haunted sky-scraper, haunted airplane or even haunted space capsule. And there's no question that the movies have made the modern underground parking lot a near-archetypal haunted house as a setting of urban and other-world terror. Where terror takes full shape, there is your haunted space.

Character: Today's wandering spirits may be flesh-and-blood creatures reborn into this world from hell—or as a test-tube experiment, or simply carrying the "killing gene." Today a hellion may look like a pleasant neighbor, and the pit he's crawled from might be his mother's womb. Cemetery fog might today be replaced with choking pollution lying over the land, and the distant howling of an animal in the dark woods replaced by the whine of a particularly annoying, nerve-grinding generator. The classic (and alliterative) "cold, clammy crypt"? Let's substitute sterile cold storage facilities or the hallways of modern hospital wards.

Plot: The protagonist of my *Instinct* series, medical examiner and FBI agent Jessica Coran, has no mystical visions or encounters with spectral finger-pointing ghosts, but she does have evidence and a very real talent—a psychological-artistic *instinct*, if you will—not unlike that of psychologists Carl Rogers and Fritz Perls, for getting inside the minds of her quarry.

If you look closely, it's not difficult to see Gothic roots in most of today's horror. By linking our age and archetypal convention, we can turn the old into the new. It's the same tune underneath, still as haunting as ever and just waiting for us to sing it again.

On Horror
A Conversation With Harlan Ellison

Richard Gilliam

Editor's Note: Harlan Ellison has, for more than a few years, been openly critical of some of the commercial and artistic aspects of the horror genre. Yet during this period, he has received four Bram Stoker awards plus the Horror Writers Association Life Achievement award. The following interview was conducted in December 1996, shortly before this book went to press.

You were Toastmaster at the 1996 Horror Writers Association banquet and delivered a surprisingly well-received speech that attacked the amateurism of a large segment of horror writers. It's been called a "ferocious" speech . . . What prompts this passionate assault?

HE: My feeling about contemporary horror writing is that it suffers from the same malaise that is suffocating *most* art forms in our time: widespread and deep-seated illiteracy on the part of the body politic and a lack of historical memory. People apply for editorial positions at fantasy magazines and book publishers, and when asked for their credentials as evaluators of the genre, they declare themselves well-versed, call themselves "big fans" of the field, and then they list having watched *The X-Files* as a qualification.

This wouldn't matter so much if they said they watched *The X-Files and* read books, but watching idiot television is what passes nowadays for an education in the genre. Ill-informed and semiliterate amateurs pollute the market and downgrade the literature. They make it impossible to reach, or create, a smarter audience.

But it isn't just The X-Files *influence. You've been aggressively critical of the horror genre for the past seven or eight years.*

HE: In my view, the horror story has *always* been a constrained form, even though the definition of "horror" has been expanded to include straight suspense or mystery fiction featuring serial killers. For years I've been cautioning writers not to cling to a sinking ship; and even after one disastrous season atop the last, validating my observations, I'm witness to the ongoing uproar from people who don't want to hear that the engine room is filled with water. "How *dare* Ellison piss on the parade yet again!" they bleat. I don't much like being the specter at the banquet, but I *do* keep my eyes open and I *do* listen. And as a consequence I do think that in many instances writing horror became an activity for people who were better suited to be in other occupations. Check it out: all the pointless vampire novels that get published. The whole vampire *idea* is one of the dumbest that's ever come down the pike. Once you've read *Dracula* and Suzy McKee Charnas's *The Vampire Tapestry* and seen George Hamilton in *Love at First Bite*, what further is there to say about vampirism? It always boils down to "may-I-suck-your-neck?" No wonder—employing such creaky, familiar, dopey materials—that there's a record number of good writers in bankruptcy, and less-good ones who have had to take jobs at fast-food joints to survive in a time of desperation. The bad writers have driven away the readers. There's just too much imitative, semiliterate, in-joke *crap* out there. Excuse me if I display almost *no* compassion for people who are simply under-talented, jumped-up amateurs!

A few writers continue to have success. Stephen King, obviously.

HE: Stephen King single-handedly resurrected the horror novel. He's an unprecedented force in literature, *sui generis*, and there just isn't *anyone* in the history of American letters who has had that sort of success.

That didn't stop people from trying to jump on the King ship, though. When Stephen became a publishing phenomenon, through dint of hard work and by demonstrating a singular, universally accessible talent, a great many parvenus of limited ability, who were doing other things, fled across, slavering with greed—with not much else to recommend them—into horror. Fantasy writers came; science-fiction writers came; romance writers came; mystery writers and suspense writers and true crime writers . . . and most of them not much of a writer to begin with. Purveyors of derivative *crap*.

In only a very few cases were any of them successful. Dean Koontz, as a diametrically opposed exception, is a fine example of a *real* writer because Dean is an accomplished storyteller who has a fecundity of imagination. And he's paid his dues. He has spent years learning to write well. But I could also list dozens of others, of less talent, who failed to fear the iceberg even after their personal Titanic hit it. The smart ones knew the ship was sinking and took to the lifeboats, most often into suspense and mystery. The others got drawn down into the whirlpool and didn't get away from the genre quickly enough before it sank. The people who insist on calling themselves "horror writers" exclusively have stifled themselves; they're like the those tunnel-visioned superannuated fanboys who write "science-fiction" exclusively or write "westerns" exclusively. It's an amateurish way for someone who thinks he or she is a Writer to run a career. If you're a *writer*, you should be able to write more than just one type of fiction . . . which is also smart from a commercial perspective since it opens additional markets, opens the world, for the writer!

Those who have been earning a living for many years as professionals already know these truths in their blood and bones. Amateurs who stumble about and get published occasionally . . . and think they're writers . . . do not. They just ain't got a clue.

You also dislike the term "horror fiction."

HE: Jeezus, yes! What an off-putting appellation. I would *much* rather use the phrase "fiction of the macabre." Consider: *most* people, what we like to call "normal people," spend most of their lives trying to *avoid* horror. The six car pile-up on the freeway with beheaded corpses is horror. The mother who straps her children in a car and drowns them . . . that's horror. Bosnia, O.J. Simpson, church bombings by skinheads, all of that. It's horror. Sickening, paralyzing, horror, worse than splatterpunk shockstuff.

What I write is "fiction of the macabre," not horror.

And yet you've continued to maintain connections to the genre, mentoring new writers who want to write horror.

HE: Correction: I support writers of talent who fight the odds in order to create Art. My connections are with writers, not with some bullshit category designation. Just because I visit a whorehouse to deliver succor and medicine don't make me no whore. I look at the horror field with a jaundiced eye, and I say this having read much of the recent work published in the field, including a great many of the anthologies and the semiprofessional magazines. Most of what gets published these days as *horror* writing is just *bad* writing. Sincere, maybe, but bad. Amateur. But the good news is that it isn't much worse than what's being published in *other* fields and there are occasionally writers who deliver something good enough to make wading through the crap worthwhile. When working with new writers, a mentor who means well *must* be selective and not profligate with his aid. Compassionate but tough . . . and pragmatic. You have to be able to differentiate: between the ones who aren't threatened by constructive criticism, who are not in the game for self-aggrandizement and that fantasy lure, Success, but are in the game to write what no one else has written, and those who are simply looking for undiscriminatory praise, or validation. As long as the latter continue to seek that useless pseudoconfirmation, they're going to have a tough time getting any better. Get this: writers *always* control their destiny. It's one of the few professions where a person can program him- or herself into being at the right place at the right time. There's no such thing as luck. It's how well you run your life—run this cottage industry you call your writing career. It's the one great secret of writing that I've learned over the years, and the secret is not how to *become* a writer. If you look at the crap Judith Krantz writes you'll know that ants or aphids can do it, paramecia can become writers. The secret is *staying* a writer. And staying a writer is hard. To stay a writer you have to keep growing, have to be flexible, have to be able to recognize when the world has gone on and changed without asking your opinion. Do that, and you can not only *become* a writer, you can *stay* a writer.

MARKETING
HORROR

Sharing the Creeps
Marketing Short Horror Fiction

Edo van Belkom

You've just finished writing a horror story that's so scary it even gives you the creeps. Now you want to share your work with as many readers as possible.

The conventional wisdom for marketing short stories is to create a list of the best-paying markets and submit from the top down, sending the story to the highest-paying market first. If the story is rejected, you send it to the *second* highest-paying magazine, gradually working your way down the list until the story finally sells.

Unfortunately, horror doesn't have the high-paying, prestigious markets that we find in, say, science-fiction and fantasy. Horror currently has nothing comparable to magazines like *Asimov's* or *Science Fiction Age*, established magazines that pay well and have high circulation. There *were* several top-flight horror magazines in the mid-1980s, such as *Night Cry* and *Twilight Zone*, but sadly they are no more.

Despite the demise of some top horror markets, there are still a number of well regarded magazines publishing horror. In the most recent *Writer's Digest* "Fiction 50"—an annual list of the top fifty magazines publishing fiction in the United States—three "horror" magazines were included in the list. *The Urbanite* was ranked number 22, *2 AM* was ranked number 23 and *Worlds of Fantasy and Horror* (formerly *Weird Tales*) came in at number 50.

It's important to note that the markets listed in the "Fiction 50" are judged on a range of criteria, from "rate of pay" to the number of "stories published in a year," from "personalized rejections" to "range of interest." Therefore some highly respected, albeit low-paying or low-circulation magazines in the horror genre did not make the list.

These magazines are generally known as semiprofessional and small-press magazines. Some prestigious horror magazines such as *Cemetery Dance* and *Deathrealm* are considered semiprofessional (though *Cemetery Dance* pays at the three-cents-a-word rate the HWA sets as "pro" level), but have nevertheless published some of the finest short fiction and the biggest names in our field: Jack Ketchum's short story "The Box," first published in *Cemetery Dance*, won the 1994 Bram Stoker Award for best short story.

Market Information

So, if there *are* horror markets out there, how do you find them?

Fortuately, the horror genre is blessed with many excellent sources of market information, covering everything from small-press magazines to anthologies from major publishers.

Best of them all is *Scavenger's Newsletter*, which has been published monthly by writer Janet Fox for over ten years. Each issue contains timely information on new markets, updated guidelines for established markets and all sorts of market news shared by other writers who are regularly submitting to the magazines. Perhaps because Janet Fox is herself a fine writer, she knows how to provide the info writers need.

Another worthwhile publication is *The Gila Queen's Guide to Markets*. Published on an infrequent schedule by Kathryn Ptacek, also a fine writer and reviewer, each issue of the newsletter focuses on a specific genre—romance, westerns, mystery, erotica—in addition to providing up-to-date information about new and established markets.

These newsletters are invaluable if you have several stories to market or if you feel more comfortable breaking into the horror field at the ground level and slowly working your way *up* to professional ranks.

Other worthy publications which *sometimes* provide market info for horrorists are *Science-Fiction Chronicle* and *Locus*. Their focus is, of course, on science fiction, but with genre overlap, if not always crossover, seeming to be a trend, these monthlies are helpful.

The Small Press

If you've sent your story to all the top markets without any luck, or have been discouraged by countless impersonal rejection slips, you might want to consider sending your story to some lower-paying markets or even those that pay in contributor's copies.

Publishing in small-press magazines can be an excellent starting point for several reasons. First, there are many small-press horror magazines, most of which are eager to publish new writers. Second, the contact you have with editors is quite often on a more personal level than can be had with editors at the top magazines. And finally, making a sale, even to a pays-in-copies magazine, can give you some much-needed confidence as you work toward more professional markets.

Not so much of a digression: That's how it worked for me.

My first story, "Baseball Memories," was published in a pays-in-copies literary magazine called *Aethlon*. After the story appeared there, it was selected by Karl Edward Wagner for the twentieth installment of his *Year's Best Horror* anthology series.

Luckily for me, the story found its own top market. However, I should point out that *Aethlon* was not the first place I'd sent the story, but rather the fourth after it had already been rejected by some of the top magazines of the day. Would it have sold to a top market if I had continued to use the "top down" method of marketing? Perhaps, but selling to small press magazines, with the occasional submission of a story I thought of outstanding merit to the top markets, seemed the best route for me early in my career.

The Pro Markets

While the small press is a great place to learn the craft of writing, it is not a place to forge a professional horror writing career. Although the small press represents a large market for horror fiction, many of the publications operate on shaky ground in terms of financing and personnel. Not infrequently, small-press magazines fold after a single issue. Sometimes a small press might hold onto stories literally for years— before deciding not to print another issue—often without notifying the story's author!

Yes, the small press can be aggravating. The "big press" might frustrate you, with its greater likelihood of rejection, but at least you'll know that when a story is accepted it will end up being published— usually. (After all, even the Big Boys can go bust.)

Information about professional markets is just one of the advantages of joining a professional writer's organization, such as the Horror Writers Association. As well as providing new writers an opportunity to make contacts within the field and learn from established pros, each HWA newsletter includes listings for horror markets paying professional word rates for fiction. As a bonus, some of these markets, such as the HWA's anthologies *Under the Fang* and *Robert Bloch's Psychos*, are open exclusively to HWA members.

Of course, being a professional-writer's organization, HWA mainly focuses on professional-rate horror markets. Another writer's (and artist's) organization that provides its members with all kinds of market information, pro *and* small or even minuscule press, is the Genre Writer's Association (formerly the Small Press Genre Association). In addition to a quarterly newsletter with market info, members also receive two issues of *The Genre Writer's News Market Supplements* each year.

Mainstream Markets for Horror

But what if the horror-focused magazines all reject your story? What do you do then?

Submit it to mainstream or other nonhorror *markets.*

Obviously some mainstream markets like *Redbook* or *Cosmopolitan* won't be receptive to stories about zombies, ghouls and vampires, but other top magazines might. For example, *The Magazine of Fantasy and Science Fiction*, number 9 in the last "Fiction 50," sometimes publishes horror stories, and contemporary horror often finds its way onto the pages of *Alfred Hitchcock's Mystery Magazine*, which hits the list at number 25.

But many professional magazines outside of the top 50 will also consider horror fiction. For years, the slick men's magazine *Cavalier* routinely published the horror fiction of Stephen King, Dennis Etchison and Mort Castle. Sadly, *Cavalier* is no more, but there are still countless other magazines that will consider publishing a horror tale if it conforms to the overall needs of the magazine.

I once read a posting on an electronic bulletin board about a magazine for truckers called *RPM*. The magazine published *fiction* and that got me thinking: *RPM* . . . trucks and trucking . . . my story, "Death Drives a Semi."

Why, yes, *RPM* wanted my story, my *horror* story, and paid me five cents a word, eight contributors copies and (all right!) an *RPM* baseball cap for one-time rights. To top it all off, the magazine had a circulation of 120,000.

It doesn't get much better than that.

Study the Market

While sales like that don't happen all the time, they are possible if you keep your ears and eyes open and study the market.

An excellent source for finding alternative horror markets is the annual *Novel and Short Story Writer's Market* published by Writer's Digest Books. Each year *Novel and Short Story Writer's Market* lists hundreds of professional, literary and little (small-press) magazines and journals, as well as contests, agents and book publishers. You'll have to spend considerable time studying the reference book to find markets right for your horror, but once you do, you'll have a great list of possibilities.

Finally, there's one more tried and true method of finding markets for your horror. It's called firsthand market research and it's done at your local newsstand or bookstore.

Say yours is a literary horror story, heavy on atmosphere and mood. You might want to take a look at several of the literary magazines on the shelf and give them a try. And if your horror story features a serial killer, you might try sending it to a mystery or crime magazine. If you can't make up your mind about which of the magazines you want to submit to, there's no better way to determine what kind of fiction a magazine publishes than by buying a copy and reading it cover to cover.

This last point you've probably heard before, but it's something that bears repeating because ...

The best way to market your short fiction is to know your short-fiction markets.

Scavengers Newsletter
Janet Fox, Editor
519 Ellinwood
Osage City, KS 66523-1329

The Gila Queen's Guide to Markets
Kathryn Ptacek, Editor
P.O. Box 97
Newton, NJ 07860-0097

Horror Writers Association
P.O. Box 50577
Palo Alto, CA 94303

The Genre Writer's Association
P.O. Box 6301
Concord, CA 94524

Novel and Short Story Writer's Market
Writer's Digest Books
1507 Dana Avenue
Cincinnati, OH 45207

Locus
34 Ridgewood Lane
Oakland, CA 94611

Science-Fiction Chronicle
P.O. Box 022730
Brooklyn, NY 11202-0056

Dark Light Focus
Cemetery Dance

Gary A. Braunbeck

Richard Chizmar says that he began *Cemetery Dance, the* leading horror magazine, to "fill the void" left by the demise of David Silva's *The Horror Show.* There are marked similarities, to be sure, but the last four years have seen *CD* create its own identity by expanding its focus to include not only horror, but also dark mystery and suspense, as well as everything from traditional hard-boiled *noir* fiction to wildly surrealistic fantasy, not to mention the good old-fashioned ghost story.

"I do my best to make sure each issue of *CD* offers a disparate selection of stories," says Chizmar. "While the magazine will always keeps its roots firmly planted in horror, the cross-genre movement of the last few years has produced several writers whose work encompasses more than one aspect of imaginative fiction (*CD* regular Norman Partridge being a prime example), and it makes for a richer, more challenging and rewarding reading experience. People have been very supportive of the direction *CD* has taken. I hope they stick with us."

Chizmar needn't worry about readers sticking with *CD*; the magazine (a World Fantasy Award winner) recently hit a landmark with the publication of its twenty-fifth issue, and has seen its circulation jump from 500 to well over 5,000, publishing such luminaries as Stephen King, Dan Simmons, William F. Nolan, Ray Garton, Chet Williamson, Joe R. Lansdale and Ed Gorman, plus dozens of other well-known writers. Its contributors make up a virtual "Who's Who" of the contemporary horror/dark suspense field, and each new issue attracts a fresh batch of readers and writers.

"I've been lucky," Chizmar says. "I've found that readers are willing to allow you room for experimentation when editing a magazine. I suppose it's because no one wants to plunk down four bucks for one hundred pages of the same type of story told over and over again in the same old way. I don't like to see that in other magazines as a reader, and as an editor *I will not* allow that sort of stagnation to set in at *CD*. I strive to make every issue fresh and exciting. While the majority of each issue is and always will be devoted to fiction, we've had great success with our various columnists and reviewers; people want a good mix of material. They've come to expect it from *CD*, and that's what I'll do my best to give them."

In 1993, Chizmar (along with his wife, Kara L. Tipton) launched CD Publications, a book line that stemmed directly from the success of the magazine. Publishing both trade and limited hardcover editions, CD Publications has enjoyed tremendous success and more than a few triumphs—not the least of which was publishing a deluxe, signed, slip-cased limited edition of Dean Koontz's *Strange Highways*, the only edition of its type, with the enthusiastic approval of the author.

"Dean was great to work with," Chizmar recalls. "A true professional and one hell of a decent human being. We were all proud of the way the book turned out, and I hope to do more like it in the future while continuing to publish original novels and short-story collections."

The list of authors who have published original novels and collections with CD Publications includes Ed Gorman, Rick Hautala, Joe R. Lansdale, Norman Partridge, William F. Nolan and Charles L. Grant. Each CD edition is printed on acid-free paper and is smythe-sewn.

"I decided to publish the types of books that I would want to read, of course, but," Chizmar adds, "I also wanted to publish the types of books I'd want to *own*, an edition that would appeal to both the reader and hard-core bibliophile. Because the print run of most small-press trade and limited hardcover editions is so small (usually around 500), you're looking at a minimum price of thirty-five dollars for the trade edition, sixty dollars or more, limited. For that kind of money, you'd better damn well give your readers not only good material, but *fine craftsmanship*, as well; a book that is a pleasure simply to hold and look at, one that's going to last forever. I'm a collector of books myself, and I want good value for my money, and that's what I strive to give people who buy CD books."

Judging by the reception of the CD line of books, Chizmar and Tipton have established and maintained high standards; a good majority of the CD books have sold out, some even before the galleys went to print.

But unlike some editors who *claim* to understand how writers feel, Chizmar knows that "writing is a lonely life"; whenever he can grab a few hours for himself, he "steals away" to his desk to pen lean and mean dark suspense stories, many of which have recently been assembled in *Midnight Promises*, his first short-story collection, from Gauntlet Publications.

The book has garnered critical praise and may very well put a few more awards on Chizmar's shelf.

"That would be nice," he says, laughing, "but I don't think about things like awards or other accolades—that's not why I write and it's not why I started *Cemetery Dance* or CD Publications. I do it because I love the genre—what it has been, what it is at the moment, and what it's evolving into. The idea of awards never enters into it. It's the story that matters—this one, the next one, the one after that—and doing your part to ensure that the genre you love doesn't croak from a prolonged case of arrested literary adolescence. It's the power of the story, period. 'It is the tale, not he who tells it,' as Stephen King wrote."

"The next few years—despite what the doomsayers will tell you—are going to see exciting changes in the field of horror and dark suspense, and I'm glad that *Cemetery Dance* and CD Publications are around at this time."

Does he think that he's had a hand in bring about these exciting changes?

"Only the readers can answer that," he replies. "When it's all been said and done, the readers are the ones who show you how well you have done, what influence you might have had. As a rule, I try not to dole out advice to new writers, but when I break that rule I always say the same thing—never, *never* underestimate the readers. They know when they're being conned."

Which is why they keep coming back to *Cemetery Dance* and CD Publications. Rich Chizmar doesn't run a con on the readers; he deals only from the top of the deck, as editor, writer, human being.

Cyberhorror
Online Resources for the Horror Writer

Paula Guran

The Internet! The World Wide Web. The Information Super-highway. Cyber Times have arrived—

And the only constant about the Web is change. That's both its advantage and disadvantage. Up-to-date information and content derived from essentially infinite sources is an undeniable plus. But it is difficult to provide a guide to the Net in a static print publication. What is there today may be gone tomorrow—or enhanced, refocused, moved, regenerated or otherwise not available in the form I could cite here.

So I am going to try to stick to *some* generalities that *should* remain *somewhat* unchanged.

Maybe.

For any writer, the Internet is a valid tool. It offers (1) communication and networking, (2) promotional possibilities, and (3) research potential. More and more it is also offering opportunities to write (or provide content) for it. Working in a small genre like horror, writers need every advantage they can easily and inexpensively access. Cyberspace is now both affordable and technically effortless.

Communication and Networking

E-mail is an important avenue of communication and the cyber address *name@whatever.com* is no longer proprietary to the technogeek. At bare minimum, writers should have electronic mail. Cost these days is negligible as various "free e-mail" services are now common. It can bring you information through newsletters, market listers and private correspondence; manuscripts can be transferred in electronic form; queries, guidelines, acceptances and rejections are quickly handled with e-mail. E-mail is integral to the cybernetwork of horror writers.

E-mail and Editors

Despite the world becoming more and more cyber, many editors dislike e-mail submissions and will so state in guidelines. Some start out taking e-mail submissions and then stop. Follow guidelines. Never assume e-mail is desirable. Most publications do accept e-mail questions and requests for guidelines, however. Short messages back and forth between writer and editor are also handled most efficiently and cheaply with e-mail. Moreover, e-mail is a sure way of getting a story to an editor in a usable electronic format. Once a hard copy of a story is accepted, editors often ask for an electronic version. E-mail dispenses with sometimes incompatible disks that have to be "snail mailed" (using the postal service).

E-mail and Writers

Another aspect of e-mail is the more personal one of writers networking with one another. One can find background, friends, support, others with the same interests, even criticism of stories and learning opportunities thorough e-mail. In the often isolated world of the writer this can be important. Horror writers sometimes have no one in their immediate geographical area who easily accepts that "they write that *weird* stuff." To find others of "your kind" and exchange ideas is often an inspiring and sanity-preserving accomplishment. Many writing partnerships and other business relationships were established and are now maintained almost exclusively online with the help of e-mail.

Other than e-mail, the online horror network consists of individual writers and editors connected by workshop situations (on commercial services or the Net), live chat areas, various netletters and web sites. Communities of writers developed first on individual commercial services, like Genie and America Online, but the Internet itself is beginning to offer similar cyberspace colonies for horror writers.

Cyberspace breeds an easy familiarity. You get to make contact and connect with other writers and editors to whom you might not otherwise have access. Conventions are now full of people meeting long-time friends in "real life" that have, up to then, shared a great virtual-only friendship. In many ways the writing network on the Web is a type of ongoing, virtual, worldwide con in which contacts and information are constantly exchanged.

Market Lists

Markets are now frequently heard of first online. Janet Fox's *Scavenger's Newsletter* and Kathryn Ptacek's *Gila Queen's Guide to Markets* are not electronic, but they do swap and obtain news via the Net for their print market listings. Chris Holliday offers an electronic Market List for SF/H/F and Cynthia Ward's *Speculations* column, "The Market Maven," is also on the Web. Various newsletters/netletters are available for delivery right to your virtual door. Lisa Jean Bothell produces an abbreviated free e-mail version of her bimonthly print 'zine *The Heliocentric Network*. I do a weekly, exclusively electronic newsletter that deals with matters of interest to horror writers.

Whether posted or found in netletters, you will find early notice of anthologies, magazines, openings, closings, special needs, updates and editorial dislikes. Many small-press and major magazines now offer guidelines right on Web pages. Publishers have developed informative sites as well, often with their guidelines and current editors. The network of writers will often clue you in on anything you missed.

Is there any advantage over the traditional print market listers? Time.

The first issue of a magazine I was editing was filled almost entirely by authors who initially learned of it online. It was close to full before the guidelines ever became ink on paper. *Any* advantage in marketing your work is an advantage worth taking!

Promotional Possibilities

Promoting via cyberspace takes on various aspects. There are Web pages and sites for authors established commercially or by the authors themselves or their avid fans. Some sites are connected directly to booksellers. No matter the approach, the Web is fast becoming a fascinating way to make contact with readers and buyers of horror. Having one's own URL (universal resource locator) is becoming as common as an eddress (an e-mail address).

Virtual "personal appearances" are also now daily fare on the commercial services and soon more and more on the Net itself. Authors and others in horror can be guests in several different ways online through real-time "live chat." You may not be able to sign autographs, but it's a practically free way to "meet" many readers. You reach people all over the country and can do it from the comfort of your own home wearing your pajamas.

The cybernetwork of horror writers also provides promotional possibilities. Once F. Paul Wilson e-mailed me about a friend who was working on a story for *Writer's Digest* and wanted to interview first-time novelists who were contracted but not yet published. I recommended two he used, but they weren't horror writers. W.C. Stroby, who was writing the article, e-mailed me that he really wanted some horror writers who would fill the bill. It was a slow year in horror for first-time novelists and I was stumped. I e-mailed Jim Moore, a writer friend with connections to White Wolf Publishing. White Wolf was putting out a number of new books and I thought they might have an author with the proper prerequisites. He could think of only one author at White Wolf who qualified and another two with specialty-press books. I e-mailed Stroby the White Wolf author's name and asked if specialty press would work. He replied that specialty was fine and that he really wanted a female horror author to help balance the story. One of the specialty-press authors mentioned was Caitlin Kiernan. Stroby got his story; Kiernan got a fine slice of PR.

None of that took more than a minute or two of anyone's time at any point. My time invested overall was probably less than it took to write the paragraph above, and three authors I know got a nice write-up in *Writer's Digest*. I hadn't even met Caitlin at the time. But, that's how it can work.

Interviews are commonly done via e-mail these days, as well. The interviewer gets easy-to-edit electronic copy and can quickly ask for more information, replies to expanded questions or updates. The interviewee is comfortable actually writing the replies instead of having to verbally reply within a limited amount of time.

Newsgroups and Message Boards

Usenet (postings within established categories) and newsgroups also provide ways to get the word out about your most recent achievement. (You'll know you have "made it" when you have your own Usenet group.) Even if you are not *alt.books.stephen-king* or *alt.books.clive-barker* you can post in various groups or carry on a thread of conversation.

Services and now Net sites also have message boards to post on. Sometimes files are set aside for individual authors, books are reviewed, discussed or recommended. It's like virtual handbill posting in thousands of towns at the same time.

Research Potential

Research through online sources is another advantage for the writer. Writing a story about voodoo? A comprehensive list of *loa* is at your fingertips, as are dictionaries in a vast range of languages. Information on just about any subject exists—and if you can't find what you need, you will find an expert who might be able to help you. Want to use your local library? Many libraries' catalogs can now be directly accessed through your modem. You can determine what is in the system, what is checked in and where.

Other ways of searching for Internet files, like Archie, Gopher and WAIS provide more information direct to your computer through FTP (file transfer protocol).

Sites on the Internet or areas on services provide resources specifically for the writer and even more specifically the horror writer. Using one of the "search engines" (Yahoo, Excite, Lycos, Alta Vista, etc.), just key in the word "horror." Then you can try "writers" or "writing." Often one site leads, via links, to another.

The Web itself is becoming a market for writing. E-zines already exist as a small but growing market for horror fiction and articles. Some e-zines pay rates comparable to small-press.

You aren't wired yet? Access is getting easier and less expensive all the time. If you have a computer and a phone line you just need to add a modem and decide what entries to the Internet you want. Commercial services like America Online, Compuserve and Microsoft Network all offer a friendly, easy-to-use, organized starting point with their own content and access to the Net. Both local internet service providers (ISPs) and national ones offer unlimited use of the Internet that is now almost as simple to use as a commercial service. Web pages can be set up through your server or you can have them done for you. E-mail is offered as part of virtually any provider's package—and can even be established alone for as little as $1 a month.

Besides, doesn't "Web" sound like a place just made for horror writers?

Whither Horror
The Editors Speak

Benjamin Adams

Multiple choice: Selling an adult horror novel in the current publishing climate is (A) just about impossible; (B) extremely difficult; (C) an attainable goal; or (D) pretty easy— if you are Stephen King or Anne Rice.

Publishing moves in cycles. Boom! And then bust. According to most Keepers of the Conventional Wisdom, horror is presently in the "bust" phase of its cycle, following its phenomenal growth during the 1980s. Some predict horror will never return to the huge popularity it enjoyed during that heady decade, while others see encouraging signs in television programming, motion picture production and multimedia entertainments with strong horror leanings; much of pop culture "science fiction" is nothing but horror created by pseudoscience.

As an editor at Dell for seven years, Jeanne Cavelos launched the successful Abyss line of horror novels. This is her take on the horror market:

"Part of the job of an editor is guessing what will sell a year or two down the line, says Cavelos. My sense is that the publishing world has gone through a lot of changes in the past ten years or so and the horror field has changed along with every other field. Niche publishing is much more the way things are done now, and similarly in horror you have different niches; the biggest one is the Young Adult (YA) market, which is huge and has developed relatively recently. So I think part of what you see as a downturn in horror is simply a change in the *marketing* of horror. Instead of fifth graders reading *The Exorcist*, which is what I did, today's fifth graders read YA horror, like R.L. Stine."

Unfortunately, according to Cavelos, that doesn't necessarily mean the kids who are reading Stine will graduate to adult-level horror novels.

"Now that I'm teaching college, I have college students who are *still* reading Young Adult titles by R.L. Stine, believe it or not! I find that a little scary, myself. But they read the Stine books and enjoy them, so you have people up to twenty years old reading books that are really written for early teenagers. These people are reading these books to a much older age than expected."

"There was undeniably a surge of interest in horror in the early 1980s, which is not happening right now, except in this younger age group. Whether it's ever going to come back again—hey, *everything* comes back again. *When* it will come back, I don't know."

Cavelos also suggests that perhaps a boom isn't always the best thing to happen to the field.

"I'd love it if ten times the number of horror novels were being published, because it would give a lot of new writers a chance, but, frankly, some of those writers who had their chance in the early 1980s boom maybe didn't quite deserve it, or weren't quite ready yet and got rushed out."

Ginjer Buchanan of Berkeley Publishing, an editor for twelve years, has blunter words on whither horror.

"Mass-market horror publishing is not viable, except for the Young Adult market. I don't see a change in the near future."

According to Buchanan, the way around this impasse is "stealth" horror—suspense and thriller works with a dark edge are still being bought. But the supernatural angle doesn't seem to cut it any more.

"Major hardcover breakout attempts have been made, but nothing has really worked," says Buchanan. Another possibility is attempting to sell your novel outside of the North American market. "England is open to horror," says Buchanan, citing examples such as Phil Rickman, Elizabeth Massie and Jay Bonansinga, who have enjoyed more success with a British audience than in North America. "It's a fluke that [the British] Rickman made it in America, and his next novel may not sell here," she says.

For those who feel their talent lies in ghoulies and ghastlies, there is hope. Don D'Auria, editor for Leisure Books, says that Leisure will continue a schedule of one horror novel a month for the foreseeable future. He's been an editor for ten years, and has seen trends come and go.

D'Auria's prognosis for horror? *Stable!*

"Leisure is going to continue with horror," says D'Auria. "We do very well with it, so we have no plans to discontinue it or cut back. In terms of horror we do about one title a month.

"There has been a decrease in horror sales since the 1980s. I think right now the market is dominated by just three or four obvious names: King, Koontz, Barker, Anne Rice. I think its really just a question of readers wanting to read other things. Unfortunately for the market—very fortunate for those authors, but unfortunate for other writers—King is very prolific, and Anne Rice is very prolific, so there's no shortage of books by them for people to read. Its not like while folks are waiting for the next Stephen King, they'll turn to something else.

"We've been doing well with supernatural horror, but now we're shifting a little to include more dark suspense/thriller-type things as well to try to balance it out. For a while we were doing almost exclusively supernatural material. Now we're trying to broaden it, increase the mix a little bit to get more non-supernatural suspense and horror in there as well."

But, according to D'Auria, certain kinds of supernatural beasties are out. Forget about your plans for a sequel to *The Blob*, or a grand Lovecraftian opus.

"The only thing we're probably not going to do as much is 'monster' type stuff. Supernatural will still be involved, but not the large pulsing Jell-O that ate Miami. We're going for more mainstream horror: ghosts, vampires and haunted houses."

Why does Leisure have a different take on the current state of the market? Its size that counts, D'Auria says.

"Leisure is a relatively small house compared to Bantam or Pocket or any of the larger houses. I don't think any genre really dies; the market just shrinks to a point where it becomes unprofitable for the larger houses to do. But because we're relatively small, we can address more specific, smaller markets like horror. The readers are still out there, and they're never going to go away, and we're just giving the readers who are still out there what they want.

"I can only speak authoritatively for how Leisure is doing, and horror does well for us."

D'Auria *does* have specific desires for manuscripts that come in over the transom.

"We're looking for originals, primarily; the occasional reprint if its something that hasn't been in paperback before, or for a long time. Mostly we're interested in original novels, generally 90,000 words or thereabout. Once you get over 140,000 words, it just becomes almost physically impossible to print books in mass quantities, and ultimately that's our concern, that we have to do it in mass-market. We don't tend to do well with anything shorter than 80,000 words. Readers want to feel like they're getting something when they buy the book!"

Value for the readers money: Now *there's* a concept!

Leisure isn't the only publisher that's continuing with horror. Many authors are excited about White Wolf Publishing's Borealis line. The Borealis books are imaginatively designed and produced with great sympathy toward the writer and are being compared favorably with Jeanne Cavelos Abyss line for Dell. Also, White Wolf is continuing with production of novels set in its World of Darkness role-playing universe.

Currently, series novels are preferred for the World of Darkness line, with interlocking events and characters between some of the series, to create a cohesive whole.

White Wolf and Leisure are small publishing houses and can devote concerted energy to horror. Indeed, horror is White Wolf's *raison d'etre*; the company was built on its World of Darkness role-playing games, such as *Vampire: The Masquerade* and *Mage: The Ascension*. By focusing on horror and dark fantasy, White Wolf has emerged as a force which bears reckoning, as exemplified by their project of reissuing Michael Moorcock's and Harlan Ellison's vast oeuvres.

But at this stage in the game there doesn't appear to be enough demand for new horror to allow many other publishers to continue issuing it. Zebra Books, one of the mainstays of the 1980s horror boom, recently ceased production of its horror line entirely—shocking some authors, who abruptly found orphaned the books they had under contract with Zebra.

This business of writing is volatile. Editors don't have a crystal ball that allows them an accurate glimpse of the future. Perhaps, despite the worst fears of Jeanne Cavelos and Ginjer Buchanan, horror will once again roar back from the dead, showing there's still life in the old corpse yet. Or, as Leisure Books and White Wolf Publishing show, it will continue at a steady pace, allowing a climate in which authors with strong material are able to sell their books.

It all comes down to this: Before you pack up your horror novel and send it out, make sure its the best you can possibly produce. These are lean times for horror, so be prepared for the worst, no matter the quality of your work.

Selling a novel is tough.

But nobody ever said it was supposed to be easy.

From the HWA's FAQ Folder on "Agents"

Lawrence Watt-Evans

Editor's Note: FAQ stands for "Frequently Asked Questions." This is only a brief excerpt from the HWA's FAQ folder on agents, which was prepared by Lawrence Watt-Evans with the assistance of members of the Science Fiction and Fantasy Writers of America and the HWA. By this stage of the game, you know what HWA stands for.

Do I need an agent?

The short answer is, "No." Plenty of successful writers have managed just fine without them. Isaac Asimov's last agent left the business in 1953, which didn't prevent Asimov from selling hundreds of books and thousands of articles over the next forty years.

But if we rephrase the question as, "*Should* I have an agent?" it gets much trickier, and the answer becomes, "It depends on your exact circumstance—who you are, what you write, and what you want."

Some writers will do better with an agent, some will do better without. To quote writer and critic Gregory Feeley: "Writers who market their own work do it energetically and diligently, and know what's up with their submissions' status. If they are incompetent at it, they shall have to learn; it isn't too hard. A professional and professional-looking submission will look a lot better than a submission from an agent that the editor knows to be hopelessly small-potatoes."

So we'll have to look at other questions to decide whether you need an agent.

What does an agent do?

Beginning writers often misunderstand just what an agent does. They hear about agents selling first novels for huge sums of money, and assume that with the right agent, they could do just as well.

That isn't the case. An agent cannot sell a story that the author would never be able to sell. What an agent *can* do is sell it faster, and get better terms for it.

If an editor would reject a story when the author submitted it, that editor will still reject it when an agent submits it. Agents aren't magic; they can't *make* an editor buy anything. No agent has so much clout that he can force an editor to publish a bad story.

What an agent *can* do is find the right market. A good agent knows the tastes of all the editors in the business. A writer wouldn't know that Editor A has an obsession with stories about moths, while Editor B hates the fluttery little things; but an agent might, and when a client sends him a novel about giant telepathic moths he'll know to skip Editor B and send it to Editor A.

But he can't make Editor B buy it, any more than the author could.

So if you have an agent, one of the things you're paying your 10 or 15 percent for is *expertise*, for knowing what can sell where, for finding markets you'd never have thought of.

If you know the markets as well as your agent does, or even better—it is possible—then you aren't getting your money's worth in this department, and you don't need an agent for this.

The second major function of a literary agent is getting the best possible deal for the client. This isn't just a matter of getting the highest advance; it's also negotiating royalty rates, subsidiary rights and so on. A book contract is fairly complex; if you have trouble with tax forms, if you're in the habit of signing things without reading the fine print, you'd be better off with an agent.

On the other hand, if you're a Hollywood accountant in your day job, your main problem with a book contract might be that it's so simple you keep looking for more booby-traps than are actually there, and you probably don't need an agent.

Or if you're selling to markets where nothing's negotiable, every contract is take-it-or-leave-it—as is the case with many magazines, most anthologies, and several licensed, work-for-hire deals—an agent can't do much for you.

Those are the two primary purposes of an agent—knowing the market and making the deal. Everything else is secondary.

Probably the most important of the secondary functions is selling those subsidiary rights that the agent talked the publisher out of—foreign rights, movie rights, and so on. Bestselling author Raymond Feist points out that "foreign sales are nearly impossible without a good agent."

If you can *reasonably* expect these to be profitable for you, then you do want an agent. I take in an average of three or four thousand dollars a year from foreign sales, and I don't think I'd have *any* of that without an agent!

(I've never had a movie deal, though, or even come close. And some writers have Hollywood come looking for *them*, with no agent involved.)

As Feist says, "Good agents develop careers, not just make sales, and while the first commission may not be much, the view should be long-term."

Some agents provide editorial services. I, and other established writers, tend to be wary of this. Sometimes it's legitimate; more often it's a scam. The top agents do not rewrite stories or refer their clients to "book doctors." If an agent offers editorial services, approach with extreme caution, especially if up-front fees are involved. This is *not* something you should expect an agent to do; you should find a collaborator, or a good workshop, or some other way to handle technical problems in your work.

Having an agent can speed things up and smooth them out. A good agent, one editors respect, can send a manuscript to an editor and get it read relatively quickly, bypassing slushpiles and first readers; also, agents can nag editors to make decisions, where many writers are too timid, too afraid they'll just annoy the editor into rejecting the work. The agent provides a buffer between author and editor and keeps them from aggravating one another. Sometimes, especially if either the editor or author is short-tempered or socially inept, this is important.

And that's really about it; some agents might provide other special services, but there you have the major ones. If you think you could use these services, then you could probably use an agent.

Specialists in Fear
The Small and Specialty Presses

James J. Gormley

Who are "the specialists"? Smaller, smaller still, and really small "specialty publishing" houses. Their logos are not kangaroos or roosters, and their editorial board is frequently one person.

The publishing industry would say that anything under 20,000 copies of a given title is a small-press run (and therefore denotes the product of a small press), yet there are no absolutes here. In practice, a small-press horror publisher is one that prints from one to several titles a year, with press runs ranging from several score to several hundred to several thousand (almost never larger than 5,000 copies), with the smaller quantities dedicated to signed, limited-edition runs. Typically, the larger runs (trade editions) are first-edition small trade printings (signed or unsigned, usually not numbered), usually slipcased. Prices for any stitched hardcover in these groupings would start at approximately double the normal mass-market hardcover price.

One view has it that the small presses are like independent film-makers—they can take the kinds of chances that bigger houses can't, and can put out material from new authors that is more powerful, and riskier, than that produced by the huge mass-market and mass-trade firms. The other position is that since small presses often only put out one title a year, two or three "dogs" (sales-wise) in a row would damn a small house to bankruptcy and oblivion; therefore, big-name writers with proven commercial worth have to be the mainstay of a small-press operation.

Smaller presses are usually swamped by unsolicited manuscripts. A number of the publishers profiled in this chapter specifically asked that their addresses not be listed. In part, a small press must maintain a "don't call us, we'll call you" attitude.

Yet the right small press can be well suited to the horror writer who is not a "brand name"—and who may never prove to be one. If you become established enough in little magazines, you could be invited to contribute to a short story anthology. By making contacts within the "horror business," attending conventions, cyber-networking, etc., you can knock on small publishers' doors and have a chance of being welcomed.

Let's take a look at some "specialists in fear":

Donald M. Grant, Publisher, Inc.
Hampton Falls, New Hampshire

Grant's first, early publishing effort dates to about 1945, when Donald Grant and Thomas Hadley published *Rhode Island on Lovecraft*. Due to military service, Grant left, later reentering the publishing scene in 1949. In 1964, he began selling books under the Donald M. Grant imprint, starting with *A Golden Anniversary Bibliography of Edgar Rice Burroughs*. As of 1993, Grant had produced about one hundred titles in trade and limited edition quantities.

According to Grant's Robert Weiner, sales really peaked in the mid-1970s, when Robert E. Howard's novels were especially popular, although sales have dipped since the late 1970s.

"The 1990s have been tough," says Weiner. "In 1991/1992, we had a sharp drop in sales—but this was not just in the horror market—book dealers in that period had a 25 to 35 percent drop in sales," although he adds that "horror may have been hit harder."

In fact, Weiner adds, "most of our books lose money. We sometimes know this in advance, and we obviously try to keep this to a minimum."

Known more for first limited and trade editions of works by Stephen King, Grant's recent offerings have included first editions of *Desperation* and *Insomnia*. In terms of press runs, for *Desperation*, 2,000 signed traycased editions were produced and 4,000 slipcased gift editions. Recent trade and limited editions include Peter Straub's *Mrs. God* and David Morrell's *The Totem*.

Tips for writers? "Start out in magazines," Weiner recommends.

Maclay & Associates
Baltimore, Maryland

Founded in 1981 by John and Joyce Maclay to publish books on Baltimore history and architecture, it was only in 1984 when the company switched (almost accidentally) to horror fiction, producing the first *Masques* anthology, edited by J.N. Williamson. In 1990, with the first *Borderlands* anthology, edited by Thomas F. Monteleone, the Maclays began issuing only signed, limited edition, slipcased horror titles.

Other Maclay & Associates titles in print include *Haunted Castles*,

Ray Russell; *Logan: A Trilogy*, William F. Nolan; *Voices From the Night*, a horror anthology, John Maclay, editor; and *St. Louis Blues*, Rex Miller.

"I enjoy publishing anthologies because you get to include a lot of different writers," says John Maclay. "I love to write short stories myself, so that's why I lean towards anthologies." Although Maclay points out that "there's nothing in the pipeline right now," we can be sure that "more anthologies will be published in the near future."

Why limited-edition? "For the love of it," says Maclay. "It's better, in horror, to cater to the specialty market; many of our buyers are fairly serious collectors."

Tips for writers? "Sell your short stories and build some credits. If you also join some of the organizations and make contacts, you will get noticed. At that level, you'll know which anthologies are open to submissions; in fact, you might, at that point, even be asked by an anthology editor to participate."

Silver Salamander Press/Darkside Press
Seattle, Washington

Is horror publishing in trouble? "Not for small presses, it isn't," shoots back publisher John Pelan. "The reality of it is, we are probably in the midst of a revival. There was a lot of damage done by and to specialty horror publishers in the 1980s. In the rush to meet the demands of a boom, the New York publishing establishment, in particular, did a disservice to our industry in that much of what was published didn't merit limited-edition release, or printing at all, for that matter."

"We're in the midst of an upswing," says Pelan. "If we keep even 10 percent of the kids who grew up reading *Goosebumps*, that will do more for us than Stephen King and Clive Barker did for us over the last twenty years.

Pelan has two imprints. "Under Silver Salamander, I do short story collections of 50,000 to 60,000 words. Darkside Press exists to do reprints of novels which merit hardcover presentation, or important new short-story anthologies, such as *Darkside: Horror for the Next Millennium*, which I edited."

Pelan grants, "I have to be lot more careful than the big houses. Two bad books in a row would kill me. Compare this with mass-market paperbacks, which sell for $5.95 and cost the publisher (including royalties) about 75 cents. In comparison, my costs on a signed trade paperback amount to significantly more."

Silver Salamander's available titles are: *I, Said the Fly*, Michael

Shea; *Close to the Bone*, Lucy Taylor; *Lost in Booth Nine*, Adam-Troy Castro; and *The Flesh Artist*, Lucy Taylor.

Tips for writers? "Research the market you are submitting something to," cautions Pelan, "and don't send a small press an unsolicited short story when there's no open anthology in the works."

Borderlands Press
Grantham, New Hampshire

In *Cemetery Dance* magazine (Spring 1994), Borderlands Press publisher Thomas F. Monteleone described his 1991 entry into book publishing this way:

> I had no idea what I was going to publish, but I was talking to Joe Lansdale and I told him that I was starting this small press and asked him if he had anything [of his] that he would like to see in print. He mentioned *The Magic Wagon* . . . It sounded like an interesting project, so I rented a few mailing lists, printed up a flyer on the Lansdale book and sent it out . . . I didn't have enough money to typeset it and print it until . . . about April of 1991. So there was the initial delay, because I frankly didn't know what the hell I was doing.

Today, Borderlands Press's titles include: *Borderlands II*, edited by Monteleone; *No Doors, No Windows*, Harlan Ellison; *Under the Fang*, the first HWA shared world anthology, edited by Robert R. McCammon; *Cut! Horror Writers on Horror Films*, nonfiction; *Batman: Captured by the Engines*, Joe R. Lansdale; *The Throat*, Peter Straub; and *The Beast That Shouted Love at the Heart of the World*, Harlan Ellison. The newest anthology is a collection of stories by Whitley Streiber.

Often cited for excellence, the *Borderlands* anthologies publish "stories that (are) not the usual; that series has been about stretching the boundaries."

Tips for writers? Monteleone, an award-winning horror novelist himself, has plenty. In a *Writer's Digest* profile, he said: "I tell proven professionals that I only want to see their best work . . . so consider this (Borderlands) an extremely tough market to crack."

CD Publications
Baltimore, Maryland

CD stands for *Cemetery Dance*, the name of the horror magazine publisher Richard Chizmar founded in 1988. CD's publication list is rather evenly divided between anthologies and novels: *Prisoners and Other Stories*, Ed Gorman; *The Definitive Best of the Horror Show*, edited by David B. Silva; *Act of Love*, Joe R. Lansdale; *Slippin' Into Darkness*, Norman Partridge; and *Second Chance*, Chet Williamson. CD's newest titles are *Strange Highways*, Dean Koontz; *The Mountain King*, Rick Hautala; and *Things Left Behind*, Gary A. Braunbeck.

Tips for writers? "There's no reliable formula for breaking in, aside from establishing a credit list," Chizmar offers. "I try to buy the best possible fiction I can; if it turns out to be from a new writer, I get that much more excited." (For more information on CD Publications, see the Dark Light Focus on page 177.)

Mark V. Ziesing Books
Shingleton, California

"For the most part, what has changed is how this kind of fiction [horror] is marketed," states publisher Mark Ziesing. "We're dealing with a specialized market here—specialty book buyers and collectors, consisting of eclectic readers, loyal patrons—people who share our passion for this literature."

Ziesing's horror or horror-related books include: *Lot Lizards*, Ray Garton; *Still Dead*, edited by John Skipp and Craig Spector; *Alarms*, Richard Laymon; *Insomnia*, Stephen King; *Black Leather Required*, David Schow; *Dirty Work*, Pat Cadigan; *Walking Wolf*, Nancy Collins; and *Hunger and Ecstasy of Vampires*, Brian Stableford.

Tips for writers? Ziesing observes that "traditionally new writers first start working, then later hope to get included in a couple of anthologies. Once one has amassed a significant amount of work, then that makes the prospect of a publishing contract more realistic."

Gauntlet Publications
Springfield, Pennsylvania

Having started in 1990 with a no-holds-barred fiction and exposé magazine, *Gauntlet*, publisher Barry Hoffman began putting out books in 1993. A teacher by profession, Hoffman's focus on quality, limited editions of "books that have stood the test of time" and newer works by proven writers is "what keeps Gauntlet Publications alive."

Hoffman is keenly excited about his "fine reprint" series, which he calls "Classics Revisited." Having "forged a niche for myself with Robert Bloch's *Psycho*, I look forward to doing this sort of thing for years to come." Gauntlet Publications's current list/backlist of "signed limiteds" includes *Nameless Sins*, Nancy Collins; *Shadowland*, Peter

Straub; *The Illustrated Man*, Ray Bradbury; and *I Am Legend*, and *Hell House*, Richard Matheson.

Tips for new writers? Hoffman is not ready to take on new writers at this point. "Since I have been doing 90 percent of the work myself, I can only do two or three new books a year. Aside from not having time, costs make it too prohibitive to take chances with unknowns."

TAL Publications
Leesburg, Virginia
"The feeding frenzy of the 1980s did a lot of damage to the field, since some books were just doomed for failure, not being backed by marketing and quality packaging," says publisher and literary agent Stanislaus Tal. "Then the bottom fell out.

"Even bigger-name authors took a beating in the long term. High advances and zero marketing were part of the problem. What author was going to turn down a $75,000 advance, even though the publisher wouldn't then invest any money in the marketing of the book? Over the long haul, that spells doom."

Tal has pretty much limited his publishing to chapbooks. "I originally picked up a lot of novelists," says Tal. "Those who were willing to branch out have done better—to cross subgenres or types, for example. In terms of what I'm doing for my writers, I'm going to be doing film projects through a company I'm forming, Extreme Entertainment. The publication list will be tied to the literary agency, independent filmmaking and the entertainment business, including multimedia."

Tal chapbook titles include *Shrines and Desecrations*, Brian Hodge; *Unnatural Acts*, Lucy Taylor; *Stephen*, Elizabeth Massie; and *Sex and the Single Vampire*, Nancy Kilpatrick.

Tips for writers? "I think that the small press is a good place for writers to hone their skills and gain experience."

Subterranean Press
Flint, Michigan
When the business gets tough, the tough start up a small-press horror house; that's the way Subterranean Press came into being, say Bill Schafer and Tim Holt of this specialty publisher. Very new on the scene, Subterranean released its first book (a chapbook) in 1995.

Shafer is both realistic and ambitious: "Small and specialty presses are cropping up and dying off very quickly. Nobody's going to get rich here."

How did Shafer get started? "I called Richard Chizmar (of CD Publications) hoping he would talk me out of it—and he didn't. In fact, he and Bob Morrish have been two of my biggest supporters."

Subterranean Press can offer authors a chance to produce works of theirs that aren't likely to find a home at a mass-market house. "As with other small presses, we have more of a hands-on approach, seeking authors' input in a variety of areas, including cover art, dust-jacket design and overall book design."

Shafer admits, "I didn't start reading horror until the mid-1980s, when I was old enough to appreciate it. There was, at that time, a lot of really awful stuff published. The big names from that period, whose work was good, have more or less gravitated to thrillers. What's left are the good ones who stuck around. Where do we fit in? Simply speaking, we cater to a certain market of collectors. When we're more established, we can then attract more authors and readers."

Titles include *Spyder*, Norman Partridge; *Out There in the Darkness*, Ed Gorman; *Bad Intentions*, Norman Partridge; and *Blood Brothers*, Richard Chizmar. There's even a limited edition of a western written by Joe R. Lansdale under the pen name Ray Slater: *Texas Nightriders*.

Tips for new writers? "Don't quit your day job," says Tim Holt. "I understand that it's a very tough field." Shafer suggests that writers read a lot, write a lot and "submit to the better horror magazines, such as *Cemetery Dance* and *Deathrealm*."

Charnel House
Lynbrook, New York

Started in 1989 by Joe Stefko and Tracy Kocaman, Charnel House's first release was a fantasy novel by Tim Powers, *The Stress of Her Regard*. Horror titles include *The New Neighbor*, Ray Garton; *Last Call* and *Where They Are Hid*, Tim Powers; and two novels by Dean Koontz, *Beastchild* and *Dark Rivers of the Heart*.

Stefko, who's a drummer for The Turtles, got the idea to start Charnel House while touring in Southern California, where he met Tim Powers.

Like other specialty publishers, Charnel cannot take chances on new writers. Stefko says, "We don't publish anthologies and we make very expensive books. Customers aren't going to spend $125 or $750 on an unknown, so I need authors with followings. I frankly go after people I like—whose work I know."

Tips for new writers? "Go to conventions, and talk to everybody . . . Mingle, get names and make contacts."

So there you have, in brief, the specialists in fear. If you're looking for an alternative to the big houses and you want a little personal attention, give them a try.

AFTERWORD

Quiet Lies the Locust Tells

Harlan Ellison

She thinks we were all killed when they made the Great Sweep, but I escaped in the mud.

I was there when the first dreams came off the assembly line. I was there when the corrupted visions that had congealed in the vats were pincered up and hosed off and carried down the line to be dropped onto the rolling belts. I was there when the first workmen dropped their faceplates and turned on their welding torches. I was there when they began welding the foul things into their armor, when they began soldering the antennae, bolting on the wheels, pouring in the eye-socket jelly. I was there when they turned the juice on them and I was there when the things began to twitch.

No wonder She wanted all of us dead. Witnesses to their birth, to their construction, to their release into the air—not good. The myrmidons were loosed on the Great Sweep.

I think I am the last one left alive. The last one who can create dreams and not nightmares. I am the locust.

The reversal is sweet. What we always knew to be nightmares—the empty lives, the twisted language, the squeezing of the soul—they now call dreams. What we looked high to see as dreams—silliness, castles in the sky, breathing deeply on windy afternoons—She has commanded be termed nightmares, lies. I am the locust. I tell quiet lies. Called nightmares. That are truly fine dreams.

I swam in the mud till I was the color of the land. And made my escape. Overhead I saw the corrupted things soaring off to spread their rigor of obedience and fear and hatred. For many days I lay there, hidden, turning on my back for the rain, trapping small fish and insects for my food. Finally, when the Great Sweep was done and all my brothers and sisters were dead or locked away in madhouses, I went to the forest.

But like the locust that the Middle Ages saw as the symbol of passion, I will live forever. I will tell my quiet lies and no matter how blindly the people follow their instructions, in every generation there will be a hundred, perhaps a thousand, if chance is with them even a hundred thousand, who will keep the quiet lies alive. To be told late at night to the children. With their bright eyes they will pay attention, and the dreams that have been outlawed, now called nightmares, will take root and spread.

And fifty years from now, a hundred years from now, when She thinks all courage has been drained out of the people, the children of the locust will be retelling the quiet lies. We will never be eradicated. Decimated, yes, but still we survive.

Because in us lives the noblest part of the human experiment. The ability to dream.

I've watched, since the Great Sweep. Oh, what wonders She has given them in place of what they had. They have no real freedom, they have no genuine control of their lives, their days and nights are set down for them though they don't even perceive it that way. But She has given them endless flickering images on screens: surrogate dreams (the real lies, the true nightmares) that make them laugh because they hear laughter behind the flickering images, and scenes of death and destruction that they think are representations of the real world that She commands be termed "news." She has given them more and greater sporting events, young men and women hurling themselves at each other in meaningless contests She tells them represent survival in microcosm. She has given them fashions that obsess them—though they do not understand that the fashions are one more way of making them facsimiles of each other. She has given them acts of government that unify them into hive groups, in the name of removing responsibility from their daily lives. She has taken control completely, and now they believe that the grandest role they can play is that of cog in the machine of Her design. In truth, what they have become are prisoners of their own lives.

All that stands between them and the shambling walk of the zombie are the quiet lies the locust tells.

Because I keep on the move, I have come to miss two aspects of human congress more than all the others combined. Love and friendship. Before the Great Sweep I never had the time or the perseverance to discover what raids love can make on the boredom of silent days spent alone. Nights are worse, of course.

I long to share confidences with a friend. But because I have placed myself outside the limits of their society, I fear striking up acquaintances. Who would be my friend, in any event? I live in the last of the forests and I sleep in caves. The countryside is best for me. The cities are like the surface of the sun: great flares blast off the concrete; there are no places to hide, no cool corners in which to wait. Geomagnetic storms, sunspot occurrences, enormous air masses. I am wary of the cities. She rules without mercy there. And the people do not touch each other. Like those who are terribly sunscorched they avoid each other, passing in silence but with their teeth bared.

A day's walk from the forest, there is a small town. I began going to the town innocently, making myself known by showing only that edge of myself that would not alarm anyone. And after a time I came to know a small group of young people who enjoyed hearing my stories.

Now they come to the small cave where I sit cross-legged. They do not tell their parents where they're going. I think they gather roots and herbs as a cover for the afternoons in which they sit around me and I tell them of transcending destiny, of the three most important things in life, of true love and of my travels. They lie about having gone on many picnics. And each time they bring one of their friends who can be trusted—one of the ones with that special sly, impish smile that tells me the flame burns steadily. Inside. Where She cannot snuff it out. Not yet. (I do not believe in Gods, but I ask God never to let Her discover a way of reading the inside of the people. If She ever finds a way to probe and drain the heart, or the head, then all hope will be lost.)

The young people surprised me. The last time they came, they brought a much older woman to the cave. She was in that stretch of life somewhere between seventy and the close of business. For an instant I cursed their enthusiasm. It had blurred their judgment. Now I would have to run again and find a far place to begin again.

But the sly smile was there on her wrinkled face as she stooped to enter the cave. Firelight caught my wary expression as she entered, she drew a pinback button from the pocket of her padded jacket and clipped it on the left breast. It read: *Étonne-moi!*

She grinned at me as she sat down on the other side of the fire. "I read French imperfectly," I said.

"Diaghilev to Jean Cocteau in 1909," she answered. "*Astonish* me."

I laughed, as the children settled down around us. How long had this woman kept her badge of defiance secret? Surely since the Great Sweep. Fear dissolved. The old woman was not one of Her subjects. This dear old woman, corpulent and cat-eyed, pain in her joints, was determined to live every moment with sanctification until the end. So I spun spiderwebs about looking for true love, about transcending destiny, about the three most important things in life, about times before the Great Sweep, and about just desserts.

"You're a Calvinist," she said. "Irreducible morality." But she said it with humor, and I shrugged, feeling embarrassed. "I don't think you really like shouldering the burden, even if you do it."

"You're right," I answered. "I would gladly lay it down; if I knew others would carry it."

She sighed. "We do, friend. We do."

I learned later that She had sent myrmidons against the old woman and her brother; and they were killed. They had tried to lead a strike. No one joined them and they were caught out naked in the daylight. And were killed. The children told me. The terrible sight of it had not been wasted on them. They were angry when they told me.

I loved her, that old woman. She was the locust.

I heard the sound of the locust from the hills one night. It was a man with an alto saxophone playing all alone, long after midnight. He was playing the kind of music I haven't heard in years. It was jazz. But it was the kind of sky-piercing jazz that long ago I had resisted, wondering if it was jazz at all. It had been rooted in the old order of what "Negroes" were lauded for playing, but as intense as steel, passionately soaring, the breaker of the circle. It had manifested radical inclinations; and I had refused to hear it.

But hearing it now, a solitary corner of one man's loneliness, afloat in the night, I longed to hear more. To return in time to that place where the music had been new, and I swore if the miracle of transport could be done, I would listen without insisting memory be served. I would hear it without narrow judgments. The locust played "Green Dolphin Street" and "Since I Fell For You." I remembered the name of the man who had played those tunes, years before the Great Sweep. His name had been Eric Dolphy, and I wished he would come down out of the far hills and travel with me.

I miss friendship. I miss music. What She gives them now, what She has led them to believe they want to hear, is as empty of human concern or enrichment as the fury of a thunderstorm.

It made me so sad, hearing him up there against the sooty night sky in which no stars had shone for a time beyond my recollection; a sky through which Her myrmidons flew to find old women and their brothers; a sky that would soon enough drop on the man with the horn. So sad I packed my few belongings in the rucksack . . . and I went away from the forest; from the cave, from the hills, and from the children. They would either hoard the quiet lies the locust had told, against the day when such tales would be needed, or they would follow their parents into the mouth of the machine She had oiled and set running.

Even I grow tired.

I warned them not to follow me. I am not the Pied Piper. They said, "We'll go with you. We can trust you." And I said, "Where I go there is no following. Where I go there is no mother, and no father, no safe days and no safe nights; where I go I go alone, because I travel fast." But they followed. They hung back and I threw stones at them, then ran as fast as I could to lose them. But they kept coming. Three of them. Two boys and a girl. I wouldn't let them sit with me when I rested, and they stayed out of range and yelled through the forest to me.

"Our parents stood by and watched. They didn't lift a hand. When those things fell out of the sky and took the old woman and her brother, they didn't do a thing. When they set fire to them, no one tried to stop them. We can't live with people like that. You told us what that means."

I tried not to listen. I am not their leader. I am just the locust. I cannot even lead myself. I cannot do what they think must be done. All I can do is tell them quiet lies.

That isn't enough.

Some among them have to take the strength upon themselves. Some among them must rise up from their midst to lift the real burden. *Must I do all the work?*

I can tell them of the night of black glass, and of the hour that stretches, and of the visionary . . . but I am no one's hero.

I waited behind a tree and when they passed I stepped out and explained my limitations, the amount of burden I was prepared to carry. They smiled the impish smiles and said I was better than that; I could beat off myrmidons with my bare hands; I was their inspiration. I slapped one of the boys. He took it and looked hurt, but they wouldn't leave me.

A man hides in the far hills and plays slow soft melodies. Nothing more is asked of him. Until he goes to the final sleep. That is a peace greatly to be desired. Why can't they hear the message? Do any of them really listen?

I struck out again and let them fend for themselves.

And when She sensed our movement, because there were four of us, unauthorized, moving at random, She sent the nightmares on their night flight, like bats that see in the dark, and they fell upon us. I did not stay to help them. In the chaos I escaped, went into the ground and hid. I tried not to think about the sounds the children made. And finally there was silence.

There are no leaders. There are only terrified souls trying to live till the day when She loses control and the machine turns on her. Until that day, unless I find a distant hill where the final sleep will free me, I will tell my quiet lies. There is nothing more to it than that.

There are no heroes of my generation. That role has yet to be filled. For my part, I am just the locust.

I speak of dreams called nightmares. No more should be expected, at risk of driving the reflection so deep into the mirror it will never emerge again.

The ability to dream is all I have to give. That is my responsibility; that is my burden. And even I grow tired.

The HWA Members Who Contributed to This Book

Benjamin Adams has work appearing in *Blood Muse; 100 Vicious Little Vampire Stories, Miskatonic University, Return to Lovecraft Country, Singers of Strange Songs* and "others." He lives in Seattle with his wife, Erin Ward, and two cats, Salem and Heinz.

Jay R. Bonansinga earned a reputation as a new master in horror and suspense writing with his first novel, *The Black Mariah*, a 1994 finalist for the Stoker award. Other novels include *Sick, The Killer's Game* and *Head Case*. He earned his masters degree in film in 1986 and his script, *ManSlayer*, is to be directed by Mary (*Pet Sematary*) Lambert. The author resides with his wife Jeanne and three antisocial cats in Evanston, Illinois.

Gary Brandner has published twenty-eight novels—yes, *The Howling* one of them!—about one hundred short stories, six screenplays (two produced, the others paid for), and "a handful of nonfiction hardly worth mentioning." He lives with his wife, Martine, in the San Fernando Valley above Los Angeles.

Gary A. Braunbeck, a former actor, became a full-time writer in 1992. Among the magazines and anthologies his work has appeared in are *Cemetery Dance, The Horror Show, The Magazine of Fantasy & Science Fiction, Masques, The Year's Best Fantasy and Horror* and *Murder Most Delicious*. His first story collection, *Things Left Behind*, was released by CD Publications in early 1997. He lives in Columbus, Ohio, with his wife, Leslie, and two cats, Tasha and "The Winnie."

Richard Lee Byers holds bachelor's and master's degrees in psychology. He worked for over a decade in an emergency psychiatric facility, then left the mental health field to become a writer. A resident of the Tampa Bay area, he is the author of such novels as *The Ebon Mask, On a Darkling Plain, Netherworld, Caravan of Shadows; Dark Fortune* and *Dead Time*, as well as the Young Adult books *Joy Ride, Warlock Games* and *Party Till You Drop*.

Dominick Cancilla's fiction has appeared in *Robert Bloch's Psychos, The Best of Cemetery Dance, Bending the Landscape* other anthologies, and in numerous magazines. He lives in Santa Monica, California, with his wife, Deborah.

Jeanne Cavelos is a former senior editor at Dell Publishing, where she created the Abyss horror line and ran the science-fiction/ fantasy program. She has published short fiction, nonfiction and numerous reviews in a number of periodicals. Cavelos serves as the director of Odyssey, the annual six-week summer workshop in speculative fiction at New Hampshire College, and teaches writing and literature at Saint Anselm College.

D.G. CHICHESTER is a ten-year comics vet, earning his stripes as an editor at Marvel. Since then, his writing career has included comics, screenplays, video games and Internet Web sites. Recent comics include *King Tiger/Motorhead*, *Elektra: Root of Evil*, and *Batman/Daredevil: Eye for an Eye*. He lives in upstate New York with his wife, Jennifer, her feline, Slashing Claw, and a free-range rabbit named Sabretooth.

MATTHEW COSTELLO wrote the Gothic horror script for the award-winning *The 7th Guest*, a Virgin/Trilobyte "Interactive Drama," which has become a best-selling CD-ROM with over two million copies sold. He also scripted its sequel, *The 11th Hour*, as well as other CD-ROM projects, including *The Dark Half*, based on Stephen King's novel. An acclaimed novelist as well as a "multimedia man," Costello lives in the Westchester suburb of Katonah, New York, with his wife and three children.

HARLAN ELLISON has been called "one of the great living American short story writers" by the *Washington Post*. He has won the Hugo eight and a half times, the Nebula three times, the Stoker five times (in 1996, Ellison received the HWA's Lifetime Achievement Award), the Edgar Allan Poe Award twice, and many, many more such honors. Ellison has won more awards than any other living fantasist for the sixty-four books he has written or edited, the more than seventeen hundred stories, essays, articles and newspaper columns, the two dozen teleplays and a dozen motion pictures he has created. He lives with his wife, Susan, in Los Angeles.

ELIZABETH ENGSTROM fled the Midwest and eventually settled in Hawaii. Her first book was published in 1985. Among dozens of short stories, articles and essays in print, Engstrom has written five novels, among them *When Darkness Loves Us*, *Black Ambrosia* and *Lizard Wine*. She moved to Eugene, Oregon, in 1986, where she teaches classes in novel writing and holds workshops for women on writing erotica.

RICHARD GILLIAM worked his way through graduate school at the University of Alabama as a freelance sportswriter. After a career in the financial services industry, he began writing full-time in the early 1990s. His 1993 novella "Caroline and Caleb" was a finalist for the Bram Stoker Award, and in 1996 he co-edited the critically acclaimed *Phantoms of the Night*, an anthology of ghost stories featuring more than two dozen of the field's leading authors.

OWL GOINGBACK has written and published everything from poetry to self-defense articles. His novels include *Crota* and *Shaman Moon*. A frequent lecturer throughout the country on the customs and folklore of the Native American, he makes his home in Winter Park, Florida.

JAMES J. GORMLEY is the editor-in-chief of *Better Nutrition*, but his passion for "things fantastic and macabre" is nearly as great as his interest in "not just good, but good for you" food. Gormley lives in Manhattan with his wife, Dr. Juana Gonzalez Gormley (a researcher in immunology), and their two children, Julian and Natalia.

PAULA GURAN, aka DarkEcho, brings marketing news and more to the horror community via her Web site and *Omni* online. The editor of a magazine once called *Bones*, then *Bones of the Children* and soon to be *Wetbones*, she admits to spending more time in cyberspace than she probably should.

NANCY HOLDER has sold twenty-two novels; over one hundred short stories, articles and essays; computer game fiction; and Japanese manga and TV commercials. She has received four Stoker awards, three for short stories, and one for the novel, *Dead in the Water*. A charter member of the HWA, Nancy lives in San Diego with her husband, Wayne, their brand-new daughter, Belle, and their pack of Border collies, Mr. Ron, Maggie and Dot.

TINA JENS currently serves as Chairman of the Board of Trustees for the Horror Writers Association and is also a member of the World Fantasy Convention Board of Directors. Her stories have appeared in numerous anthologies including *Diagnosis: Terminal, Phantoms of the Night, Miskatonic University* and *The Secret Prophecies of Nostradamus*. Living in Chicago with her husband, Barry, she spends most of her days in neighborhood coffee shops writing, and most of her nights in blues clubs wishing she could sing.

JACK KETCHUM is the pseudonym of a former actor, teacher, literary agent, lumber salesman and soda jerk who grew up in New Jersey, lives in Manhattan and writes mostly about rural New England. In the words of Stephen King, "no writer [who has read Ketchum] can help being influenced by him . . . [He] is a genuine iconoclast, a writer who is really good, one of the few outside the Chosen Circle who really matter." His books include *Off Season*, *The Girl Next Door*, *She Wakes*, *Joyride* and *Red*.

NANCY KILPATRICK, under the pen name Amarantha Knight, has published five novels in the erotic *Darker Passions* series from Masquerade, exploring the sexual desires and practices of such archetypes as Dracula, Frankenstein and Dorian Gray, and has edited several anthologies with sexual themes. Her novels *Near Death* and *Child of the Night* are more mainstream horror. A Stoker award winner, Kilpatrick has taught fiction in the university classroom and online and has written nonfiction for newspapers and magazines as well as scripts for comic books.

STEPHEN KING is acknowledged by his peers and his readers as the most influential and successful horror writer of modern times. His novels and short stories have been translated into virtually all the world's languages and have been presented in every medium. King plays guitar, works hard, and lives in Bangor, Maine.

TRACY KNIGHT is a clinical psychologist who practices in rural Illinois. His short fiction in the horror/suspense/mystery and science-fiction genres has appeared in numerous anthologies, including *Werewolves*, *Murder for Father*, *Whitley Streiber's Aliens*, *The UFO Files* and three of the books in the "Cat Crime" series. He claims to be the only human being to have had his work published in both the *Journal of Abnormal Psychology* and *Grue* magazine.

JOE R. LANSDALE is best known for horror and suspense/mystery writing, but his work regularly crosses all genres. His novels include *Act of Love* and *The Two Bear Mambo*, as well as a Batman novel, *Captured by the Engines*. He's published well over one hundred short stories and has brought his "weird western" take to comics with the *Jonah Hex* series for DC. A Stoker winner, Lansdale lives in Texas.

JOHN MACLAY's seventy-five-odd horror and supernatural stories have appeared in such magazines as *Twilight Zone*, *Night Cry*, *The Horror Show*, *Cemetery Dance*, *Pulphouse* and in the anthologies *Stalkers*, *Urban Horrors*, *Vampire Detectives* and others. He and his wife and partner, Joyce, as the publishing firm Maclay and Associates, have put into print some of the genre's finest books, including the four-volume *Masques* series, *Voices From the Night*, Rex Miller's *St. Louis Blues* and Ray Russell's *Haunted Castles*.

JILL M. MORGAN, Texas born, is the author of eighteen novels—ten for adults and eight for young adult and middle grade readers. Her adult novels, published under the pseudonym Morgan Fields, include *Shaman Woods* and *Deadly Harvest*, while her most recent book for younger horror fans is *Blood Brothers*. In addition to her novels, she has co-edited an anthology with Martin H. Greenberg and Robert Weinberg, *Great Writers and Kids Write Spooky Stories*.

DAVID MORRELL is the award-winning author of *First Blood*, the 1972 novel in which Rambo appeared. He holds a Ph.D. in American literature from Pennsylvania State University. From 1970 to 1986 was a professor of English at the University of Iowa until he resigned to devote himself to a full-time writing career. Morrell has written numerous best-selling thrillers, including *The Brotherhood of the Rose* (the basis for a highly rated NBC miniseries); *The Fifth Profession*, *Assumed Identity* and *Extreme Denial*. His horror novel, *The Totem*, has been described as "one of the finest horror novels of the past 20 years" (*The Washington Post*) and "one of the scariest of all time" (*The Denver Rocky Mountain News*). Of his many horror short stories, two were nominated for World Fantasy Awards, two were nominated for Stokers, and two others received awards from the HWA.

GREGORY NICOLL has had three stories in *The Year's Best Horror Stories*. Recent tales appear in the anthologies *Gahan Wilson's Ultimate Haunted House*, *It Came From the Drive-In*, *Blood Muse* and *100 Vicious Little Vampires*. Frequently cited as the nation's "best rock music journalist," Greg owns several weird vintage guitars. He presently writes full-time, dividing his efforts between fiction and journalism.

JOYCE CAROL OATES is the prolific author of novels, essays, short stories, poetry and plays. She has received the National Book Award and the HWA's Lifetime Achievement Award. The range of interests and expertise in her writing attracts a wide audience: her work *On Boxing* is ranked with the best ever written on the sport, while her short story "Martyrdom" from the aptly named anthology *Metahorror*, proves that stomach-wrenching horror can do far more than simply shock. Her novels and short story collections include *Upon the Sweeping Flood*, *Do With Me What You Will*, *By the North Gate* and *Zombie*. She is presently the Roger S. Berlind Distinguished Professor in the Humanities at Princeton University.

DAVID QUINN is best known as the co-creator of *Faust*, the dramatic, ultraviolent "modern Gothic romance" which set high standards of story, art, character and psychosexual excess for contemporary outlaw comics. Quinn, raised in Ann Arbor, Michigan, studied literature at Amherst College and acting, writing and music at the National Theater Institute (Eugene O'Neill Theater Center) before settling in New York City, where he continued his writing training as a playwright. In addition to his "borderlands" material, Quinn has kicked a provocative sense of wonder into a diversity of "mainstream" comics, like *Doctor Strange*, *Night Man/Gambit* and *Carnage*.

NORMAN PARTRIDGE has published more than fifty short stories. He won a Stoker for his first collection, *Mr. Fox and Other Feral Tales*, and co-edited *It Came From the Drive-In*, an anthology of B-movie fiction. Stephen King called Partridge's first novel, *Slippin' Into Darkness*, a "five star book." A second collection of stories, *Bad Intentions*, was published by Subterranean Press in 1996.

ALAN RODGERS is the author of *Bone Music*, *Pandora*, *Fire Night*, *Blood of the Children* and *New Life for the Dead*. The Horror Writers Association nominated both *Blood of the Children* and *Bone Music* for Stokers; his first story (actually a novelette), "The Boy Who Came Back From the Dead," won a Stoker. During the mid-1980s, Rodgers edited the fondly remembered horror digest *Night Cry*. He lives in a small city in the Northwest with his wife, Amy Stout, his two daughters, Alexandra and Andrea, and his son, Abram. The author can be e-mailed at the Internet address alanr@greyware.com.

WAYNE ALLEN SALLEE refers to himself as the Susan Lucci of horror fiction, having been a Stoker nominee in four categories in as many years without winning. More than 130 of his short stories have appeared in anthologies and in magazines ranging from *Grue* to *2 AM*, including *Nightmares on Elm Street*, *Little Deaths* and *Masques*. His short fiction was included in the final ten volumes of *Year's Best Horror*, from DAW, edited by the late Karl Edward Wagner. In 1992, Sallee's novel, *The Holy Terror* (Ziesing Books) was published. In 1996 a story collection, *With Wounds Still Wet*, was published by Silver Salamander.

KAREN E. TAYLOR lives in Maryland with her husband, two sons, two cats and a dog. Best known for her three-volume *Vampire Legacy* series—*Blood Secrets*, *Bitter Blood* and *Blood Ties*—she has also had short fiction published in anthologies such as *Love Bites*, *100 Vicious Little Vampires* and *100 Wicked Little Witches*. When asked why she writes horror fiction, Karen pleads a lifelong fascination with the supernatural; she first conceived of writing a vampire novel while living across the street from a large cemetery.

EDO VAN BELKOM's first short-story sale in 1990, "Baseball Memories," was reprinted in *Year's Best Horror Stories XX*. Since then, he's sold over one hundred other stories to a wide variety of markets. His first novel, *Wyrm Wolf*, was a *Locus* bestseller and a finalist for the 1995 Stoker Award. Other novels include *Lord Soth*, *Army of the Dead* and *Mister Magick*.

ROBERT W. WALKER grew up in Chicago and attended Northwestern University, earning a master's in English education. He has published over twenty-five novels in a variety of categories, including YA, mystery and thriller, but his best-known work has been in the *Instinct* series, whose central character, medical examiner and FBI agent Jessica Coran, regularly meets (and defeats) the most bizarre serial killers. Walker currently teaches writing classes at Daytona Beach Community College in Daytona Beach, Florida.

LAWRENCE WATT-EVANS is the author of some two dozen novels—most of them fantasy or science-fiction, but one, *The Nightmare People*, deemed sufficiently horrific that *Fangoria*'s book reviewer thought it "too extreme." About a third of his one hundred-plus stories have been horror as well. He lives in the Maryland suburbs of Washington with his wife, two kids and an assortment of small animals, and he served as president of HWA from 1994 to 1996.

ROBERT WEINBERG is the author of thirteen novels, six nonfiction books and numerous short stories. As an editor, he has compiled over 120 anthologies in the horror, mystery, western, fantasy and romance fields. He has been nominated five times for the prestigious World Fantasy Award, winning twice. Weinberg served as Vice-President of the Horror Writers Association from 1994 to 1996.

STANLEY WIATER is the author of four books and the editor of two acclaimed anthologies of short fiction. He is widely considered the premier interviewer in the fields of horror and dark suspense. His first book of interviews, *Dark Dreamers: Conversations With the Masters of Horror*, won the Stoker Award for nonfiction. The second collection, *Dark Visions: Conversations with the Masters of the Horror Film*, was a 1992 Stoker nominee. Wiater's first published short story was the sole winner of a competition judged by Stephen King in 1980.

J.N. WILLIAMSON, with nearly forty novels and over one hundred short stories to his credit, is known in the horror community as a